American Opera Librettos

by

ANDREW H. DRUMMOND

The Scarecrow Press, Inc.
Metuchen, N.J.   1973

Library of Congress Cataloging in Publication Data

Drummond, Andrew H
    American opera librettos.

    Bibliography: p.
    1. Opera, American--History and criticism. 2. Opera
--New York (City). 3. Libretto. I. Title.
ML1711.D8   782.1'2'0973   72-8111
ISBN 0-8108-0553-7

ACKNOWLEDGMENTS

The author wishes to thank the following people for their generous assistance: Dr. John L. H. Stigall and Dr. Merrill Skaggs for invaluable editorial assistance; Miss Ruth Hider of the New York City Opera for assistance in locating materials concerning productions at the New York City Opera; Dr. William P. Sears, Dr. Walter Kob, and Dr. Charles N. Schirone of New York University for their expert guidance; Dr. Alfred Borrello; and my wife, Maria.

CONTENTS

INTRODUCTION

In a recent article in the New York Times, Ezra
Laderman, a composer of five operas, expressed the following opinion:

> Of all the arts today, the one held in lowest esteem
> by audience, critic, colleague and impresario
> throughout the world is contemporary American
> opera. Our dance, our theatre, our artists, our
> poets, our musicians are welcomed, imitated,
> sought after and admired universally, and rightly
> so. Not so our composers, particularly those who
> are involved with the lyric stage.[1]

This is a harsh judgment and, like all such sweeping statements, a dangerous over-generalization. Although American
opera is a recent development, it has grown in the twentieth
century into a mature and serious genre, worthy of systematic study.

The history of opera in America is a history of bor-
rowings, mainly from European sources, but with an increasing awareness of the native material that can be treated. The ballad opera form of the eighteenth and nineteenth
century was adapted by American composers and librettists
in an attempt to inject music and dramatic forms distinctive
to America. Then, at the end of the nineteenth century,
with a surge of activity, mainly in New York, the recognized
operatic center of America, opera became an important, if
mainly imported, cultural expression. As is indicated in
this study, this great activity gave rise to a conscious attempt on the part of American-based artists to create a distinctive American opera. The results, although of wide
diversity, did succeed in bringing to the opera public the
recognition of the possibilities of opera native to America.
Perhaps this new country could make a valid contribution to
a form intimately associated with European culture. To
this end many artists gave and have continued to give serious attention.

1

Since World War II, New York has supported two
opera companies, the Metropolitan Opera Company and the
New York City Opera Company. The Metropolitan is the
older of the two houses and has been one of the leading
opera houses in the world since its establishment in 1883.
It is, however, primarily European-oriented with respect to
repertoire. Created in 1943, the New York City Opera has
established the more consistent record for production of
American opera. From 1948-1971, the span of this study,
the New York City Opera produced forty American operas.[2]
It is the librettos of these forty operas on which this study
concentrates. In 1958 and in 1959, the Ford Foundation
supported two all-American opera seasons, and subsequently
it established a grant to the New York City Opera to commission the writing and production of ten new American
operas. As to the efforts of the New York City Opera in
producing American opera, Howard Taubman commented:

> The City Center has completed its first season of
> American opera. This week's extra performances
> of Lost in the Stars are an unexpected dividend of
> a daring enterprise that has been carried to frui-
> tion. One's admiration is almost as great for the
> City Center's discharge of its self-imposed obli-
> gation as for the caliber of some of the American
> operas.[3]

A basic problem for composers of opera is obtaining
an effective libretto. As Virgil Thomson has written,
"Librettists, of course, are a scarcity everywhere."[4] The
earliest Italian opera librettos were standardized in their
exclusive consideration of mythological and historical subjects. Later these stories were modified and more contemporary subjects were treated. A more honest relationship
between the libretto and the music, making a more dramatic
whole, was a contribution of Gluck and his librettist Calza-
bigi.[5] Then Mozart brought a psychological treatment of
character similar to twentieth century concepts. This is re-
flected in the librettos he used as well as in his music.[6]
In the nineteenth and twentieth centuries, subject matter for
librettos has ranged widely over historical and contemporary
subjects. Wagner wrote his own librettos, as have Menotti
and Floyd, composers whose works are included in this
study. Throughout the history of opera, a lengthy discussion has ensued concerning the importance of the libretto as
compared to the music. The controversy has proved so per-
sistent that Richard Strauss, in 1942, wrote Capriccio, an

opera on the subject of the poet versus the composer. In
Scene Six, the Countess sings of words versus music:

> The poets pleading, how brilliantly clear! Yet what
> was hidden from one, the other reveals. Where
> lies the answer? Was it through the words that
> he found the key to his music? Was our language
> always fraught with song or does music gather its
> lifeblood from words? One holds the other and
> needs the other. In music, emotions are yearning
> for language--in words there's a craving for music
> and sound. [7]

And later in the opera:

> In angry disputes you argued and struggled; vainly
> you tried to vanquish one another. Now leave
> your wilderness of thinking! Feel this with me:
> that all the arts have only one home and one de-
> sire. [8]

It is not the object of this study to engage in the
argument over the relative importance of libretto or music.
As Joseph Kerman has written:

> Of the many current partial attitudes toward opera
> two are most stultifying: the one held by musi-
> cians, that opera is a low form of music, and the
> one apparently held by everybody else, that opera
> is a low form of drama. These attitudes stem
> from the exclusively musical and the exclusively
> literary approaches to opera. [9]

He adds: "Opera is excellently its own form." [10]

This study seeks to determine which elements are
dramatically valid and positive in librettos of American
operas performed at the New York City Opera Company
from 1948-1971. Using an historical and critical approach,
the investigation surveys briefly the development of the American opera libretto from the late nineteenth century to 1948.
Following this historical background is an identification of
the "dramatic elements" of librettos as defined in historical
dramatic criticism. The dramatic elements in the librettos
of American operas performed at the New York City Opera
from 1948-1971 are then identified. Following this, a survey of critical appraisal is given to American opera

librettos to ascertain additional dramatic elements, and the
study concludes with the author's final appraisals of the
librettos in the study.

Certain terms for this investigation should be defined
clearly. "The New York City Opera Company" and "City
Center Opera" are both used to indicate the New York City
Opera Company located at the New York City Center, 131
West 55th Street, New York and later at Lincoln Center,
during the period under study. Since operas are usually
identified by composer, rather than librettist, the term
"American Opera" is used to denote operas written by American composers.

The study is not concerned with an appraisal of costumes, settings, and general visual, vocal and musical effects.

The brief survey of American opera from the late
nineteenth century to the time of the study (1948) in Chapter
I poses several questions. What was the state of American
opera at the close of the nineteenth century? What American operas were produced at the Metropolitan and which outside New York? Finally, what was the critical response to
these productions of American opera? Immediate "first
night" criticism in periodicals was considered as well as
long-range opinion. Newspaper criticism from the New York
Times and other periodicals was especially valuable as were
works on the operatic activity of the period. These included
Henry Krehbiel's Chapters of Opera and More Chapters of
Opera; Irving Kolodin's The Story of The Metropolitan Opera;
David Ewen's Encyclopedia of the Opera; Donald Grout's A
Short History of Opera; John Tasker Howard's Our American
Music; and John Frederick Cone's Oscar Hammerstein's
Manhattan Opera Company.

Chapter II identifies characteristics of dramatic elements. Employing Aristotle's canons as well as nineteenth
and twentieth century critical statements on operatic form,
"dramatic elements" were isolated for the examination of
the librettos of American opera. Many theatre critics and
practitioners have been concerned with the problem of adequate definition of drama. Stanislavsky, G. B. Shaw, Ibsen,
Pirandello, and Brecht in theatre, and Wagner, Verdi,
Strauss, and Menotti in opera have all addressed themselves
to critical analyses of the dramatic form and its twentieth
century metamorphosis.

In Chapter III, the forty American operas of this
study are analyzed under three headings: plot, characterization, and style.   First, characteristics of plot are considered: form, content of the libretto, central statement,
and clarity of focus.   The use of plot devices such as dramatic irony and reversal of fortune is also considered. Concerning elements of characterization, one must/ ask if the
characterization is believable and to what extent it is dominant over plot.   One must also ask what types of people are
treated in the work--their social strata, their psychological
situation.   Lastly, the elements of literary form were stud-
ied--is the libretto written in prose or poetry?   Is the style
appropriate to the plot, the characterization, and the theme?

Finally, the study surveys contemporary critical appraisal of American opera librettos under consideration.
Here the concern is particularly with the criticism of dramatic elements in the librettos.   Can a consistent critical
standard be discerned in contemporary criticism?   Does this
offer new insights into the nature of modern opera criticism?
Newspapers and periodicals were the main source for this
information as many of the operas have not been treated ex-
tensively in scholarly criticism.

Several unpublished works were consulted in this
study.   The Aufdemberge dissertation[11] examines sixteen
American operas on American themes and discusses each
one in musical and dramatic terms.   His list begins with
The Scarlet Letter by/Walter Damrosch (1896) and ends
with The Ballad of Baby Doe (1956), and discusses seven of
the works included in this study.   It is the conclusion of
Aufdemberge that, in general, American opera is developing
toward making opera better drama and better theatre. He
bases his conclusion on the fact that/ there has been an improvement in dramatic structure in opera composition, with
a greater simplicity of dramatic line.   Also, it is Aufdemberge's conclusion that characters exist as people and not as
excuses for song, and that there is a closer collaboration
between composer and librettist in the later works.   He discusses the increased use of native musical materials such
as ragtime, jazz, hymns, and the folk song.   From these
elements he traces the beginnings of a more "grand" opera
in such works as Moore's The Wings of the Dove, Menotti's
The Last Savage, and Barber's Vanessa.   He also touches
on opera subject matter and current production methods.   It
is in this latter category that he commends the New York
City Opera for its efforts in producing American opera.

The purpose of Casmus' study[12] was to analyze Menotti's dramatic technique and to determine the principles of libretto writing employed in his works. Eight operas were selected by Casmus, of which seven are used in this volume. The Casmus study is important in suggesting the critical criteria that are valuable for an examination of librettos.

In a study by Ruth Katz[13] the origins of opera in relation to the "disposition of its creators and to the aspirations of their society at the moment of its birth" are examined. Katz traces the increasing lyricism, the rise of middle class individualism, and the changing idea of the role of the artist in society. Camerata as a social institution and its relation to the humanistic tradition is discussed. This cultural atmosphere led to the crystallization of sixteenth century aesthetic ideals and to the rise of beautiful singing as an independent art. The point is also made that the Italianate basis of opera emphasizes an appeal to the senses through song rather than an appeal to the intellect. An example of this last point is the opera, Orfeo, which is characterized by the investigator as crude intellectually but extremely refined in its sensuous aspects.

The period covered in a dissertation by Davis[14] is from the beginnings of American opera in the west to 1961. The study surveys opera in Chicago, New Orleans, and San Francisco, and at the end mentions the tradition of opera in Dallas. French opera was predominant in the New Orleans tradition until the Opera House fire in 1919. Since that time the tradition of opera has never regained its importance, and it was subsequently replaced by jazz in the city's musical life. The current conditions in these different cities are a major concern of the study. San Francisco and Chicago today steer a course independent from New York, and Davis believes it a healthy development. He also believes that the Metropolitan Opera in New York is far too conservative in its policy. Dallas has a new tradition, but it is one in which the attempt is made never to produce a routine performance, but rather to integrate all elements of opera into a meaningful and fresh approach.

A final unpublished work consulted was the investigation by Crooker[15] into the roots of the American musical play, which concludes that tried and true theatre techniques are the basis of the American musical play. It is not a completely new form, but rather a combination of techniques that have proved themselves with audiences over the years.

Opera, in conclusion, although it often promises more than it gives, attempts to fulfill the requirement of the complete or total theatrical experience better than any other form. Through its combination of music, drama, dance and spectacle, opera most nearly synthesizes the performing arts.

In America this form is now beginning to show signs of maturity. Tyrone Guthrie recently, in Opera News, described opera in these terms:

> We 'believe in' opera because of the four or five great performances we have experienced. Their effect has been so thrilling, so uplifting, so life-giving that we go back again and again, hoping each time that the angel will trouble the waters . . . how impossible it is to achieve a great performance. But when it is achieved, is there anything to compare with it this side of Jordan?[16]

With the growing interest in opera in America, the rapidly increasing professional activity and the number of opera workshops found on college campuses, opera will inevitably assume increasing importance in America's artistic life. It is hoped that this book will provide guidelines for developing librettists as well as teachers of opera technique. It also may give added relevance to a performing art now receiving an increased measure of serious attention in America's cultural activity. To know opera is to know the fullest possibilities of the theatrical form, and its finest moments speak uniquely to the human spirit.

Notes

1. Ezra Laderman, The New York Times, June 16, 1968. © 1968 by The New York Times Company. Reprinted by permission. [All other New York Times quotations in this volume are also copyrighted by the New York Times Company and are reprinted by permission.]

2. See Chapter III.

3. Howard Taubman, New York Times, May 4, 1958.

4. Virgil Thomson, New York Times, June 16, 1968.

5. Donald Jay Grout, A Short History of Opera (New York: Columbia University Press, 1965), II, pp. 236-245.

6. Ibid., p. 282.

7. Libretto by Clemens Krauss and Richard Strauss, c. 1942 by Richard Strauss, English translation by Maria Massey, c. 1963 by Franz Strauss, Capriccio (Boosey and Hawkes, Inc.), p. 24.

8. Ibid., p. 53.

9. Joseph Kerman, Opera As Drama (New York: Vintage Books, 1959), p. 21.

10. Ibid.

11. Leon Maurice Aufdemberge, "Analysis of the Dramatic Construction of American Operas on American Themes, 1896-1958," (unpublished Ph.D. dissertation, Northwestern University, Evanston, Ill., 1965).

12. Mary Irene Casmus, "Gian-Carlo Menotti: His Dramatic Techniques: A Study Based on Works Written 1937-1954" (unpublished Ph.D. dissertation, Columbia University, New York, N.Y., 1962).

13. Ruth Torgovnik Katz, "The Origins of Opera: The Relevance of Social and Cultural Factors to the Establishment of a Musical Institution" (unpublished Ph.D. dissertation, Columbia University, New York, N.Y., 1963).

14. Ronald Leroy Davis, "A History of Resident Opera in the American West" (unpublished Ph.D. dissertation, University of Texas, 1961).

15. Earle T. Crooker, "The American Musical Play," (unpublished Ph.D. dissertation, University of Pennsylvania, 1957).

16. Tyrone Guthrie, "Out of Touch," Opera News, Vol. 31, No. 16, February 11, 1967, p. 11.

Chapter I

AMERICAN OPERA FROM THE
LATE 19TH CENTURY TO 1948

The opera tradition in America began with liberal bor-
rowings from Europe. Record of the first opera performances
in America is sketchy, but the first performance reputedly
took place in a courtroom in Charleston, South Carolina, on
February 8, 1735,[1] a production of an English ballad opera,
Flora. Ballad operas were the most popular form until 1791
when French opera was introduced in New Orleans. Italian
opera was first done in Baltimore in 1794--Paisiello's The
Barber of Seville--and Rossini's Barber was given in New
York City in 1819. Both of these operas were sung in
English translations. In 1825, Rossini's opera was first
sung in Italian in New York. Lorenzo Da Ponte, Mozart's
librettist, was instrumental in encouraging opera in New
York, and he was responsible for New York's first permanent opera house, the Italian Opera House, built in 1833.
German opera was first heard in the original tongue when a
visiting troupe gave Der Freischutz in 1855. In 1850 opera
was first performed in Chicago with a production of La Son-
nambula, and in 1852 in San Francisco this same opera was
the first performed.[2]

To find American opera in these early records is not
always easy. The first American operas were based on the
ballad opera genre of which Gay's The Beggar's Opera was
a popular example. This opera was often performed but
altered "with characters and dialects appropriate to the
American locale."[3] These operas were a mixture of spoken
dialogue and singing. Toward the end of the eighteenth
century several "opera" are mentioned, but Donald Grout in
A Short History of Opera remarks:

The first publicly performed opera with continuous
music by a native American composer was Leonora
by William Henry Fry (1813-64), given at Philadelphia in 1845 and in a revised version at New
York in 1848--a work of considerable competence

9

and musical interest, modeled on the styles of
Donizetti and Meyerbeer. [4]

In 1855 George Frederick Bristow's Rip Van Winkle
was performed in Niblo's Garden, New York. [5] Again it was
in the style fashionable for European light opera, although
with subject material drawn from a native writer, Washington Irving.   Also in 1855 the celebrated violinist, Ole Bull,
then manager of the Academy of Music of New York offered
a prize of $1,000 for "the best original grand opera by an
American composer, upon a strictly American subject."[6]
However, the Academy closed soon after this announcement
and the prize was withdrawn.

Still, there continued to be considerable operatic activity in the United States in the last half of the nineteenth
century.   In New Orleans there was a long history of successfully produced opera.   In fact, throughout the whole of
the nineteenth century, New Orleans was considered an opera
center, and, by some, the opera capital of the United States.
Before 1850 "dozens of European singers came to New Orleans to display their talents and returned to the Continent
without having sung a note in any other city in the United
States."[7]   The French Opera House, built to succeed the
Theatre d'Orleans in 1859, stood for sixty years until it
burned in 1919.   Since jazz had replaced opera in the musical
life of New Orleans by that date, the long tradition of opera
production ended. [8]   In New York the Academy of Music,
built in 1854, succeeded the Astor Place Opera House and
served as the principal opera house until the opening of the
Metropolitan Opera House in 1883 successfully challenged the
Academy artistically and socially as New York's first permanent home for opera.   Many American premieres took place
at the Academy, including Andrea Chenier, Otello, Rigoletto
and La Traviata. [9]

During the same period the operatic activity in other
areas of the country consisted of standard European reper-
tory furnished by travelling companies.   Philadelphia,
Boston, and Washington saw many such troupes.   In 1865,
St. Louis had its first real season and in the same year
Chicago's Crosby Opera House opened.   In both cases Jacob
Grau's Grand Italian Opera from New York provided the
productions. [10]

It was not until 1896 that a significant American work
appeared.   This was Walter Damrosch's The Scarlet Letter.

The reasons for this lapse in operatic composition is explained
thus by one writer:

> The Civil War disrupted much of the established
> musical culture in the United States. However, the
> primary reason lies perhaps in another direction.
> There were a number of American composers ac-
> tive during the period of 1860-1900, but most of
> them used their talents on other forms of music.
> The cantata and the song form were especially
> popular during the period. And, because of the
> growing nationalism in America, there seemed
> to be no room for what was looked upon as a for-
> eign pleasure. [11]

The events surrounding the production of The Scarlet
Letter are informative of the state of operatic production in
New York at this time. When the Metropolitan Opera House
began its first seasons of production, the emphasis was almost entirely Italian. Then, during the period when Leopold
and Walter Damrosch were general managers, 1885-91, the
House became very German. Even the non-German operas
were sung in German. Upon the end of the Damrosch administration, German opera passed from favor. In 1894
Walter Damrosch organized the Damrosch Opera Company
primarily to present German opera--more specifically,
Wagner--as a corrective. Through six seasons German and
eventually Italian and French operas were presented. There
were extensive tours, and the company is credited with re-
storing German to a place of importance in New York's
operatic life. In 1896 Damrosch presented his first opera,
The Scarlet Letter, in a fully staged version after a first
presentation in concert form by the Oratorio Society of New
York the year before. [12] The libretto was by George Par-
sons Lathrop, a son-in-law of Hawthorne, author of the novel
on which the opera was based. Henry Krehbiel writes of the
libretto:

> The book of the opera proved to be undramatic in
> the extreme, a defect which was emphasized by the
> execrable pronunciation of nearly all the singers at
> the performance on the stage at the Academy. [13]

There were many Wagnerian elements to this opera.
The music was in the style of Wagner, and Krehbiel remarks
on the " . . . nixies of the Rhine [which] peeped out of the
sunflecked coverts in the forest around Hester Prynne's hut."

He also noted, " . . . the sinister Hunding was heard mut-
tering in the ear of Chillingworth, and Hester wore the badge
of shame on the robes of Elsa, washed in innocency."[14]
The opera was later characterized because of these Wagnerian
elements as "the Nibelungen of New England."[15] Another
phase of Wagner's style is seen by one writer in the similarity of the libretto to that of Tristan und Isolde: the pair of
guilty lovers who meet secretly, the adulterous affair, and
the death of both at the end of the opera.[16] It was, however
derivative, a serious attempt to present an opera based upon
an American theme.

     At the Metropolitan Opera during the time of the Dam-
rosch Opera Company, a balance--German, Italian, and
French works--was regained, in part due to the outstanding
initial success of the German repertoire of the Damrosch
company. The Metropolitan now sang the French and Italian
repertoires in the original languages, but the occasional German offerings were sung in Italian. A reorganization of the
Company followed the 1897-98 Season in which no opera was
performed at the Metropolitan, and Maurice Grau became
manager. The next five years, under his leadership, were
outstanding and have become known as the "golden age of opera."[17] Some of the greatest singers of the generation were
presented and the era is remembered for its all-star casts
which brought outstanding artistic and financial success to the
Metropolitan. This, however, was not a period of performance of American opera at the Metropolitan, or for that matter, at any other opera house in the United States.

     Interest in opera was extremely high during this period,
probably higher than any other period. During and immediately
following Grau's administration, increased operatic activity
developed. Oscar Hammerstein, a New York opera producer
of some repute, had been presenting opera independently for
some years, and it was his ambition to achieve a consistency
and scale equal to that of the Metropolitan. In fact, Hammerstein felt he could do much better: "Hammerstein believed that opera as given at the Metropolitan Opera House
was a disgrace and that Heinrich Conried, the director since
1903, was incompetent, 'not equal to the occasion.' "[18]
(Heinrich Conried's work was not without merit. He was
responsible for the introduction of Enrico Caruso to the
American public, and for the first full production of Wagner's Parsifal, despite the strong objection of Cosima Wagner at Bayreuth. His later initial production of Strauss'
Salome was a sensation.)[19] When, in 1906, he opened the

Manhattan Opera House on Thirty-Fourth Street, Hammerstein
proved equal to the challenge of the Metropolitan and assem-
bled what proved to be one of the most artistically exciting
series of opera seasons in America. Krehbiel writes of the
first season:

> A company gathered together from the ends of the
> earth succeeded in giving one hundred and thirteen
> performances of really remarkable excellence.
> The reason was obvious at nearly every presenta-
> tion; from the principals down to the last person
> in the chorus and orchestra, everyone had his
> heart in his work.[20]

The result of these four seasons from 1906 to 1910
at the Manhattan Opera House was to heighten the interest in
opera in New York and to introduce to its opera public many
new operatic works, mainly French. Mary Garden was imported with a French cast to present Debussy's Pelléas et
Mélisande, and such outstanding artists as Nellie Melba, Lillian Nordica, Luisa Tetrazzini, Ernestine Schumann-Heinck,
John McCormack, Alessandro Bonci, and the conductor Cleofonte Campanini also appeared.[21] Hammerstein was so successful that upon the resignation of Heinrich Conried at the
Metropolitan in 1908, an extensive reorganization directed to
improvement of the financial and artistic standing of the Metropolitan resulted. The Manhattan Opera House closed in
1910 rather mysteriously, but later it was revealed that a
financial agreement had been reached with the Metropolitan
by which Hammerstein agreed for a consideration not to produce opera in America for a period of ten years--further
proof of his successful efforts. He had competed with the
Metropolitan not only in New York but also in Philadelphia
and Boston and in extensive tours around the country, and
in doing so had raised the standards of opera production in
America.[22] Irving Kolodin writes in summary of Hammerstein's efforts:

> The excitement and interest that Oscar Hammer-
> stein contributed to opera in New York can be
> gauged not only from the operas and artists he in-
> troduced, but also from the powerful forces he set
> in motion. First in Philadelphia and Chicago, then
> with Chicago as base, they continued to fertilize
> the operatic soil in a way unmistakably his for a
> full twenty years.[23]

Hammerstein also wanted to encourage American opera and, to this end, he announced a $1,000 prize to be given for a libretto, preferably written by an American.[24] He also commissioned Victor Herbert, already known for his operettas, to write an opera, but the Manhattan Opera closed before it could be presented. It opened, however, on February 25, 1911, under the management of the Philadelphia-Chicago Opera Company which was the artistic child of the Manhattan Opera Company and which had been formed in 1910. The opera, entitled Natoma, written by Herbert, with a libretto by Joseph Redding, starred Mary Garden and John McCormack and was conducted by Cleofonte Campanini, former artistic director for Oscar Hammerstein.[25] It was well received in Philadelphia and three days later was performed in New York, a climax to the great anticipation that preceded its opening. It was greeted as the arrival of great American opera.[26] In the Public Ledger of Philadelphia the review read in part: " . . . the crowd was delighted beyond all expression and today the country is throwing out its chest and saying: 'At last we have it--the American opera by an American composer, and it was sung in English.'"[27] But other reviews were not so generous. Lawrence Gilman wrote in Harper's Weekly:

> The libretto of Mr. Joseph Redding should go down into operatic history as one of the most futile, fatuous, halting, impotent, inane and puerile ever written. Its dramatic development is totally wanting in sense and logic, its situations have been worn threadbare by convention, its characters are sawdust-stuffed marionettes and its verbiage, cheap colloquialism or jingling balderdash.[28]

So, too, Mrs. Parker of the Boston Transcript agreed in an opinion summary in the Literary Digest. "From beginning to end, equally in text and music 'Natoma' is an utterly mediocre opera."[29] And the Musical Courier offers this opinion:

> What ails the opera? A tedious and endlessly long and generally uninteresting first act; a brilliant, but light and rhapsodic second act, and an ineffective third act. That is a catalogue of its ills generally . . . the plot is foolishly weak . . . and its end is an anticlimax.[30]

Again, Irving Kolodin's much later estimate of this opera

concerned with an Indian maid "done wrong" by a white man reads:

> Book trouble was a disturbing liability of Natoma
> when it was heard on March 1, though Henderson
> could not grant the admired operetta-composer
> credit for more than a 'sorry assault on this puer-
> ile nonsense.' What stands out now, stood out
> then: the same critic found the Dagger Dance
> 'really excellent.' Garden made something thrill-
> ing of Natoma, for all its weak music, but Mc-
> Cormack's Lieutenant Paul Merrill was not merely
> as bad as the role: it was worse.[31]

It is interesting to note that at the time of this production of Natoma, Victor Herbert's operetta, Naughty Marietta, was playing very successfully in New York.[32]

He tried again to write an opera, Madeleine, with a libretto by Grant Stewart based on a French play. A one-act opera, the New York Sun called it an "operetta," rather than the more substantial genre title of opera comique. The piece was characterized in Current Opinion as "a charming but unexciting story . . . in the musical manner of Strauss."[33] It was presented for a total of four performances in the 1913-14 Season at the Metropolitan.

At the Metropolitan Opera, under the new management of Giulio Gatti-Casazza, starting in 1908, there was a re-newal of interest in American opera. Under Gatti's manage-ment the first American opera was performed at the Metro-politan. This was Frederick Converse's The Pipe of Desire, produced in 1910, after almost a generation without American opera produced in America. Gatti began by offering a $10,-000 prize for an American opera. The Converse work did not win the prize but was put into production as a stimulant for further native works. It did not receive a favorable critical reception, however, for Kolodin wrote:

> It had first been given downtown on March 18,
> with a critical reaction that foreshadowed a pattern
> of reaction to such works to come: the handicap
> of a 'hopeless text' (Henderson's estimation) ex-
> pressed through a melodic invention sometimes
> pleasant, but more often 'wanting in rhythmic con-
> tour.'[34]

Another American opera, Twilight, by Arthur Nevin, was projected for performance at the Metropolitan but was withdrawn. Twilight was produced in 1918 at the Chicago Opera, conducted by Campanini under the title A Daughter of the Forest. The scene was western Pennsylvania during the Civil War. Johnson remarks: "the work is entirely lacking in dramatic motivation." It was given only once.[35]

The period showed other favorable signs for opera. An opera company had been formed in Boston in 1909 to give the city, in addition to the tours of the Metropolitan Opera or other travelling companies, a troupe of its own. In the same year one of the most long-lived travelling companies of opera was formed: The San Carlo Opera Company, from which San Francisco eventually gained the founder of its own opera company in Gaetano Merola, who visited San Francisco with the San Carlo as conductor, and remained to form a company in 1923.[36]

Another American opera achieved a performance in Boston in 1910. This was Poia by Arthur Nevin, with libretto by Randolph Hartley in German translation by E. von Huhn. It concerned the Blackfoot Indians of Montana and had been first performed in Pittsburgh in 1906 in concert form. There, according to H. Earle Johnson, ". . . the press considered it 'destined to take its place among the greatest of the world's classics'" (Pittsburgh Dispatch).[37] Later, the opera had a different reception in Berlin. According to the Boston Herald, "No onslaught in all past history of savage musical and dramatic criticism in Berlin has ever excelled in downright abuse and violence the treatment accorded Arthur Nevin's American opera Poia."[38] Johnson suggests that this anger resulted from the strong feeling of Germans against a foreign interloper in a field they felt was their own.

The second American opera that Gatti-Casazza offered at the Metropolitan Opera was entitled Mona, with score composed by Horatio Parker and libretto by Brian Hooker. This first opera to be awarded the $10,000 prize was a story of a British princess, Mona, set in the first century A.D. during the Roman conquest. Although generally praised by public and critics the opera was dropped after four performances. The libretto was praised for its literary qualities, but not as a model of dramatic writing.[39] Krehbiel thought that with revisions the opera might well be retained, but he believed there was need for more dramatic variety in both music and libretto.[40]

An opera, his second, by Walter Damrosch produced
during the 1912-13 Season at the Metropolitan was entitled
Cyrano de Bergerac, with libretto by W. J. Henderson based
on the Rostand play.   Several reviewers noted that the story
is one calling for operatic treatment.   In the New York Tribune, Krehbiel remarked it was a setting that "might even be
said to cry out for an operatic investiture [and it] has been
turned into an attractive musical drama."   He thought that
the work did not offer a solution to the problem of opera in
English, but he believed this production might encourage other
aspiring American operatic writers.[41]   The Evening Post
held that not enough cuts had been made "to make the score
sufficiently compact" and that "it was generally felt that the
work was too long . . . with the result that only a rather
pale replica remains as an operatic portrait of the original
Cyrano."[42]   The opera had five performances during the
season and it was not revived.

Much later, in 1937, Walter Damrosch wrote a third
opera, also produced at the Metropolitan, entitled The Man
Without a Country, with libretto by Arthur Guiterman from
the story by Edward Everett Hale.   Aufdemberge's study of
this opera indicates Damrosch's motives in writing the opera:

> Damrosch's purpose in writing this opera was two-
> fold.   First, he wanted to write a popular opera,
> full of tunes which the audience could sing.   Sec-
> ond, he wished to pay tribute to his adopted coun-
> try, writing a patriotic opera which could assert
> some sort of basic patriotic ideals which were un-
> der attack at the time he wrote it.[43]

Aufdemberge also points out that "the structure of the
libretto is that of the German singspiel, a form used by
Beethoven in his opera [Fidelio]."   (This form employs
spoken dialogue as well as musical numbers.)   Aufdemberge
concludes: "the libretto he chose is somewhat better in
construction than in versification."[44]

Olin Downes, however, in the New York Times,
thought there was "no distinction in the Libretto," and that
the "style of the opera wavers between comedy and melodrama."[45]   Lawrence Gilman, in the Herald Tribune, on
the other hand, considered the opera a "Damroschian apotheosis," commenting further that "His newest opera is, it
may be affirmed at once, not only the best that Mr. Damrosch has given us, but it has an astonishing freshness of

feeling, an infectious gusto."[46]   All the reviewers remarked
favorably on the Metropolitan debut of Helen Traubel in the
role of Mary Rutledge.   Still, it is for his services to American music rather than as an opera composer that Walter
Damrosch is remembered today.   He furthered the cause of
American composers, notably George Gershwin, and devoted
many years as radio commentator on symphonic music after
retiring in 1927.[47]

Reginald De Koven was the composer of two operas
that were produced during this period.   The first, The Canterbury Pilgrims, appeared at the Metropolitan during the
1916-17 Season.   The second was Rip Van Winkle, performed
by the Chicago Opera in 1920.   Earlier in his career De
Koven had established himself as the composer of the operetta, Robin Hood, in which appear the songs "Brown October
Ale" and "Oh, Promise Me, " following the path set earlier
by Victor Herbert.   After Robin Hood (1890) De Koven continued to compose, and he also served as music critic of
the New York Herald from 1898-1900 and again from 1907-
1912.[48]   His two operas had librettos by the poet, Percy
MacKaye.   The Canterbury Pilgrims was greeted as a comic
opera in the best tradition.   Rip Van Winkle, which De Koven
termed an American "folk opera,"[49] however, was considered
by the World reviewer as a libretto that "contains nothing
startlingly novel; nor for that matter is the music epoch making."[50]   These two operas did not endure more than one
season, and a second attempt to set the Rip Van Winkle story
to music was unsuccessful.   In this version Rip is the victim
of a sleeping potion with no longer a nagging wife but a
sweetheart.[51]

In the same seasons (1917-18 and 1919-20) another
American composer offered two operas, one at the Metropolitan and one at the Chicago Opera, respectively Henry
Hadley's Azora and Cleopatra's Night.   The librettist for
Azora was David Stevens and Current Opinion captioned its
article on this opera as "The First Genuinely All-American
Operatic Production, " indicating that the cast, authors and
subject matter were all American.   The setting was the con-
quest of Mexico by Cortez, with Azora the daughter of Monte-
zuma, and the New York Times referred to the opera as "a
frankly American cousin of Aida."[52]   The libretto was not
praised generally.[53]

On the occasion of the second opera, Cleopatra's
Night, with a libretto by Alice Leal Pollack, Richard Aldrich,

of the New York Times, reported:

> Cleopatra's Night is the tenth American opera given
> at the Metropolitan Opera House under the present
> management; and it may be said at once that it is
> the best of the ten; the most competent, the most
> skillfully made and the most 'viable.' " [54]

Charles Henry Meltzer wrote under the headline, "Four un-
known operas in one crowded New York week," that this opera had "an unusually good libretto . . . if not quite so dramatic as it might have been, [it] was sane and singable."
He concluded that "the opera forms a real and pleasing
whole." [55] On the other hand, the Sun reported: "doubtless
much will be said about Miss Pollack's libretto but it hardly
seems worthwhile.   The style is stilted and unnatural throughout." [56] The Musical Courier was more specific in its criticism:

> . . . the story is interesting but its action is
> spread out too thinly, or rather, not enough inci-
> dents are devised to succeed the very rapid de-
> velopment of plot in the early moments of the op-
> era. [57]

The opera remained in repertoire a second season and had a
total of seven performances.

During this particular period, when the Chicago Opera
was most active with Cleofonte Campanini as conductor,
Andrew Dipple as artistic director, and Mary Garden as an
outstanding star, new operas were staged in Chicago and
then were brought to New York and to other eastern cities.
The Metropolitan also travelled.   The Metropolitan and Chicago encouragement of American composers was an interesting development in opera, even if the results were not always significant.   Several composers had works performed
in both houses, and the public was not averse to novelty.
Often composers conducted their own works and the press
was favorable to the idea of American opera.   It was a chau-
vinistic period when much was said about "American" culture
and when "the great American opera" was eagerly awaited
with several premature acclamations.   Results were often so
disappointing that press notices by necessity were unfavorable.
With the enlightened attitude of Gatti-Casazzi, Dipple, and
Campanini, new works were commissioned and performed,
and American composers were encouraged.   This was a de-

cided change from the attitude of earlier artistic administrations.

A third American composer whose works were performed at both opera houses was Charles Wakefield Cadman. His previous success was in music based on Indian themes, for he had spent time among the Omaha Indians studying their dances, ceremonials, love calls, and songs.[58] Shanewis was an opera with an Indian theme, and William Chase, writing in the New York Times in 1934, gave the following criticism:

> Shanewis . . . may be recalled as the first opera to deal unaffectedly with the raw material of American places and people. Mrs. Nelle Richmond Eberhardt of Pittsburgh supplied the sketch of 'Shanewis' which Mr. Cadman developed from a single scene of an Indian girl singing in a California drawing room to a tragic sequel on an Oklahoma reservation. A new designer of that Indian scene was Norman Bel-Geddes.[59]

A review of the opera in Musical Courier following its performance commended "the very serviceable book." The review continues to praise the libretto:

> . . . some have objected to the always commonplace, and sometimes even colloquial, language in which the story is told, it is just in this point that Mrs. Eberhardt's libretto is a decided improvement on what other American librettists have turned out. The book of Mona, to refer to that unhappy creation . . . was capital from the literary standpoint, but its philosophy and high flown language, impossible for the stage.[60]

On the other hand, Krehbiel wrote quite another estimate of the libretto: "The plot of the opera was generally voted about the stupidest that could be conceived for such purpose and the dramatic construction of the score betrayed the hand of the apprentice."[61] It was performed eight times in two seasons.

In 1926 A Witch of Salem, also by Charles Cadman, was performed at the Chicago Opera. Not on an Indian subject, it was concerned with the early history of New England. Again with a libretto by Mrs. Eberhardt, the opera prompted the opinion of Felix Browski that, although the book was not

"as technically adroit as the libretti of many authors of
European fame, it is at least much more skillfully contrived
than the books of Victor Herbert's Natoma and Madeleine."[62]
The New York Times praised the use of this ancient story
"mellowed by glamour and romance." The story was written
in "sufficiently broad outlines" and the "end climax delayed
more through music than dramatic design."[63] It was only
performed one season at Chicago but enjoyed numerous performances in amateur and semi-amateur productions.[64]

Two short pieces offered at the Metropolitan on March
12, 1919 were American one-act operas forming a triple bill
with Shanewis. These operas were presented three times in
one season. They were entitled The Legend (music by Joseph
Breil and libretto by Mme. Jutta Belle-Ranske based on the
religious rites of the Hindus) and Temple Dancer (music by
John Adam Hugo, libretto by Jacques Byrne, with the scene
in a mythical Muscovite country). Breil had previously written the score for The Birth of a Nation "and other pictures
and plays when they couldn't afford to hire Victor Herbert."[65]

An American opera first heard in the Chicago Opera
House in 1923 was Theodore Stern's Snowbird. It was repeated in the next season. Aldo Franchetti's Namiko-San was
produced in 1926. Franchetti had had a considerable career
as an opera composer in Italy before coming to America, and
the opera had a Japanese subject. Wl. Frank Harling's A
Light from St. Agnes was also produced in Chicago that same
year with a libretto set by Minnie Maddern Fiske. The
score makes "incidental use" of jazz with saxophones, ban-
jos, and snare drums. It is the story of a philanthropist in
a small Louisiana community. The composer was wildly ac-
claimed by the audience who "pursued, hugged and kissed the
composer in a near-riot."[66] It received, however, only one
performance.

Eagerly awaited, Deems Taylor's opera, The King's
Henchman, was produced at the Metropolitan Opera in 1927.
It was the first of two operas he brought to the Metropolitan.
His second, Peter Ibbetson, was produced in 1931. Both operas were well received, but Peter Ibbetson received generally less enthusiastic critical response. Despite the early
acclaim of The King's Henchman, it is the second that has
been revived recently. Both operas were repeated in subsequent seasons, with The King's Henchman appearing fourteen
times in three seasons and Peter Ibbetson sixteen times in
four seasons. When the latter was revived at the Empire

Festival in 1960, Ross Parmenter commented that "the opera
was worth reviving, and the festival deserves credit for doing it so well."[67] In a long article summarizing American
opera, William B. Chase stated in 1934 that "Deems Taylor
was the only man to strike the popular fancy twice."[68]

One of the most interesting features of the production
of The King's Henchman was the libretto written by the poet-
ess, Edna St. Vincent Millay. The setting was not American
but rather England in the tenth century, and the story was a
variation on the Tristan-Isolde theme. Olin Downes praised
the libretto for its "prevailing beauty and expressiveness of
. . . text." He noted that Miss Millay brought to opera an
"eloquence, dignity and dramatic existence nearer realization
than it has ever been before in this country."[69] Pitts Sandborn, however, felt that the libretto was cast in a "quasi-
Elizabethan idiom" and concluded that "there still seems to
be a haunting futility about the American opera libretto."[70]
There was a touring company for this opera, so as a result
it was presented widely.

With its favorable response, Otto Kahn, President of
the Board of Directors of the Metropolitan Opera, soon announced that Taylor had been commissioned to do a second
work. This was Peter Ibbetson, with libretto by the composer in collaboration with Constance Collier, who had fashioned a play from the Du Maurier novel of the same name.
Again the libretto was adjudged worthy of commendation.
Olin Downes commented that "the libretto of the opera was
its principal strength."[71] The opera's story is that of a
man victimized by a tyrant uncle and who finds escape in
dreams. Musically the opera was not too well received;
what "the critical listeners found wanting was a musical development, a personal accent, which would justify reference
to a Taylor Style."[72] Although Taylor was accused of borrowing too many styles ("Taylor-made"), Peter Ibbetson, on
December 26, 1933, became the first American opera to open
a Metropolitan season.[73]

The first American opera of the new Civic Opera
House in Chicago was Hamilton Forrest's Camille, suggested
by Mary Garden and performed on December 10, 1930. It
was a reworking of Dumas' famous story, so successfully set
to music by Verdi in La Traviata. In Mary Garden's Story
the comment on this opera is as follows: "There were other
people who thought there were a few good moments in Camille,
but I'm afraid none of those people were in Chicago. It was

a pretty dismal failure there.   I just wanted to give an
American a chance and I wanted an American grand opera. "[74]

        Hitherto in the development of American opera, the
form was more or less traditional, following the lines set
by nineteenth century European styles.   Wagner, Puccini,
Verdi, Debussy, Musorgski were the operatic models for inspiration.   American thematic material in the form of Indian
legend, literary themes, or historic incidents constituted the
most "native" aspect of American opera at this time.   With
the 1930's, there developed in American opera an attitude
much more experimental, colloquial, and socially aware.
New operas written by Americans were produced in Europe
and America which indicated both a distinctive maturity and
a concern for indigenous story elements, and particularly
for "American" musical rhythms.   Such composers as George
Antheil, Virgil Thomson, Howard Hanson and Louis Gruenberg, closely followed by George Gershwin and Marc Blitzstein, established firmly the distinctive elements in American
operatic expression.

        Several of the composers who were to figure promi-
nently in the coming years studied abroad.   In Paris in the
1920's American artists, writers and musicians studied under recognized masters in the various disciplines.   Nadia
Boulanger was one such teacher, and under her guidance
Douglas Moore, Virgil Thomson, Aaron Copland, George
Antheil and Marc Blitzstein developed their talents as composers.   Howard Hanson studied at the American Academy
in Rome.   As a result, the music of such composers was
often performed in Europe before it was given in the United
States.   Despite European training, the net result was a distinctive and decidedly "American" contribution.   It was in
Paris that Virgil Thomson (and so many other American
artists) met Gertrude Stein, another expatriate American,
and it was she who provided the libretto for his first opera,
Four Saints in Three Acts.

        George Antheil has been characterized as the enfant
terrible of music.   His experiments with jazz, mechanical
noises and dadaist-surrealist effects outraged or met with
wild enthusiasm, but his opera, Transatlantic (the Hamburg
Opera Company gave the only performances), is regarded
as an important work.   Aufdemberge, in his study of American operas on American themes, writes that "one hesitates
to pronounce it a failure."   He continues:

It is a <u>zeitgeist</u> work, a work which summed up the
whole of a period, but . . . it has not weathered
very well.   But it is an important work, not so
much for what it did, but for what it influenced.
Antheil's importance lies in his bringing coals to
Newcastle, re-importing jazz into American music,
particularly symphonic music, back from Europe
where composers had been incorporating jazz rhythms into their scores.   In this he undoubtedly influenced his friend George Gershwin.   In his use
of opera for satirical purposes, he seems to have
influenced several American musical writers with
Gershwin as perhaps the best example.[75]

The libretto, also written by Antheil, is in thirty-five
scenes, and it presents a caricature of American life with
Helen, a beautiful woman, who tries to attract Hector, a
candidate for the presidency.   Howard describes the plot as
follows: "There was a feverish struggle for power and for
love; scenes at dances, booze parties, political meetings,
attempts at murder, until finally Hector rescued Helen from
suicide on the Brooklyn Bridge and was elected president."[76]
It has an aria sung in a bathtub (à la Hindemith's <u>News of
the Day</u>), scenes in a descending elevator, the use of a movie
screen (which recalls Brecht and Piscator), a scene in a
"Child's" restaurant, and a full ballet.   Needless to say, the
production of the opera would be complex since the third act
alone has twenty-seven changes of scene.[77]   It is an opera
of an "almost tabloid realism" that represented an absolute
break with previous subjects of romantic opera.[78]   The music
was generally considered less striking than the libretto since
it appeared to many critics to be a confusion of styles.   The
plot was difficult to follow, and because of its political satire
some doubted that it could be produced in America.[79]

A second opera by Antheil, <u>Helen Retires</u>, was produced in 1934 at the Juilliard School.   It has a libretto by
John Erskine.   Again there is a mixture of styles, but Gilbert Chase says that:

> . . . with its blend of disparate styles ranging
> from musical comedy to modern dissonance, its
> pseudo jazz effects, its deliberate banality, its
> tunefulness and topicality, deserves, I believe, a
> place with the developing tradition of realistic op-
> era in America. . . .[80]

Later Antheil wrote movie scores in Hollywood and also the opera Volpone, The Brothers, and The Wish. The latter, in a more classical style, has been equated with the music of Shostakovitch. [81]

An experimental opera by an American composer was Virgil Thomson's Four Saints in Three Acts, produced in 1934 by the "Friends and Enemies of Modern Music" in Hartford, Connecticut, with an all-Negro cast. It created a sensation. Later in the month it was brought to New York where it enjoyed a six-week run and was subsequently revived in 1952 in New York and in Paris. [82] Although the libretto by Gertrude Stein was enigmatic, Gilbert Chase termed the opera "a lovely work" and "a masterpiece in originality and invention." [83] Olin Downes in the New York Times, writing under the headline "The Stein-Thomson Concoction," added the sub-heading which read "Despite faddish preciosity, 'Four Saints in Three Acts' Amusing and Absurd, has certain merits." He remarked: "The text is extremely flexible. It has rhythmic and syllabic design." Also he felt that the libretto "genuinely was written to be sung." He concluded that "All this is nine-tenths farce and exhibitionism, but there is a little truth in it, and there are some lessons that American opera composers could well take to heart." [84] It was difficult to make the text "mean something" in traditional terms, for even the stage directions were set to music. Critics were alternately charmed and angered. Aufdemberge equates the lack of characterization and conventional motivated plot structure to a "landscape with figures" attitude of Gertrude Stein--a kind of panoramic view of sainthood. [85] The composer has commented thus on the design of the opera:

> Please do not try to construe the works of this opera literally or to seek in it any abstruse symbolism. If, by means of the poet's liberties with logic and the composer's constant use of the simplest elements in our musical vernacular, something is here evoked of the child-like gaiety and mystical strength of lives devoted in common to a non-materialistic end, the authors will consider their message to have been communicated. [86]

There was a second collaboration by Thomson-Stein in 1947 when Columbia University presented The Mother of Us All under the auspices of the Alice M. Ditson Fund. [87] The opera treats, rather loosely, the life and career of Susan B. Anthony, the feminist leader. Nineteenth century

American figures as widely diverse as General Grant, Daniel
Webster, Lillian Russell and Andrew Jackson appear in the
cast.   Again the effect is panoramic--a landscape with figures
in a libretto without conventional development with "Virgil T."
and "G. S." as narrators.   The opera begins in 1820 with
John Adams and Daniel Webster defeating male suffrage in
Massachusetts, and ends in 1920, a century later, with the
Nineteenth Amendment granting women the right to vote. 88
Near the end a chorus sings what is probably the basic theme
of the opera:

> Susan B. Anthony was very successful we are very
> grateful to Susan B. Anthony because she was so
> successful, she worked for the votes for women and
> she worked for the votes for colored men and she
> was so successful they wrote the word male into
> the constitution of the United States of America,
> dear Susan B. Anthony. 89

The opera received a special citation from the New
York Music Critics Circle after its initial production, and in
1959 was again revived in New York.

In the 1932-33 Season of the Metropolitan Opera a new
work was presented: Louis Gruenberg's The Emperor Jones,
based on Eugene O'Neill's play.   The operatic possibilities
of this expressionist play of an American Negro against a
continual drum-beat background are readily apparent.   However, the opera had no great success.   It included spoken as
well as sung portions, and Pitts Sandborn felt that the spoken
portions were more successful.   "The orchestral commentary,
for the most part, sounded less like the issue of an inspired
imagination than like a remembered convention."90   Gilbert
Chase praised the whole project, declaring that Gruenberg
showed an instinct for theatre, drew on Afro-American rhythms and songs, and wrote an opera concerned with recog-
nizable human beings in a contemporary situation involving
psychological tensions.   He concluded: "the significance of
Emperor Jones is that here at last an American opera appeared that was both musical and dramatic."91   It had nine
performances in two seasons at the Metropolitan and was revived in Chicago in 1946.   In 1930 Gruenberg's opera Jack
and the Beanstalk was performed at the Juilliard School. His
setting of Hudson's novel, Green Mansions, appeared in operatic form on the Columbia Broadcasting System radio performance of September 17, 1937. 92

The next season (1933-34) at the Metropolitan a new
work by Howard Hanson was presented. It was Merry Mount
with libretto by Richard L. Stokes based on a New England
legend and Hawthorne's short story, "The Maypole of Merry-
mount." Lawrence Gilman commented on the libretto in the
New York Herald-Tribune:

> Let it suffice to say that Mr. Stokes has accom-
> plished one of the few opera books to which a self-
> respecting mind can address itself--a libretto of
> strength and dignity and skill, often impassioned
> and glowing in its imagery and rich in its invita-
> tions to the composer. [93]

Olin Downes liked some of the libretto but felt "the story
. . . too cluttered up with incidental diversions." Also he
felt that "Bradford is nothing but a maddened and perverted
sadist who becomes a figure of melodrama, set up to be
knocked down." [94] The story develops the conflicts between
Puritan and Cavalier in New England (the authors of the opera favor the Cavaliers). It had six performances in one
season, and has been revived by other producing groups since.

On the occasion of the premiere of Merry Mount,
William B. Chase in the New York Times summarized twentieth century accomplishments of American opera. In the
article entitled "15th Native Opera in Gatti's Regime," Gatti-
Casazza was credited with extending a "generous gesture toward the forgotten man of music, the American composer."
It was a careful cataloging of American operatic productions,
and not those of the Metropolitan alone. The article ended
with the announcement of the Stein-Thomson opera scheduled
for performance in Hartford: a "futurist" opera. [95] The
article is further evidence of the support that American opera has usually received from the press.

One American opera--a disputed label for this work--
has survived to take its place in American lyric theatre as
a permanent contribution to American opera: Porgy and
Bess, by George Gershwin with libretto by Du Bose Heyward
and lyrics by Ira Gershwin. It initially received a Broadway
production of sixteen weeks and a road tour of three months,
and has been revived several times since--in 1938, in 1942,
and in 1952 when its tour of Europe and South America met
with great acclaim. In 1962 it was revived at the New York
City Opera. Critics have disputed as to the exact genre of
the piece and some characterized it a "folk opera" or a

Broadway musical, but Gilbert Chase pointed out that Gershwin does not use folk tunes to any great degree. Chase concluded that it is "simply an American opera in three acts
and nine scenes. If anyone doubts its operatic proportions,
let it be observed that the manuscript score contains 700
pages of closely written music." [96] Gershwin spent time in
Charleston, South Carolina, studying the "Gullah" dialect and
took part in the "shouting" of the religious services. He also noted the cries of the street vendors of Charleston and
incorporated these effects in his score. Aufdemberge remarks that the Musorgskian influence in this work is similar
to that in Merry Mount in that the chorus serves as the real
protagonist of both operas. He is also enthusiastic about the
quality of the libretto, and holds that the story provides most
of the dramatic interest since the music is largely lyric and
undramatic. [97] The characters are all Negro, and Ewen
states: "Its roots are in the soil of the Negro people, whom
it interprets with humor, tragedy, penetrating characterization, dramatic power, and sympathy." [98] In 1942, during the
long revival of the work, it was given special praise by the
New York Music Critics' Circle.

        Gershwin brought folk elements to America's lyric
stage in a rather romantic light, but it remained for Marc
Blitzstein to provide the bitter social commentary of the
1930's. In The Cradle Will Rock (1937) and No For An Answer (1940) Blitzstein's operas of "social significance" center
about trade unions and social injustice. Gilbert Chase commented on these works as follows:

> Regardless of the ideological content, these operas
> had the merit of coming to grips with problems of
> our times and in the musical language of our times.
> Moreover, they revealed a flair for the theatre that
> was further manifested in a later, non-political
> work: Blitzstein's operatic version of Lillian Hell-
> man's play The Little Foxes, produced in 1949 at
> the New York City Center under the title of Re-
> gina. [99]

In the opinion of Aufdemberge, Blitzstein paves the way for
the direction of the future Broadway musical and serves as
the "musical father of West Side Story and others." [100] His
use of colloquial speech, popular musical language and concern for the social scene gives his work an immediate and,
in the opinion of some critics, a strictly contemporary quality which tends to date his works.

The production of The Cradle Will Rock was an adventurous affair. Written as the Federal Theatre project, it
was censored by government officials for what they considered
politically inflammatory material. On opening night, without
official sanction, its director, Orson Welles, and producer,
John Houseman, and Blitzstein led the audience and actors to
a new theatre and presented the opening performance with only a piano on stage played by Blitzstein and with actors scattered through the audience.   Nineteen performances followed.
When it was revived in 1960 at the New York City Opera,
Winthrop Sargeant objected to the piece as an opera:

> My main objection to the appearance of the work in
> the New York City Opera's repertoire, however, is
> that it is not by any stretch of the aesthetic defini-
> tion an opera, and therefore ought to have been left
> to Broadway (if Broadway wants it), since the re-
> sources of a fine operatic-repertory company are
> completely wasted in its presentation.[101]

One of the strongest influences on Blitzstein can be
traced to his contemporaries, the German composer, Kurt
Weill, and the German playwright, Bertolt Brecht.   Brecht
and Weill first collaborated in Germany on Aufstieg und Fall
der Stadt Mahogonny (Rise and Fall of the City of Mahagonny)
in 1927.   "Borrowing from elements from the political cabaret
and the satiric review, he fused those into the new genre of
topical opera that pungently hit off the temper of the time,"
according to Joseph Machlis.[102]   Following this work came
the most famous piece from this partnership, Die Dreigros-
chenoper (The Three-Penny Opera), in 1928.   It was introduced in August of that year and ran for over 4,000 performances in some 120 German theatres.[103]   After fleeing Germany in 1933 for Paris, Weill came to the United States in
1935 and quickly established himself on Broadway with new
collaborators in such works as Johnny Johnson with Paul
Green in 1935, Knickerbocker Holiday with Maxwell Anderson
in 1938, and Lady in the Dark with Moss Hart in 1941.   But,
with Elmer Rice's Street Scene in 1947, Down in the Valley
in 1948 with Arnold Sundgaard, and Lost in the Stars in 1949
with Maxwell Anderson, Weill gave the American theatre
"works that transcended the level of popular entertainment."[104]
Weill had always been concerned with American themes.   His
first opera, Mahagonny, is set in the state of Alabama where,
in a kind of modern morality play, he exposes corruption and
hypocrisy.   Writing in Modern Music in 1937, Weill expressed
his hopes for American opera and that the American musical

would replenish and revitalize the opera form. He was enthusiastic about the Federal Theatre and also felt that films
offered many new opportunities. He used the term "musical
theatre" in this article and stressed that opera was originally
a folk art form. [105] His whole career points to this belief.
His work, Down in the Valley, which includes several authentic Appalachian folk songs written especially for school performance, was performed widely, and Street Scene and Lost
in the Stars were both revived in Ford Foundation-sponsored
seasons of American opera by the New York City Opera in
1958 and 1959.

        Several operas appeared which retain traditional forms
and stylistic content. In 1935 John Lawrence Seymour's In
the Pasha's Garden opened at the Metropolitan. It was the
final American opera premiere produced by Gatti-Casazza.
This was a one-act opera with libretto by H. G. Dwight, and
it appeared on a double bill with La Boheme and starred
Lawrence Tibbett. It had three performances in the season. [106] An opera based on Browning's poem, The Ring and
the Book, was produced at the Metropolitan in 1937. It was
written by Richard Hageman with libretto by Arthur Goodrich.
There were only two performances at the Metropolitan, after
it had been performed in Freiburg, Germany, five years
earlier. [107] As previously mentioned, Damrosch's The Man
Without a Country, which received an enthusiastic audience
reaction, was only performed three times in one season.
In 1947 Bernard Rogers' The Warrior was a new work offered at the Metropolitan, but it had only two performances
that year. This one-act opera with libretto by Norman Cor-
win was based on the Biblical story of Samson and Delilah.
It had received the Alice M. Ditson Fund Prize of 1946. [108]

        Gian-Carlo Menotti, of Italian birth but with American
musical training (Curtis Institute), produced his first opera,
Amelia Goes to the Ball, in 1938. He has subsequently en-
riched the literature of opera with a number of widely performed works. Menotti has held to a lyric, romantic opera,
drawing heavily on the verismo style and musical cliches of
Puccini, despite the widespread experimentation of other
composers. Whether he is Italian or American is often
posed and Pitts Sandborn remarks:

        To make an end of it all, Amelia is an agreeable
        example of modern Italian opera, vivacious and
        tuneful, sung in English. American it is not, ex-
        cept through geographical accident. [109]

Following the success of Amelia the National Broadcasting Company commissioned Menotti to write an opera,
The Old Maid and the Thief, performed in 1939. Then,
again, in 1942, the Metropolitan presented an opera of Menotti's, The Island God, which appeared only three times in the
season. After winning a Guggenheim Fellowship in 1945,
Menotti composed a new opera, The Medium, which resulted
in a Broadway production in conjunction with another one-act
Menotti opera, The Telephone. These two operas have been
widely done since throughout the United States. In 1950 the
well-received The Consul was awarded the Pulitzer Prize
and the New York Drama Critics' Award and was even produced at La Scala, the first work written in America so to
be honored. Other operas of Menotti's which have met with
considerable success are Amahl and the Night Visitors, a
one-act nativity opera, and The Saint of Bleecker Street, an
opera about Italian-Americans, which won for the composer
his second Pulitzer Prize. Menotti writes his own librettos
and often serves as his own director. Ewen comments on
Menotti's musical style, characterizing it as "eclectic": "It
can be popular or esoteric, realistic or romantic, cacopho-
nous or lyrical, poetic or sardonic--in any case it meets
demands of good theater with remarkable effectiveness."[110]

Two composers who enjoy high esteem in American
music complete this early twentieth century survey of American opera. They are Aaron Copland and Douglas Moore.
Copland has not contributed to operatic literature so much as
to symphonic work, but, like Douglas Moore, he has drawn
on American folk music strongly. Copland's first operatic
work, The Second Hurricane, was entitled "a play-opera for
school performance" and was set in the Middle West. It was
first performed in New York in 1937. His much more ambitious The Tender Land was first performed by the New
York City Opera in 1954. It was coolly received, and Time
magazine declared that the music "held as little punch as the
libretto."[111] Aufdemberge wrote of the libretto:

> Its plot comes out of the West, a region Copland
> has treated often in the past. It is a twentieth
> century pastoral opera, the New York sophisticate
> paying tribute to the past, to the folk without folk-
> siness.[112]

The libretto was written by "Horace Everett," a pseudonym,
and his identity has remained a well kept secret. The opera
was revised from two to three acts, and in this form it is

now performed.   The original idea for the opera was based
on the collection of photographs taken by Walker Evans and
James Agee and published in Let Us Now Praise Famous
Men, concerned with rural conditions of the Southern and
Western areas of America in the 1930's.113

        Douglas Moore's contribution to American opera has
been large, and he has attempted to deal with American
themes and situations.   His The Devil and Daniel Webster
was favorably received in New York in 1938.   The libretto,
by the composer, is based on Stephen Vincent Benet's short
story of a man who makes a pact with the Devil.   It is in
one act and was revived successfully in 1959 at the New York
City Opera.   It has been popular in college opera workshops.
His next opera, written in 1950, is entitled Giants in the
Earth, and is based on the novel by Rolvaag, with libretto by
Arnold Sundgaard.   It was awarded the Pulitzer Prize in 1951.
In 1957 the Central City Opera House in Colorado presented
what is probably Moore's most noted work, The Ballad of
Baby Doe.   The libretto was written by John Latouche and
the opera won the New York Music Critics' Award in 1958.
It has been repeated for several seasons at the New York
City Opera where it has remained a staple of the American
repertoire.   It has been termed "An operatic Western," and
"The Girl of the Silver West."   The New York Herald-Tribune
commented: "Apart from Porgy and Bess and The Mother of
Us All, no single American work has mirrored so clearly the
life of an era and a people."114   Moore subsequently wrote
The Wings of the Dove, based on the novel of Henry James,
which was presented by the New York City Opera in 1961.

                                Notes

1.   David Ewen, Encyclopedia of the Opera (New York: Hill
         and Wang, 1963), p. 354.

2.   Ibid., pp. 364-5.

3.   Donald Jay Grout, A Short History of Opera (New York:
         Columbia University Press, 1965), II, p. 491.

4.   Ibid., p. 492.

5.   Paul Henry Lang, ed., One Hundred Years of Music in
         America, Philip L. Miller (New York: G. Schirmer,
         Inc., 1961), p. 54.

6. John Tasker Howard, Our American Music (New York: Thomas Y. Crowell Company, 1954), p. 200.

7. Ronald L. Davis, A History of Opera in the American West (Englewood Cliffs, N.J.: Prentice-Hall, Inc., 1965), p. 8.

8. Ibid., pp. 8-13.

9. Ewen, op. cit., pp. 4-5.

10. Lang, op. cit., p. 57.

11. Leon Maurice Aufdemberge, "An Analysis of the Dramatic Construction of American Opera on American Themes 1896-1958" (Unpublished Ph.D. dissertation, Northwestern University, 1965), p. 30.

12. Ibid., p. 41.

13. Henry Edward Krehbiel, Chapters of Opera (New York: Henry Holt and Co., 1909), p. 262.

14. Ibid., p. 262.

15. Gilbert Chase, America's Music from the Pilgrims to the Present (New York: McGraw-Hill Book Co., 1955), p. 634.

16. Aufdemberge, op. cit., p. 47.

17. Ewen, op. cit., p. 318.

18. John Frederick Cone, Oscar Hammerstein's Manhattan Opera Company (Norman, Okla.: University of Oklahoma Press, 1966), p. 22.

19. Lang, op. cit., pp. 68-70.

20. Krehbiel, op. cit., p. 367.

21. Ewen, op. cit., p. 288.

22. Cone, op. cit., pp. 280-84.

23. Irving Kolodin, The Story of the Metropolitan Opera, 1883-1950 (New York: Alfred A. Knopf, 1953), p. 25.

24. Cone, op. cit., p. 102.

25. Ewen, op. cit., p. 340.

26. Aufdemberge, op. cit., p. 64.

27. Philadelphia Public Ledger, February 26, 1911, p. 1.

28. Harper's Weekly, March 4, 1911, p. 1.

29. Literary Digest, March 18, 1911.

30. Musical Courier, March 22, 1911.

31. Kolodin, op. cit., pp. 262-3.

32. Ibid., p. 285.

33. "The Hoodoo That Pursues Music Made in America."
     Current Opinion (March, 1914).

34. Kolodin, op. cit., p. 252.

35. H. Earle Johnson, Operas on American Subjects (Bos-
     ton: Coleman-Ross Co., 1963), p. 80.

36. Arthur J. Bloomfield, The San Francisco Opera 1923-
     1961 (New York: Appleton-Century-Crofts, Inc.,
     1961), p. 4.

37. Johnson, op. cit., p. 80.

38. Ibid.

39. Kolodin, op. cit., p. 268.

40. Henry Edward Krehbiel, More Chapters of Opera (New
     York: Henry Holt and Co., 1919), p. 265.

41. Henry Krehbiel, New York Tribune, February 27, 1913.

42. New York Evening Post, February 28, 1913.

43. Aufdemberge, op. cit., p. 102.

44. Ibid., pp. 103-4.

45. Olin Downes, New York Times, May 12, 1937.

46. Lawrence Gilman, New York Herald Tribune, May 12, 1937.

47. Aufdemberge, op. cit., p. 100.

48. Ewen, op. cit., p. 107.

49. Chase, op. cit., p. 619.

50. New York World, January 31, 1920.

51. Ewen, op. cit., p. 432.

52. Current Opinion, February, 1918.

53. Johnson, op. cit., p. 57.

54. New York Times, January 31, 1920.

55. Charles Henry Meltzer, Arts & Decorations, February, 1920.

56. New York Sun-Herald, February 1, 1920.

57. Musical Courier, February 5, 1920.

58. Ewen, op. cit., p. 68.

59. William B. Chase, "15th Native Opera in Gatti's Regime," New York Times, February 11, 1934.

60. Musical Courier, March 28, 1918.

61. Krehbiel, More Chapters of Opera, p. 412.

62. Christian Science Monitor, December 11, 1926.

63. New York Times, December 26, 1926.

64. Wallace Brockway and Herbert Weinstock, The World of Opera (New York: Pantheon Books, 1962), p. 380.

65. Chase, New York Times, February 11, 1934.

66. Johnson, op. cit., p. 59.

67. Parmenter, New York Times, July 23, 1960.

68. Chase, New York Times, February 11, 1934.

69. Olin Downes, New York Times, February 20, 1927.

70. Pitts Sandborn, "The King's Henchman," New York Telegram, February 18, 1937.

71. Olin Downes, New York Times, February 22, 1931.

72. Kolodin, op. cit., p. 420.

73. Brockway and Weinstock, op. cit., p. 382.

74. Mary Garden and Louis Biancolli, Mary Garden's Story (New York: Simon and Schuster, 1951), p. 239.

75. Aufdemberge, op. cit., p. 141.

76. Howard, op. cit., pp. 530-1.

77. Aufdemberge, op. cit., p. 145.

78. Joseph Machlis, Introduction to Contemporary Music (New York: W. W. Norton & Co., 1961), p. 631.

79. Johnson, op. cit., p. 29.

80. Chase, op. cit., p. 574.

81. Ibid., p. 575.

82. Ewen, op. cit., p. 162.

83. Chase, op. cit., p. 644.

84. Olin Downes, New York Times, February 25, 1934.

85. Aufdemberge, op. cit., p. 223.

86. Virgil Thomson quoted in Chase, op. cit., p. 644.

87. The Alice M. Ditson fund has provided funds for the production of a number of American opera premieres including Bernard Rogers' The Warrior (1946), Virgil Thomson's The Mother of Us All (1947), Gian-

Carlo Menotti's The Medium (1948), Douglas Moore's Giants in the Earth (1951), Vittorio Giannini's The Boor (1958).

88. Aufdemberge, op. cit., pp. 229-30.

89. Gertrude Stein, Last Operas and Plays (New York: Rinehart & Co., 1948), p. 82.

90. New York World-Telegram as quoted in The Metropolitan Opera Annals, William H. Seltsam, ed. (H. W. Wilson Company: New York), p. 563.

91. Chase, op. cit., p. 641.

92. Ibid.

93. New York Herald-Tribune, February 11, 1934.

94. Olin Downes, New York Times, February 11, 1934.

95. William B. Chase, "15th Native Opera in Gatti's Regime," New York Times, February 11, 1934.

96. Chase, op. cit., p. 638.

97. Aufdemberge, op. cit., p. 124.

98. Ewen, op. cit., p. 403.

99. Chase, op. cit., p. 646.

100. Aufdemberge, op. cit., p. 164.

101. Winthrop Sargeant, The New Yorker, February 20, 1960.

102. Machlis, op. cit., p. 566.

103. Ewen, op. cit., p. 543.

104. Chase, op. cit., p. 647.

105. Kurt Weill, "The Future of Opera in America," Modern Music, 14:183-87.

106. Brockway and Weinstock, op. cit., p. 384.

107.   Ibid., p. 385.

108.   Ewen, op. cit., p. 434.

109.   Brockway and Weinstock, op. cit., p. 384.

110.   Ewen, op. cit., p. 314.

111.   Chase, op. cit., p. 510.

112.   Aufdemberge, op. cit., p. 195.

113.   Ibid., p. 192.

114.   New York Herald-Tribune quoted in Johnson, p. 77.

Chapter II

THE CHARACTERISTICS OF DRAMATIC ELEMENTS

An essential corollary to historical study of opera
librettos is consideration of the dramatic values of the works.
By an examination of the body of accumulated dramatic criticism available, general conclusions concerning the nature and
characteristics of dramatic elements emerge.

Theatrical values have been a subject for critical discussion since the time of Plato and Aristotle. Why are plays
performed? What is the nature of artistic response? What
elements can be generalized therefrom? Do common bonds
of experience and artistic necessity unite all dramatic performances? If so, what are they? If "laws" of dramatic
construction can be isolated as valid for all drama, what attitude follows? Should these rules hold to the letter, or
should there be a continued search for dramatic values? The
connection between contemporary literary insights and those
of earlier critics is of interest, and this chapter explores
some areas of dramatic criticism to arrive at a valid definition of dramatic values.

Aristotle is the main source of Greek thought on the
subject of dramatic theory. His Poetics contain observations
of fifth century drama and that of his own time, and his
work, in many respects, is a critique of Plato's views on
art and poetry. Plato states in The Republic that poets are
moved by "divine inspiration" rather than by conscious "art"
as Aristotle later held. Poets create in a state of frenzy
and use lies, he writes. As a result, the poet's work has
no basis in reality. There is war between poets and philoso-
phers and, in the ideal state, Plato will tolerate only "manly"
poets--those who extol the "good." He refuses to be hypnotized by poets for he feels their stimulation to the passions
is basically harmful.[1]

In answer to Plato's negative estimate of the poet and
his work and, in part, to define critical terminology and to
study poetic methods, Aristotle wrote the Poetics. Unfortu-

nately, Aristotle's work has come down to us in the form of
incomplete lecture notes but, nevertheless, all later western
dramatic criticism derives from Aristotle. In the Renaissance
critical attitudes were judged valid to the extent that they
agreed or disagreed with Aristotle. Such an overriding importance of Aristotle as the basic point of departure makes
it imperative to understand him as nearly as possible. F. L.
Lucas, in commenting on the Poetics of Aristotle has written:

> But the Poetics, ill-written, incomplete lecture-
> notes as they are, provide even now the basis for
> an inquiry into the nature of drama. Those few
> pages ask, if they do not answer, much that we
> need to know.[2]

Francis Fergusson points out that the Poetics should be used
as an "aid to reflection" and should be read slowly.[3] S. H.
Butcher, in his invaluable commentary on Aristotle, says
"There is a special risk at the present day attending any such
attempt to bring together his (Aristotle's) fragmentary remarks and present them in a connected form."[4] And Gassner, in his introductory remarks to Butcher's translation,
states that the Poetics is a "fragmentary manual . . . Yet
implicated in it is virtually everything that makes esthetics
truly and deeply practical rather than an airy exercise for
life's and society's ineffectuals."[5] Aristotle, then, tried to
bring a rational approach to a process and a body of human
achievement.

What then is the nature of Aristotle's observations?
In the Poetics he discusses the general subject of poetry,
which he points out as a mode of imitation (mimesis). Poetry he sees as being of several different forms: epic, lyric,
and dramatic (tragedy and comedy). It is with this last category that this study is most vitally concerned. As Aristotle's
chapter on comedy is fragmentary, it is not possible to discuss it in detail. Tragedy, however, is more fully treated
and is the principal source of information for Aristotle's theory of drama. Here, Aristotle defines tragedy as composed
of six elements: in order of importance, plot, character,
thought, language, music and spectacle. The last, spectacle,
concerns the property-man rather than the poet. As plot is
for Aristotle of primary importance, he devotes much discussion to this element of tragedy. Structurally, plot must
be a complete whole with a beginning, a middle, an end, and
a logical unity. This unity must not be too vast and not only
a unity of the hero, but essentially a unity of action. The

subject of the plot must be an ideal truth holding in general
to figures from traditional legend. Plots are divided into
the worst, episodic and not causally connected, and the best,
those with surprise and the use of the irony of fate. Plots
are also further classified as "simple" or "complex" and
this leads to the definition of the elements of plot. These
elements are peripeteia, or reversal of the situation; anag-
norisis, or recognition of persons, things or facts; and pathos,
or catastrophe. The ideal plot is "complex" and excites pity
and fear. The unhappy ending is best, although it is certainly not the most popular. Scenic effects are an inferior method for achieving a dramatic effect and the best is the one
which arises from situations in the play. [6]

The second element, that of character, is also discussed by Aristotle. A character should be good or fine,
true to human nature, true to itself or consistent, probably
and logically constructed, and idealized. Practical rules are
also set forth by Aristotle and include a discussion of the
elements of conception and the elements of execution of tragedy. The writer must place the scenes before his own eyes
and act them out to himself to achieve sympathy with the
characters of the play. Also he should sketch a bare out-
line of the action before attempting to fill in details and episodes. A subsequent section gives additional rules to follow,
including careful attention to the complication and denouement of the plot, and attention to the overall unity of poetic
excellence to achieve an organic whole. He touches on the
thought and ideas of tragedy, diction, grammar, and style.
Mastery of metaphor is much the most important quality of
diction. [7]

It is generally recognized that Aristotle deepened and
expanded Plato's views. There are several points, however,
on which they disagree. Aristotle believes that the work itself can be judged on its merits as a work of art and need
not be judged in terms of moral standards as did Plato.
Aristotle thinks, contrary to Plato, that ugly objects can be
imitated and can give pleasure. The exciting of emotions
by tragedy is to Aristotle an agreeable circumstance in that
it allows purgation or releasing of these emotions (catharsis).
Plato, however, thinks the effect morally dangerous. Finally,
Aristotle believes the universal truth of poetry to be an
overriding consideration and, hence, a poetic treatment to
be more valid than an historical one. The ultimate truths
of poetry, then, are more valuable than the factual ones of
history. [8] Thus Aristotle sets about to analyze the pro-

cesses of artistic creation and provides a thoughtful, if incomplete, commentary and an important basis for judgment
in drama.

After Aristotle the next critic of importance is Horace
whose Ars Poetica sets forth his ideas on drama in conform-
ity with the Poetics. His influence on later Renaissance
drama was equal to that of Aristotle. His view of drama
varies in his emphasis on "decorum," whereby every aspect
of the work must be appropriate to the whole, with the choice
of subject, characterization and form, style and tone of the
expression united in a total consistency. Horace believes it
important to follow Greek models of playwrighting, advising
the poet to write for both pleasure and instruction. Genres
must not be mixed, and deeds of violence and revolting incidents should not be enacted before the audience but told or
narrated to the audience. A play should contain five acts,
with only three speaking characters on stage at any one time.
The chorus should be fully integrated into the action without
irrelevant choral interludes. These points of consistency or
"decorum" were important to French and English playwrights
and critics in the seventeenth and eighteenth centuries.[9]

From the time of the Latin writers to the early Renaissance, the amount and quality of dramatic criticism were
not significant and were chiefly to be found in the writings
of the early Church Fathers and poets, invluding St. Ambrose,
Lactantius, St. John Chrysostom, Prudentius, and St. Au-
gustine. Their attitude was almost exclusively moral, and
their works, with other scattered writings, at most indicate
a transition between Horace and the Renaissance.[10]

Horace was the most influential writer until full re-
covery of Aristotle by way of the Moslem East. In the thir-
teenth century, a Latin translation provided the first Western
contact with Aristotle, although the original text was misin-
terpreted and garbled. In 1498, Valla's Latin translation was
based on the Greek, and this was followed in 1508 by the
more accurate Aldine edition of the Greek text. In 1536,
Greek and Latin texts were published together, and in 1548
a first complete commentary on the text was published by
Robortello. Additional commentaries followed--Minturno,
1559; Castelvetro, 1570; Scaliger, 1561; and Sir Philip Sidney, 1583. Minturno emphasized the didactic qualities of poetry, stressing its unilitarian values. Castelvetro stressed
the necessity of the unities, an idea to be much debated by
Renaissance scholars, and first formulated the unity of place.

Scaliger used a Senecan approach and emphasized the violence
of tragedy and its portrayal of unsavory characters. He also
tried to harmonize Aristotle's views with those of Horace.
Finally, Sir Philip Sidney, an English poet and critic with a
wide knowledge of Italian commentators, stressed the use of
classical models in playwrighting, citing Gorboduc, an English drama based upon classical models and often called the
first English tragedy. [11]

The total effect of Renaissance criticism was a reaction against theological interpretations of drama and poetry
and a reaffirmation of the independence of the humanistic
ideal. A new classicism resulted in a new set of "rules"
in Renaissance France, with emphasis on rhetoric and dramatic form for a clarification of a poetic theory. [12] Under
the influence of these new rules, Corneille, Racine, and
Molière wrote their plays, but not always to the satisfaction
of dramatic theorists. Le Cid is an outstanding case in
point. A great controversy developed over this play and
raised the basic question of "the rules" versus probability.
The controversy became so great that when the French Academy was called upon to pass a judgment, its opinion that
Corneille should observe restraint, order and social unity
colored not only Corneille's career but those of Racine and
Molière who followed. [13]

In England, Dryden was influenced by the French, and
"An Essay of Dramatic Poesy" shows this in his discussion
of the unities and of dramatic construction. In fact, Allan
Gilbert thinks that "So well does Dryden represent Corneille
that his essay almost serves as a substitute for the original." [14]

A rewarding insight into English criticism is the attitudes of critics towards Shakespeare. Such an exploration
can also give a further definition of dramatic elements.
Shakespearean criticism has developed in two main schools:
one emphasizes and elaborates theory based on Aristotelian
thought, and the second relies on sensibility. This latter
approach is subjective and can be colloquially called "playing
it by ear." [15]

In the seventeenth century, there are glancing references to Shakespeare in a preface by Webster to The White
Devil. Ben Jonson, however, in a laudatory verse in
Shakespeare's first folio, published in 1623, calls Shakespeare
the "soul of the age . . . for all time." Heminge and Con-

dell, in the 1623 folio, write that Shakespeare never
blotted out a line. Dryden, as a dramatic critic concerned with neo-classic "rules," praises Shakespeare for
his understanding of the passions, but thinks his manner
of expression was faulty. Near the end of the seventeenth
century, in 1692, Thomas Rymer wrote a "Short View of
Tragedy" in which he also holds that Shakespeare should
have followed the rules. One of Rymer's rules was "poetic justice," or a system of rewards and punishments in
drama. He was also the first critic to return to the
sources of Shakespeare's plays.[16]

    The beginning of the eighteenth century also
marks the beginning of a change of attitude toward
Shakespeare. In 1709, Nicholas Rowe, editor and playwright, published an edition of Shakespeare in six volumes. In a second edition, published in 1714 in nine
volumes, the plays were divided into scenes, the spell-
ing was modernized, and stage directions were added.
The collection also contained the first biography of
Shakespeare which referred to him as "a child of nature." Alexander Pope, too, was concerned with the
neo-classic "rules," but in a preface to an edition of
Shakespeare in 1725, he praised Shakespeare's ability
to draw characters almost like living individuals. Samuel
Johnson in his Preface to Shakespeare (1768) stresses
an approach of Christian humanism but exempts Shakespeare from the "rules" and counterattacks. As Gassner
points out: "the freedom of Elizabethan form was no
longer considered a breach of neo-classical decorum,
requiring rigid improvement and purification by men of
sophisticated taste."[17] The emphasis upon the importance
of Shakespeare's characterization continued with such pre-
Romantic writers as Richardson, Whatley, and Morgann.

    In Germany in the late eighteenth century, Shakespeare
was much admired. Gotthold Lessing was inspired by Shakespeare, and to Shakespeare is credited much of the inspiration for the German Romantic movement. Lessing translated
twenty-two of Shakespeare's plays. Johann Gottfried Herder,
who was a Shakespearian critic, knew and influenced Goethe
in his Sturm und Drang period. The brothers August Wilhelm
and Karl Wilhelm Friedrich von Schlegel were early admirers
of Shakespeare. August Wilhelm gave a series of influential
lectures on dramatic art and literature in 1808 and also
translated Shakespeare, considering him a titanic genius. He

employed the Promethean metaphor to describe the scope
of Shakespeare's intellect. Hazlitt, in England, was
strongly influenced by Schlegel and he, too, wrote sound
criticism on Shakespeare. His reference to Macbeth as
"a huddling together of fierce extremes" is such an example.[18]

Coleridge was the origin of much of the inspiration
for modern criticism. His subjectivism and impressionism
have created a climate for modern criticism, and Clark, in
reference to Coleridge's "Lectures on Shakespeare," terms
him "all-embracing and inspirational."[19] Some critics accuse him of digressions, but his work suggests more than
it illustrates. As George Watson points out in The Literary
Critics, no English critic has so excelled at providing pro-
fitable points of departure for twentieth century critics.
Coleridge attacked the neo-Aristotelian dramatic criticism,
the concept of the three unities, and the French neo-classical
critics such as Voltaire. He defended Shakespeare against
such critics who see the plays as "irregular" and "ill-as-
sorted structures of gigantic proportions." He emphasizes
Shakespeare's "organic" structure as opposed to the "mechanical regularity of structure" sought by the earlier critics.[20]

The late nineteenth and twentieth centuries witnessed
a growth of knowledge that placed constantly greater require-
ments on dramatic criticism. When knowledge is brought to
bear on knowledge, the result can be a criticism extremely
wide in contextual reference or one excessively narrow. The
Cambridge School of Sir James Frazer, Jane Harrison, F.
M. Cornford, and Sir Gilbert Murray, with its reassessment of classical studies in the light of new knowledge of
myth, ritual and primitive societies, forms a significant approach to twentieth century criticism. This group employed
the insights of comparative anthropology to enrich literary
studies. The psychological approach, another view developed
in the writings of Freud, was followed by Ernest Jones, T.
S. Eliot, F. R. Leavis, and Robert Heilman. This "school"
has provided some of the most provocative dramatic criticism
of the twentieth century. The Oedipus Complex, developed
by Freud, has been applied with great effect to Hamlet, and
Ernest Jones in his Hamlet and Oedipus outlines the motives
of Hamlet in terms of twentieth century psychology. Hamlet's relationship to his parents is developed from textual
references in the play and Freudian psychological theory.
Often sensational, this approach has received more than its

share of popular attention, and contention, still tempestuous,
has not abated.   John Dover Wilson objects to this approach,
pointing out that Shakespeare was interested only in showing
a tragedy and in sending the audience home with a sense of
renewal.   A life antecedent to the play for a character is
not important.   He must be accepted as he is when the curtain goes up, and his life beyond his two or three hours on
the stage is irrelevant. [21]

        Modern Shakespearian criticism in the work of the
New Critics or, as characterized by the more generic term,
"the image hunters," is closely related to the psychological
approach, as it has been to earlier critical work.   Dryden
in the seventeenth century noted the images of Shakespeare
and Aristotle praised Sophocles' use of metaphor.   The New
Critics, however, renewed emphasis on the use of language.
G. Wilson Knight, I. A. Richards and Carolyn Spurgeon have
been important in this school.   Richards tested student perception and sensibility to language without traditional "tags"
of title and author, concentrating on language to the exclusion
of adventitious aids to acceptance or rejection.   Spurgeon
counted the images in Shakespeare to arrive at generaliza-
tions as to his personal and literary uses of this literary
device.   G. Wilson Knight, on the other hand, resembles
Coleridge in his attempt to "tune in" on a Shakespearian
play, distinguishing "temporal"--the unfolding tale--and "spa-
tial" elements--the spiritual atmosphere particular to each
play.   This group is also concerned with "theme" or
thought. [22]

        Another modern group, the neo-Aristotelians, with
Robert Crane as their spokesman, attempts to reconsider the
structure of drama and redress the undue influence on character.   (Aristotle considered plot of prime importance.)
Stanley Edgar Hyman distinguishes the neo-Aristotelians,
critics who induce from poetic practice, from the neo-Cole-
ridge, critics who deduce from philosophic concept. [23]

        The last group to be mentioned has a point of view
similar to that of John Dewey.   Literature should be sub-
jected to all the highly specialized tools now available to
modern criticism.   Literature and the aesthetic experience
resemble all experience, and, as a result, can be examined
in the same manner. [24]

        Hyman underlines the fact that Freud, Marx, Darwin,
and Frazer have been largely responsible for the formulation

of the assumptions of modern critics. No modern critic accepts them all, but all are influential. So much information
must be assimilated to read literature and the critics ade-
quately in a twentieth century manner that committal to an
exclusive approach proves unduly limiting. Literature is not
a body of knowledge to establish the personal life of the playwright. Nor is it a sociological tract, nor yet a political
tract nor a construction reenforcing primitive rituals. In
some way it combines all these approaches for, as Aristotle
would also hold, dramatic literature is, after all, an art.
It organizes, explores, and gives expression to human experience with a validity all its own. The proper function of the
artist is to achieve, technically, what his audience can appreciate through intelligent perception.

An approach to dramatic criticism which developed
after the neo-classic seventeenth century was connected with
domestic and bourgeois serious drama. In Elizabethan
England, the serious play on a domestic theme was not unusual; two such plays were Arden of Feversham (1592) and
The Yorkshire Tragedy (1608). This type of play, however,
developed as an important genre in the eighteenth century
and as a reaction to the immorality of the Restoration stage
and critical reassessment of neo-classic rules under the impulse of the Romantic spirit. Diderot advocated such a new
type to replace classic drama in his essay entitled "On Dramatic Poetry" in 1758. He called for prose rather than
verse and contemporary characters instead of kings. He
wanted the theatre utilitarian, and felt the theatre should replace the church and the courts as the leading moral institution. This emphasis on middle-class values bore fruit in
Germany, too, in the work of Lessing. In his Hamburgische
Dramaturgie of 1769, he rejects villain and martyr plays and
urges his contemporaries to turn from the classical standards
of France to the more flexible English drama as a model.
Beaumarchais, just before the French Revolution, also rejected heroic tragedy for domestic drama.[25] His desire was
to dramatize everyday happenings, and in his "Essay on Serious Drama," a preface to Eugenie, he states: "What do I
care of revolutions in Rome and Egypt?" He wished to por-
tray "the touching spectacle of domestic happiness."[26] He
wanted verisimilitude in every detail of scenery, and he recommended excision of act breaks and substitution of panto-
mime interludes. Here he anticipates Strindberg's theory of
uninterrupted action. Beaumarchais' two best known plays
are The Barber of Seville and The Marriage of Figaro,
whose most famous operatic settings were by Rossini and

Mozart respectively. Figaro is representative of the rising
middle class, and in the plays Beaumarchais is outspoken
against the monarchy and current social abuses in late eighteenth century France. The Marriage of Figaro, written after
the Barber, brings Figaro back to the stage--a witty, ingen-
ious, gay descendent of the servant of Spanish drama, but
far more outspoken. Louis XVI forbade it for several years,
but, when the King finally permitted a production, it appeared
sixty-eight successive times only five years before the Revolution. 27

     Following the Revolution, Napoleon lifted the restric-
tions on the number of theatres in Paris and a much freer
atmosphere developed. Music became important in the productions of smaller houses, and from such performances a
new form, melodrama--drama with music--was created.
Victor Hugo, as an exponent of Romanticism in his 1827
preface to Cromwell, attacked the classical tradition of
French drama. He urged a return to French national history
for subjects and recommended a disregard for the "unities."
He felt, too, that tragedy should mix the sublime with the
grotesque--the comic and tragic--as did Shakespeare and, in
addition, he recommended and wrote a freer verse that was
a rejection of the standard classical Alexandrine. 28

     Beside this Romantic view, a naturalist drama found
its strongest theorist in Alexandre Dumas, fils. He advocated the usefulness of drama: theatre as an end to expose
vice and remedy evil. (His father before him had been, in-
terestingly enough, of the party of Hugo's Romanticism.)
Henry Becque was a playwright of this school, and his play,
Les Corbeaux, remains an example of this more utilitarian
point of view. Emile Zola next provided the strongest theoretical basis for Naturalism. He attacked the school of the
"well-made-play," that mechanical form of Scribe and Sardou,
and spoke for greater sincerity and scientific truth about
man. On the ideas of Darwin he built a dramatic theory
emphasizing the determinist quality of man's life. For Zola,
environmental controls and scientific impersonality should
permit audiences to appreciate man's development more
clearly. If Scribe wanted to entertain, the Naturalists, under
Zola, practically ignored the audience. This led to a further
consideration of the earlier fourth-wall theory of Beaumarchais and Diderot, which was to change the style of acting
and scenic design completely. 29 With the new theoretical
basis, the theatre of Ibsen, Strindberg, and Chekov logically
followed. The work of the Duke of Saxe-Meiningen and Con-

stantin Stanislavsky put into practice these new naturalistic
theories, transforming the tone and substance of twentieth
century drama.

A number of modern critics have analyzed Aristotle's
Poetics closely. Scholarship has attempted a reconstruction
of Aristotle's text as accurately as possible. Controversy
continues, whatever the translation, but the rational attempt
has been made in this century to interpret Aristotle in ac-
cordance with his meaning. Expanded methods of research
have made scholarship more relevant, and the increasingly
precise use of mythological, archeological, psychological and
historical material have made it particularly rewarding.

Butcher's standard English translation and commentary
of the Poetics, still held in high regard, appeared in 1894.
Gassner, in a fourth edition of Butcher's translation and
commentary, 1951, praises Butcher's work. He points out
that:

> Although it is still possible to disagree on particu-
> lar readings of the text and on details of transla-
> tion, the reader can turn to Butcher's memorable
> book with confidence. As the notes show us,
> Butcher substantiated disputable points with a pains-
> taking scholarship that belongs to the grand tradi-
> tion of English learning. Moreover, Butcher's
> commentary, 'Aristotle's Theory of Poetry and the
> Fine Arts,' appended to the Greek text and the
> translation, leaves nothing to be desired; nothing
> that Butcher could have supplied without venturing
> into unresolved discussions of modern drama. [30]

Gassner in his own introduction points out Aristotle's
value for twentieth century critics: "He sets later criticism
a lesson in intelligent, systematic, and inductive procedure."[31]
Then, in an obvious reference to various "schools" of twentieth century criticism, Gassner also states:

> . . . we shall not find in his work certain refine-
> ments of the modern critical approach, such as
> 'levels of meaning,' symbolization, and chains of
> association. He treats broad and generally direct
> or objective effects. . . . Art is not a divine
> madness or a manifestation of subjective imitations.
> Nor is criticism a purely personal adventure among
> masterpieces. [32]

In summarizing some modern trends of criticism, Gassner
terms much of what is written about the Poetics as "Romantic
Aristotelianism," which he believes is a result of the "dis-
enchantments . . . and protest against a petty world and
against petty views of man . . ."[33] Tragedy for twentieth
century critics, to Gassner, is "asserting the stature or dignity of the human being in the face of the indignities of a
world of real and fancied slurs on man."[34] Finally, he
warns against either too strict or too loose an interpretation
of Aristotle.

        In 1961, Fergusson's introduction to Butcher's trans-
lation holds it to be "one of the standard texts, probably the
best now available in English."[35] He cautions the reader to
approach Aristotle thus:

> He does not intend the Poetics to be an exact sci-
> ence, or even a textbook with strict laws, as the
> Renaissance humanists tried to make out with their
> famous 'rules' of the unities of time, place, and
> action. He knew that every poet has his unique
> vision, and must therefore use the principles of
> his art in his own way. The Poetics is much more
> like a cookbook than it is like a textbook in elemen-
> tary engineering.
>
> The Poetics should therefore be read slowly, as an
> 'aid to reflection'; only then does Aristotle's co-
> herent conception of the art of drama emerge.[36]

He, like Gassner, attempts to establish Aristotle's meaning
without clouding conclusions with a particular view. Fergusson constantly tries to relate the text of Aristotle to modern
theatrical terms, pointing out the good sense of Aristotle in
play construction, the concept of the whole and the acting
method, together with references to other modern views of
Aristotle. For Fergusson, Joyce, in his characterization of
Stephen Daedalus in Portrait of the Artist as a Young Man,
casts Stephen's discussion of Aristotelian concepts of art very
soundly. "Stephen's whole discussion shows the right way to
use Aristotle's idea: as guides in one's own thinking about
art."[37] A creative relationship should exist between critic
or reader and Aristotle, neither asking total acceptance nor
a particular view. Fergusson's final remarks in this discussion treat the modern view of tragedy as involving ritual
sources. Such theories do not fully explain the Poetics, but
throw significant light on the work "by deepening our under-

standing of the art form which Aristotle was analyzing."[38]
The Cambridge School of Frazer, Cornford, Harrison and
Murray "has had the deepest influence upon modern poetry
and upon the whole climate of ideas in which we now read
Greek tragedy and the Poetics."[39]

In his The Anatomy of Drama, Alan Reynolds Thompson attempts to formulate a contemporary critical approach.
After establishing that it is worthwhile to cultivate a sound
critical judgment, he suggests the purpose of good criticism
appears in the form of three questions:

> What did the author set out to do? Did he succeed
> in doing it? And, was it worth doing? These
> questions were first propounded by Goethe in a
> slightly different form: 'What did the author set
> out to do? Was his plan reasonable and sensible,
> and how far did he succeed in carrying it out?'
> The order first given, however, is the order in
> which the critic should proceed.[40]

After discussion of various approaches to criticism and the
sources of dramatic effect, such sources as those with which
Aristotle had also been concerned--essentials of production,
conventions, plot, emotion and conflict, surprise, irony, and
suspense--he devotes an entire chapter to unity, an important
concept in Aristotle's Poetics. Here he considers unity in
connection with action, the hero, the theme, and with feeling.
The discussion explores the modern relevance of ever-recur-
ring basic ideas such as comedy, melodrama and tragedy,
the dilemma of modern tragedy, and drama and poetry, in a
reasonable book aiming at the best features of historical perspective on dramatic criticism and modern sensitivity.

The Armed Vision of Stanley Edgar Hyman, in 1955,
attempts to set forth a unified discussion of "methods of modern literary criticism."[41] Hyman surveys briefly the history
of criticism praising Aristotle throughout:

> The miracle Aristotle performed, the essential
> rightness of his criticism, based almost entirely
> on private observation and keen sensibility, is a
> triumph of critical insight hitting largely by intui-
> tion on a good deal later discovered and developed.
> Even by Coleridge's time, two thousand years later,
> not much more was known accurately about the na-
> ture of the human mind and society than Aristotle
> knew.[42]

The particular relevance of Aristotle for the twentieth century, in Hyman's opinion, is his contribution to psychological
insight: "the principal source of both psychology and the
psychological criticism of literature."[43] He notes Aristotle's
concern with dreams and memory, and his application of psychology to poetry as he expands and corrects Plato's theory
of emotional purgation.   Moreover, hamartia, the tragic flaw
of the hero; peripateia, the shock of change; and the prefer-
ence of the probable impossible over the improbably possible
are, in Hyman's opinion, "anticipations of basic psychological
truths."[44]   For Hyman, Aristotle views the poet as an "inspired psychologist." Hyman then traces the psychological
insights of Aristotle through figures whom Hyman admires,
i.e., Coleridge and Freud.   Closely connected is his interest
in the critic or symposium of critics who can present a plu-
ralistic approach to criticism which he terms "multiple-level
or plural-meaning criticism," wherein the interplay of many
critical minds--a kind of contest or agon--provides the best
possible atmosphere for achieving truth.[45]

        The discussion of Greek tragedy and of its criticism
by William Arrowsmith in the Tulane Drama Review of March,
1959, holds neither "older historical and philological criticism"
nor "New Criticism" as satisfactory.   Of Aristotle, he writes:

>   Aristotle is, I know, a rough customer: he has of
>   necessity immense authority, and one is never
>   quite sure whether one is talking about Aristotle
>   or about something that has borrowed the authority
>   of his name.[46]

Arrowsmith does admire the work of Gerald F. Else, Aristotle's: The Argument.   Else's remarks appear in an extensive footnote prepared especially for Arrowsmith's article.
Else supports, as do many of Aristotle's commentators, the
importance of action as a concept in the Poetics.   He states:

>   There is no doubt that the root and center of Aris-
>   totle's theory of tragedy, indeed of all poetry, is
>   the idea of an action (N.B. 'an action,' not simply
>   'action') . . . Without action a man can be, but he
>   can neither win nor lose; and the winning or losing
>   . . . is the tragedy.   What is tragic is neither the
>   potentiality nor the actuality or suffering, but its
>   actualization.   Tragedy cannot be displayed, but
>   only enacted.[47]

Arrowsmith appeals for a new approach to the criticism of
Greek tragedy and warns against a "crude or vulgar Aristotelianism." Tragic fall, or hamartia, has been generalized
into "something like original sin" by many critics, but he
thinks Oedipus' only specific flaws are those of his own humanity. [48] In short, look at the plays first and then look at
Aristotle, avoiding application of Aristotle's rules as a whole
to Greek plays which do not react to his categories. The
experience of the play should be primary, Arrowsmith thinks,
and he points out that we are pre-disposed to a Sophoclean
rather than to Euripidean or Aeschylean worlds when Aristotle
is the critical touchstone.

> What hinders us here, however, is the deeply Aris-
> totelian bias of our critical habits and especially
> the habit of imposing the example of the Oedipus
> Rex upon all other Greek plays. We expect unity
> to be of one kind, and missing it, we misread or
> condemn the play in order to salvage our own bad
> habits. [49]

For modern interpretations of Aristotle and the dramatic form in general, the definition of A Handbook to Literature, under "Dramatic Structure," may be helpful.

> The ancients compared the PLOT of a DRAMA to
> the tying and untying of a knot. The principle of
> dramatic CONFLICT, though not mentioned as such
> in Aristotle's definition of DRAMA, is implied in
> this figure. The technical structure of a serious
> play is determined by the necessities of developing
> this dramatic CONFLICT. Thus a well-built TRAG-
> EDY will commonly show the following divisions,
> each of which represents a phase of the dramatic
> CONFLICT: introduction, RISING ACTION, CLIMAX
> or CRISIS (turning point), FALLING ACTION, and
> CATASTROPHE. The relation of these parts is
> sometimes represented graphically by the figure of
> a pyramid, called (Gustav) Freytag's pyramid, the
> rising slope suggesting the RISING ACTION or tying
> of the knot, the falling slope the FALLING ACTION
> or resolution, the apex representing the CLIMAX. [50]

A fuller discussion of these terms follows, but the basic definition does not change with modern and more experimental
forms. "The fundamental dramatic structure seems timeless
and impervious to basic change." [51]

Joseph Wood Krutch, in 1953, opposes this view.   Concerned with what he calls the "dissolution of the ego" in
modern drama since Darwin, Marx, and Freud, as contrasted
with Aristotle's emphasis on "the fable" in tragedy, [52] he concludes:

> Many moderns, on the other hand, have insisted
> that the revelation of character through conflict is
> more important than story.   Offhand I cannot think
> of any analyst who has maintained that you could
> have a play without either action on the one hand or
> the revelation of character on the other.   Yet
> Chekhov gets rid of action and Pirandello gets rid
> of character.   One is tempted to suggest somewhat
> light-mindedly that whatever else we may not be
> able to predict about the future which lies across
> the chasm one thing seems fairly certain: There
> will not be any plays in it. [53]

This is a particularly interesting comment as it comes just
before the current theatre of the absurd, where the traditional concepts of action and character have been attacked
even more strongly.

Eric Bentley, who has exerted a wide influence through
his extensive dramatic criticism, was an early champion of
the works of Bertolt Brecht in America and was instrumental
in providing translations and, in some instances, theatrical
productions.   In his The Life of The Drama, Bentley discusses drama in two sections: "Aspects of a Play" and "Different Kinds of Plays, " treating internal organization in the
first division and genres of drama in the second.   This organization largely indicates what a modern critic considers
important in dramatic elements.   "Aspects of a Play" has
five chapter headings entitled: 1. plot, 2. character, 3. dialogue, 4. thought, and 5. enactment.   "Different Kinds of
Plays" includes chapters on melodrama, farce, tragedy,
comedy and tragi-comedy. [54]   With the purpose "to break
down prejudices against plot and prejudices against type
characters, "[55] he writes to correct modern dramatic mis-
conceptions.   He reassesses, as other critics have, the value
of "plot" and the concepts of melodrama and farce.   Plot, as
the neglected element in modern drama, for Bentley, provides
outstanding dramatists with their most effective devices.
Shakespeare and Ibsen gave importance to plot.   Bentley
points out that Ibsen, and Shaw as well, were exceptions to
the naturalistic movement of the theatre and to a drama of

character rather than of action. Brecht "rescued the idea of
plot for the twentieth-century drama"[56] and, according to
Bentley, derived his ideas from Buchner who, in his turn,
derived his from Shakespeare. Bentley states: "It may well
be that Shakespeare's plots are unappreciated precisely because they are so good--because they are invisible, because
at every point they touch the theme and the characterizations,
and we cannot discuss one without the others."[57] Bentley
underscores Lope de Vega's ability to use plot as an essential:

> Anything prophesied in Act One is going to come
> true later, and the audience knows this. Logically
> there is something childish about such a proposi-
> tion. But that is just it: it is the child in us that
> responds to stories, and the modern antagonism to
> narrative is much too exclusively adult an attitude
> for an artist.[58]

Bentley considers so many problems relevant to drama
that to discuss him fully is difficult. His sense of balance
in his discussions of form is refreshing, as is his attempt
to see modern drama in light of the history of drama and
dramatic criticism. He supports no one school and regrets
the over-literary concern of many modern critics who emphasize characterization in modern drama to the detriment
of plot. He calls for balance between philosophic statement
and the importance given to experience in the theatre. "No
doubt both (views) are perennial: but does one really have
to choose between them? To me it would seem that each
view gets less and less true as it approaches the opposite
pole." He concludes:

> Drama has to do both with conveying an experience
> and with telling truths about it. By the same to-
> ken, truth-telling is not the whole end of the drama;
> nor is the communication of an experience. Truth-
> telling--the making of statements, stating of themes,
> putting across of ideas--is indeed only an aspect;
> and there are others of comparable importance.[59]

He urges a "dignity of significance," a term which Goethe
has used.[60]

The dramatic elements of opera are mentioned by
Joseph Kerman in his Opera As Drama. This work considers a group of significant operas representative of the

historical development of the form and includes a serious
discussion of their success as musical drama.   Music is always important to Kerman, but he emphasizes dramatic elements in the libretto as well.   He writes of the tensions created by libretto and music and points out that librettos can
defeat the composer.

> In the end, the libretto is the limitation.   But from
> another point of view, it is usually true that the
> composer's powers have hardly been shown before
> hand, and come out only in the musical setting of
> the libretto.   In the beginning, the libretto is the
> inspiration. [61]

He writes of "every possible level: the plot, characterization, dramaturgy, symbolism, imagery, and diction" in a
discussion of Maeterlinck's Pelléas et Mélisande. [62]   Discussing Tristan und Isolde he lists "plot, setting, diction, imagery, dramatic rhythm and music," [63] and remarks, concerning
drama:

> Drama requires not only the presentation of action,
> but an insight into its quality by means of response
> to action.   Only the presentation of such quality
> justifies the dramatic endeavor; and in the best
> dramas, the response seems imaginative, true, il-
> luminating, and fully matched to the action. [64]

In conclusion, he remarks:

> The best operas are dramatic, and they stand with
> the best dramatic products of the modern age. . . .
> Opera . . . has shown itself to be an art-form
> with its own integrity, with its own limiting and
> liberating conventions, and with its own unique
> areas of expression.   As the dramatic form is ar-
> ticulated by music, great music is necessary, but
> only a great dramatic vision is sufficient. [65]

        If one evaluates only twentieth century approaches to
the study of drama, its critical postures are all-encompass-
ing, from great respect for the "rules" of Aristotle, to their
modification by Italian Renaissance to French neo-classicism,
to their rejection in the subjective and personal approach to
drama of the Romantics.   Each still finds critical advocates
in the twentieth century, a century unique in the respect its
critics show for the original document in every field.   George

Watson points out in The Literary Critics: "over the centuries English criticism has tended to move away from the
text and then back towards it."[66] This age attempts recre-
ation of authenticity in theatrical production to establish fidelity to author and historical period. Modern scholarship has
aided theatrical insight through more intensive use of psychology, anthropology, history, and archeology for a more
rational estimate. "A wise eclecticism" before the possibilities of the twentieth century appeals to Watson.[67] Still,
with a wider contextual knowledge of drama, much of Aristotle is still valid to what is basic in the dramatic event.
Careful modern scrutiny assures Aristotle of a high place in
dramatic criticism, and this is underlined by Gassner, Fergusson, Bentley, F. L. Lucas, Hyman, and Crane. Although
Arrowsmith cautions of the difficulty in distinguishing between
what is truly Aristotle and what appears under the authority
of his name, basic principles are unchallenged by most critics of this century. Plot, character, language, and unity are
still essential elements.

"Dramatic elements" for opera librettos concern plot,
characterization, and literary style. For plot, three aspects are particularly relevant. First is form. Does the
plot have a basic unity of beginning, middle and end? The
second is content of libretto. Is there a central statement?
Is content clearly focused? Third is plot devices. What
uses are made of dramatic irony, reversal of fortune and
discovery? A second major division of dramatic elements,
characterization, should include the following considerations.
Is the characterization believable, or are characters developed in a style and manner consistent with the social and
psychological necessities of the situation? What estimate
should be made as to domination of character over plot?
This controversy is never-ending in drama, and hence also
in dramatic opera. Finally, elements of the libretto's literary style must be considered. What is the form--prose or
poetry? Is style appropriate to plot, theme, and characterization? Such are the criteria relevant to an evaluation of
the opera libretto, American as well as European.

Notes

1. Allan H. Gilbert, Literary Criticism: Plato to Dryden
   (Detroit: Wayne State University Press, 1962), pp.
   42-55.

2. F. L. Lucas, Tragedy: Serious Drama in Relation to
    Aristotle's Poetics (New York: Collier Books, 1962),
    pp. 17-18.

3. Francis Fergusson, "Introduction," Aristotle's Poetics
    (New York: Hill and Wang, 1961), p. 3.

4. John Gassner, "Prefatory Essay" in S. H. Butcher's
    Aristotle's Theory of Poetry and Fine Art (New York:
    Dover Publications, Inc., 1951), p. 114.

5. Ibid., p. xxxvii.

6. Ibid., pp. 31-53.

7. Ibid., pp. 53-87.

8. T. S. Dorsch, Classical Literary Criticism (Baltimore,
    Md.: Penguin Books, Inc., 1965), p. 17.

9. Gilbert, op. cit., pp. 124-143.

10. Barrett H. Clark, European Theories of the Drama
    (New York: Crown Publishers, Inc., 1945), p. 41.

11. Ibid., pp. 51-52.

12. William Thrall, Addison Hibbard, and C. Hugh Holman,
    A Handbook to Literature (New York: The Odyssey
    Press, 1960), pp. 117-118.

13. Allardyce Nicoll, World Drama (New York: Harcourt,
    Brace and Company, 1949), pp. 303-4.

14. Gilbert, op. cit., p. 600.

15. A. M. Nagler class notes taken at Yale University,
    1965.

16. Clark, op. cit., pp. 171-3.

17. John Gassner & Ralph G. Allen, Theatre and Drama in
    the Making, Vol. 2 (Boston: Houghton Mifflin Co.,
    1964), p. 483.

18. Clark, op. cit., pp. 313-14.

19. Ibid., p. 422.

20. George Watson, The Literary Critics (Baltimore: Penguin Books, 1962), p. 125.

21. A. M. Nagler class notes taken at Yale University, 1965.

22. Laurence Lerner, Shakespeare's Tragedies, an Anthology of Modern Criticism (Baltimore: Penguin Books, 1963), p. 11.

23. Stanley Edgar Hyman, The Armed Vision (New York: Vintage Books, 1955), p. 387.

24. Ibid., p. 7.

25. Gassner and Allen, op. cit., pp. 462-464.

26. Clark, op. cit., pp. 305-6.

27. Nagler, class notes.

28. Clark, op. cit., pp. 363-65.

29. Gassner and Allen, Vol. 2, 464.

30. Butcher, Gassner Intro., p. xlv.

31. Ibid., p. xlix.

32. Ibid.

33. Ibid., p. lxviii.

34. Ibid.

35. Butcher, Fergusson Intro., p. 3.

36. Ibid., p. 3.

37. Ibid., p. 33.

38. Ibid., p. 37.

39. Ibid., p. 38.

40.   Alan Reynolds Thompson, The Anatomy of Drama
       (Berkeley: University of California Press, 1946),
       p. 43.

41.   Hyman, op. cit., title page.

42.   Ibid., p. 4.

43.   Ibid., p. 142.

44.   Ibid., p. 143.

45.   Ibid., p. 401.

46.   First published in the Tulane Drama Review, Volume
       III, Number 3 (T3), March 1959, copyright 1959 by
       the Tulane Drama Review.   Reprinted by permission.
       All rights reserved.

47.   Ibid., p. 337.

48.   Ibid., p. 336.

49.   Ibid., p. 330.

50.   From A Handbook to Literature by William Flint Thrall
       and Addison Hibbard, revised by C. Hugh Holman,
       copyright 1936, 1960, by The Odyssey Press, Inc.,
       reprinted by permission of The Bobbs-Merrill Com-
       pany, Inc., p. 156.

51.   Ibid., p. 158.

52.   Joseph Wood Krutch, Modernism in Modern Drama: A
       Definition and an Estimate, copyright 1953 (New
       York: Russell and Russell, 1962), p. 86-7.

53.   Ibid., p. 27.

54.   Eric Bentley, The Life of the Drama, pp. vii-ix, copy-
       right 1964 by Eric Bentley.   Reprinted by permis-
       sion of Atheneum Publishers.

55.   Ibid., p. 216.

56.   Ibid., p. 25.

57. Ibid., p. 27.

58. Ibid., p. 29.

59. Ibid., p. 145.

60. Ibid., pp. 145-7.

61. Kerman, op. cit., p. 29.

62. Ibid., p. 176.

63. Ibid., p. 196.

64. Ibid., p. 263.

65. Ibid., p. 267.

66. Watson, op. cit., p. 31.

67. Ibid., p. 227.

Chapter III

DRAMATIC ELEMENTS
IN AMERICAN OPERA LIBRETTOS
AT THE NEW YORK CITY OPERA

Forty American operas were performed at the New
York City Opera between 1948 and 1971. (These operas are
listed in a table on page 63.)

In 1948 the New York City Opera Company presented
its first American operas, Gian-Carlo Menotti's Old Maid and
the Thief and Amelia Goes to the Ball. This beginning is
significant in that Menotti offered some of the most enduring
contemporary works to the New York City Opera. Revivals
of these have often been given and public response has been
enthusiastic. In total, nine operas by Menotti have been
presented, and in each case Menotti served as his own librettist.

Menotti's librettos are the work of an artist of considerable dramatic imagination.[1] Amelia, his first work, had
its premiere at the Philadelphia Academy of Music in 1937.
Entitled as "Opera Buffa in One Act," the libretto for Amelia
was written in Italian by Menotti and translated into English
by George Mead. It is a story in the tradition of comic opera where improbable events in a farcical style are resolved
in an outlandish but happy way. The moral is stated at the
end of the opera: "If a woman sets her heart upon a ball,
the ball is where she'll go." The focus is clearly on Amelia
during the whole of the opera and she is revealed as a whim-
sical woman. She is believable in the comic opera tradition--
a commedia dell'arte figure--and the rest of the characters
are traditional. The emphasis is on plot and "what happens
next" is more interesting than the reactions of the characters.
Dramatic devices include several reversals--the husband refuses to fight his wife's lover who is larger than the husband,
and the policeman becomes Amelia's escort to the ball. The
device of discovery is used also in the letter from the lover
and again when the lover emerges from hiding to confront the
husband. The style of writing is a rather free, rhymed cou-

American Operas Performed at the
New York City Opera, 1948 - 1971

Title	Composer	Date of 1st Perf.	No. of Perfs. 1948-1971
Old Maid and the Thief	Menotti	4/ 8/48	21
Amelia Goes to the Ball	Menotti	4/ 8/48	9
Troubled Island	Still	3/31/49	3
The Medium	Menotti	4/ 8/49	15
The Dybbuk	Tamkin	10/ 4/51	8
Amahl and the Night Visitors	Menotti	4/ 9/52	11
The Consul	Menotti	10/ 8/52	14
Regina	Blitzstein	4/ 2/53	9
The Tender Land	Copland	4/ 1/54	2
Susannah	Floyd	9/27/56	19
The Ballad of Baby Doe	Moore	4/ 3/58	30
Tale for a Deaf Ear	Bucci	4/ 6/58	3
Trouble in Tahiti	Bernstein	4/ 6/58	3
Lost in the Stars	Weill	4/10/58	12
Taming of the Shrew	Giannini	4/13/58	3
Good Soldier Schweik	Kurka	4/23/58	3
Maria Golovin	Menotti	3/30/59	2
Street Scene	Weill	4/ 2/59	20
The Scarf	Hoiby	4/ 5/59	3
The Devil and Daniel Webster	Moore	4/ 5/59	3
Wuthering Heights	Floyd	4/ 9/59	3
He Who Gets Slapped	Ward	4/12/59	2
The Triumph of St. Joan	Dello Joio	4/16/59	2
Six Characters in Search of an Author	Weisgall	4/26/59	2
The Cradle Will Rock	Blitzstein	2/11/60	3
Wings of the Dove	Moore	16/12/61	5
The Crucible	Ward	10/26/61	6
Porgy and Bess	Gershwin	3/21/62	12
The Golem	Ellestein	3/22/62	4
Jonathan Wade	Floyd	10/11/62	2
Gentlemen, Be Seated	Moross	10/10/63	3
Natalia Petrovna	Hoiby	10/ 8/64	2
Saint of Bleecker Street	Menotti	3/18/65	4
Lizzie Borden	Beeson	3/25/65	4
Miss Julie	Rorem	11/ 4/65	2

Title	Composer	Date of 1st Perf.	No. of Perfs. 1948-1971
The Servant of Two Masters	Giannini	3/ 9/67	3
Carry Nation	Moore	3/28/68	3
Nine Rivers From Jordan	Weisgall	10/ 9/68	3
Help, Help, The Globolinks Are Coming!	Menotti	11/28/70	2
The Most Important Man	Menotti	3/ 7/71	3

plet form which gives an appropriate light and charming style to the libretto. The language is natural and a somewhat colloquial speech pattern is employed with a minimum of pretentiousness. The setting places the opera "about 1910," but the language reveals no particular flavor and maintains a natural and easy pattern.

The second Menotti opera of this 1948 season, The Old Maid and the Thief, had been commissioned originally by the National Broadcasting Company expressly for radio performance, and was first given by N.B.C. on April 22, 1939. "A grotesque Opera in fourteen scenes" centers on "a virtuous woman who makes a thief of an honest man." In this story Miss Todd, the "old maid," moves from a rather stereotyped figure to one of touching complexity and confusion. Her end is pathetic and leaves one feeling that perhaps this ending is too brutal for the tone of the work. Piling up of complicating incidents is similar to that of Amelia but the result is much less happy. The foolishness of the old maid is realistic and moving, and the escape of the maid and the "thief" is a good verismo touch. In this libretto irony appears first in the assumption by the two women that they have a thief on their hands and their procedure is to turn him into one whether he likes it or not. There is the additional irony of his escape with the young maid and in his robbing the old maid of everything. Also in the irony of situation is a reversal, with the old maid being completely rejected for her kindness. She is left quite alone by the end of the opera. Discovery comes when first the women believe they have given shelter to a thief, and again later when they discover this is not true. The plot is a busy one, but the characterizations come across with satisfactory credibility.

The language is a combination of prose and free verse with
some rhyming to give the effect of natural diction. The
libretto is neither heavy nor burdensome and reads with a
considerable ease. It seems appropriate to the contemporary
setting of the opera.

An American opera which received its world premiere
at the New York City Opera was William Still's Troubled Island, with a libretto by Langston Hughes, performed in the
spring season of 1949. This is a story of the leader, Jean
Jacques Dessalines, in the slave revolution in Haiti during
the Napoleonic era. The focus is on Dessalines, who is portrayed as a visionary without much development of character
detail. The opera is presented in a rather panoramic style,
as an historical pageant, which emphasizes tropical color,
voodoo rites, display of military power, and the melodramatic end of the slave leader's life. The most affecting moments in the libretto are those carried by Azelia, the rejected first wife, who remains loyal to Dessalines, and the
love scene between Dessalines and his second wife, Claire.
The plot lacks full development and motivations are not clearly explained. However, Langston Hughes does attempt to
create a sense of folk quality style in the chorus numbers,
and there are additional lyric passages written in free verse
style. The writing is not offensively pompous or "grand"
but elevation of language is attempted. Dramatic irony oc-
curs when the Emperor is killed by his own generals, and
also when his first wife, whom he rejects, tries to help him.
Implicit in these two dramatic ironies is also reversal of
fortune. Generally, then, the dramatic elements have been
employed in a workmanlike way, but the result is neither
particularly new nor startling--characterizations remain rather stock and predictable, and the principal dramatic moments
are standard.

A third Gian-Carlo Menotti opera was presented in
the same Spring Season of 1949: the two-act melodrama,
The Medium. Again Menotti furnished his own libretto and
it is one of excitement and tension. The main dramatic
conflict centers on Baba, the Medium, who holds seances
and in the course of the play confuses the spiritual world of
the seance with that of reality. The study of her growing
fear, counterpointed against her rather sweetly simple daughter and deaf-mute assistant, provides a melodramatic situation. The dramatic irony of the story is the killing of Toby
by Baba out of her intense fear of "ghosts." Reversal is
used in the effect of the seances upon Baba--she becomes a

victim of her own devices.   Although a highly colored story, it is believable because of the careful psychological study of Baba.   As is usual with Menotti, the language is colloquial during scenes of conflict and rapid exchange of dialogue, and poetic during moments of lyric reflection.   However, there is no abruptness in moving from one literary form to the other.   Finally, the underlying tone of menace, fear and suspicion created by the paranoia of Baba, juxtaposed with the simple affection displayed between Toby and Monica, provides strong and effective contrasts.

The Dybbuk, with music by David Tamkin and a libretto by Alex Tamkin based on the play by S. Ansky, was given its world premiere at the New York City Opera in October, 1951.   In this opera elements of Jewish mysticism dominate the plot.   Characterization is minimal and the theatricalism of religious ritual is emphasized.   Situation dominates character development in dramatized scenes where supernatural elements are always present.   The basic dramatic irony of the opera is that the young rabbi who initially fails to win the daughter gains her finally through the power of the Dybbuk and death.   But the conflict of the lovers is never developed and one is never given a love scene between them to establish effectively the dramatic contrast that should be present. The audience is expected to accept a series of given facts about the situation and, while the plot is believable to some extent, it lacks character development and remains essentially a series of religious tableaux.   Dramatic discovery in this opera consists of the realization by the congregation first of the young rabbi's death, second of the presence of the Dybbuk in the girl, and third of her death as the spirit is exorcized.   From the nature of the subject, it is clear that the drama offers striking visual elements, but characterization and dramatic devices are not fully realized.   The language is prose throughout the script with the exception of Biblical and religious ritual poetry.   There is effective use of chanting choruses to provide background or further comment on the dramatic situation.

The New York stage premiere of Gian-Carlo Menotti's Amahl and the Night Visitors was on April 8, 1952, following a premiere on NBC television December 24, 1951.   The two-act libretto, written by Menotti, and based upon the painting, Adoration of the Magi, by Hieronymus Bosch, is again in the poetic-prose style of The Medium and Old Maid and the Thief.   Reserving poetry for the reflective arias of the Mother and the Kings, he uses folk elements in the cho-

rus of shepherds. The blending is quite successful and the
language rarely pretends to be more than a simple, straightforward treatment of the material using somewhat formal diction. This understated development of the story adds believability and wonder to the central event in the story--the miraculous cure of the crippled boy. Presented as a commentary to the story of the birth of Christ, the story unfolds
with an added sense of mystery and strong folk tale overtones. The tone of the opera is kept light and playful, and
this counteracts to some extent an inherently sentimental situation. The mother's attempt to steal the gold of the visiting
Kings gives a realistic psychological touch to her character
and points up a strong secondary theme: i.e., the poverty
of these shepherds and the always existing distance between
the rich and poor. The believable human situation and the
touches of humor give the opera more than a pageant quality.
Its intimate and sweet quality makes it particularly appropriate for Christmas. Menotti, always aware of theatrical possibilities, uses dramatic irony, reversal, and discovery to
good advantage. Although the Mother attempts to steal the
money, the boy's willingness to take the blame for the act,
his defense of his mother, and his offer of his crutches as
a gift to the Holy Child effect his miraculous cure. The
dramatic discovery of this cure by the boy and the Kings
gives them the necessary belief to continue their journey to
find the birthplace of the Holy Child.

A fifth opera by Gian-Carlo Menotti, entitled The
Consul, was presented in the autumn season of 1952. Probably his most serious and ambitious work up to this time,
The Consul is a three-act dramatization of a Kafka-like
world where a police state has reduced its citizens to numbers and human movement has all but ceased. The focus
of the story centers on Magda Sorel, the wife of a freedom
fighter, who struggles unsuccessfully against the bureaucratic
structure of the state to obtain her passport to freedom. It
is a sound psychological portrait of a woman faced with a
terrorizing situation and her desperate solution to it. Menotti uses dramatic irony with great effectiveness here. The
husband and wife miss finding each other by minutes; she
dies, thinking it the best solution, just as the telephone
rings, in a call from her husband. The discovery of her
dead child and the discovery by her husband that he has just
missed her are the two dramatic high points of the action.
Also effective is the ironic humor of the magician who hyp-
notizes people seeking passports. Characterization is most
fully realized in Magda, while the rest of the characters

constitute a group of interesting middle-European types and
stereotypes. The result is an atmosphere of predictable menace with impersonal secretaries, trench-coated police agents,
and assorted small people crushed beneath bureaucratic methods. There is consistency but the characterization seems almost too predictable. The writing is almost totally prose,
although at several lyrical moments poetry is used. It is a
poetry expressing, in rather ordinary terms, the trials of
separation of families. The absence of a specific locale--
"somewhere in Europe"--tends to lessen the impact, or at
least generalizes the situation to give it a certain blandness
and lack of immediacy.

Marc Blitzstein, a composer who earlier established
himself on Broadway in the musical genre, was first represented at the New York City Opera in 1953 with his opera,
Regina, based on the play, The Little Foxes by Lillian Hellman. Blitzstein prepared his own libretto from the play and
retained essentially the basic conflicts presented there. He
added a prologue which set the atmosphere of the southern
American setting and effectively used jazz and hymnal references, both musical and verbal. The central theme of the
grasping, materialistic qualities of the Hubbard family which
kills its own humanity is retained, with Regina the central
focus of the action. The plot has viable complications, a
tight, fast moving plot and effective climaxes. The dramatic
irony of old values not working in the new society of the
South, the sister outplaying the brothers for financial advantage, and the dominance of evil forces are built up well in
the action. The reversals are striking--the daughter seeing
the corruption; the brothers defeated. But the discovery of
the theft of the bonds and, later, of Regina's willingness to
let her husband die before her eyes are the stuff of exciting
drama. Characterizations are well conceived, with Regina
receiving the fullest treatment. An effective contrast to her
dominant personality is that of Birdie, her sister-in-law who,
barely equal to the harsh realities of this family, escapes
into dreams of past plantations and present drinking. In fact,
the libretto is one that can be characterized by the "good"
people versus the "bad," which makes for exciting contrasts
but does not necessarily provide subtle character study. The
style of the writing is a tough, colloquial prose lifted from
Hellman's original text, plus lyric moments which have a
more poetic treatment. The stylistic difficulty encountered
in this libretto is that with such hard-hitting characters involved in such a bitter struggle, operatic treatment tends to
soften the impact and lose some of the original "bite."

The world premiere of Aaron Copland's The Tender
Land was given by the New York City Opera on April 1, 1954,
with a libretto by Horace Everett.   In this essentially lyric
treatment of a midwestern girl's maturity, the libretto does
not successfully project a dramatic situation and resolve it.
The ending is particularly disappointing as the motivations
for the girl's actions seem inconsistent with what has gone
before.   Also the characterizations are far too pat for much
individuality.   The father is stern, the mother is loving and
a good cook, the neighbors are jolly and uncharacterized,
and the central figure, the girl, develops a sudden maturity
that seems unjustified.   Dramatic irony, reversal or discovery are plot devices not developed and the main strength of
the opera lies in its creation of atmosphere and locale.   The
language is a mixture of prose and poetry and there is an attempt at regionalism in the speech with the dropping of final
"g's" and occasional use of bad grammar.   In its way, The
Tender Land suffers from too generalized a treatment as does
The Consul: the Copland and Everett "farm in the midwest"
is rather an indefinite area.

The New York premiere of Carlisle Floyd's Susannah
was given September 27, 1956, by the New York City Opera
Company with a libretto by the composer.   Using the Bible
story of Susannah and the Elders as a basis, Floyd resets
the action in a Bible-belt region of the American South.   It
is the story of a country girl whose natural response to life
is harshly judged by the strict Christian values of the community.   The focus is on Susannah and her wish to be accepted by members of the community, her involvement with
the hypocritical Reverend Olin Blitch, and the ultimate destruction of her family through community pressure.   Dramatic irony is the basis of a major motivation in the story--
that of voyeuristic "fathers" of the church watching Susannah
bathing.   The discovery of the hypocrisy of the community
and the hypocrisy of the minister who seduces Susannah provides strong dramatic focus.   A reversal is inherent in Susannah's growing knowledge of the community's true feelings and
her ultimate seduction.   Her change from a rather lively but
simple girl to one of cynical maturity is developed with considerable skill.   Despite the rather lurid dramatic overtones
to the story, Susannah's portrait is touching and consistent,
and she is the most fully developed character, only stock
figures surrounding her.   The language is a mixture of prose
and poetry, with a folk song style used at times with good
effect.   "Oh, what a lovely night," sung by Susannah early
in the opera, is one of the lyric high points in the libretto.

The colloquial quality of the language is sustained throughout the opera and the style is consistent.   The bitter ending gives the opera a heightened realism which recalls the verismo effects used earlier by Menotti.

The first of six American operas performed in the Ford Foundation-sponsored Spring Season of 1958 was Douglas Moore's The Ballad of Baby Doe, with libretto by John Latouche.   This opera, which first appeared at the Central City Opera in Colorado, used as its subject a colorful chapter from the silver mining era of the American West.   The central statement is the age-old triumph of true love despite social ostracism and financial ruin.   The focus is clearly on Horace Tabor, a wealthy silver miner, on Baby Doe, the woman for whom he risks everything, and on Horace's first wife, the austere Augusta.   The devices used in the story are rather predictable but the situation is one that, if effectively told, can hold an audience's attention.   The reversals in the dramatic action include Horace's decision to marry Baby Doe over all objections and his loss of fortune.   The discovery by Augusta of Horace's love for Baby Doe prompts her frigid behavior toward him and her refusal to grant him a divorce.   Later, Augusta relents about the divorce but warns Horace of possible financial ruin.   It is a believable story and has considerable dramatic impact.   The era of the story gives it a color, but the more grandiose aspects are played down and the primary emphasis remains on the love triangle. The confrontation scenes are particularly well handled and the pathetic figure of a broken Horace at the end is believable. Prose and poetry are both used with particular success in the love lyrics.   The style appears to be appropriate to the plot and characterization with a mixture of colloquial language and appropriate nineteenth century florid diction.   An authentic flavor of the period is one of the strongest features of this libretto.

A bill of two one-act operas was offered in this Spring Season of 1958 by two composers: Mark Bucci and Leonard Bernstein.   Bucci's Tale for a Deaf Ear features a libretto by the composer, based on the story by Elizabeth Enright.   A flash-back technique is used to develop the fantasy-reality elements of the libretto.   The central statement concerns the frustrations of marriage and the inability of husband and wife to communicate.   The dramatic device of the husband's death and miraculous revival gives the pair a chance to patch up their quarrel but it is ineffective.   The husband dies a second time and there is no revival.   Of course the ironic comment is contained in this "second

chance" situation which is unsuccessful. The reversal and
discovery device is the death and revival of the husband.
Characterizations are rather two-dimensional and give only
a stereotyped consistency. Plot overweighs characterization
as one is given an extended religious fantasy in justification
of the husband's revival in several historical scenes described
by a chorus and enacted by historic characters. The language is mixed prose and poetry with a good attempt at the
use of modern colloquial speech patterns. The style is appropriate to the piece, but the mood becomes at times too
sentimental and the attempts at serious comment appear pretentious. The opera finally lacks freshness of approach and
a depth of characterization that would make it a more compelling work.

Leonard Bernstein's Trouble in Tahiti is also about
marital difficulties, but the approach is more fully developed
and specific than that found in Tale for a Deaf Ear. The
chorus is a satiric version of television advertising, and the
fantasy life of the wife is based on an escapist film. Characterizations are more richly developed with fuller use of
satiric humor, and the action moves swiftly. The focus is
on the unsuccessful suburban marriage with dramatic irony
developed through the "commercial" chorus, the film story
and the marriage. The main discovery is in the concluding
scene where both partners realize what they already knew--
that they are unhappy. Although the conclusion is similar to
the Bucci opera, richness of detail in the Bernstein work
makes it the more appealing libretto. Liberal use of flash-
backs elaborates the character study but the effect is not un-
predictable. The language is colloquial English with catchy
rhyming and popular music lyrics as a basis for development. This style underlines the satiric quality of the work.
It is not, in sum, a wholly original work in theme, but in
treatment it has a number of cleverly worked out details.

With the production of Kurt Weill's Lost in the Stars
and the libretto by Maxwell Anderson based on the Alan Paton
novel, Cry, the Beloved Country, the 1958 Spring Season
presented its fourth American opera. The theme of this
work is the human tragedy surrounding racial strife in South
Africa. The focus is on the Reverend Stephen Kumalo and
the execution of his son for killing a white man. It is a
story of a rash act leading to death, resulting at the end in
a new understanding between men of different color. Devices
used in the story include Greek chorus effects for particularly
lyric passages that comment on the tragedy of the situation

and the beauty of the country. The dramatic irony consists
of robbers killing a man who, it turns out, is one of the few
white liberals in the community. However, the death of this
man leads to a reversal on the part of his father who is a
white man of an older tradition. This explosive situation is
characterized in a sketchy way through rather two-dimensional
situations, and the consistency of the opera is marred by too
neat an ending, at once a cliché and predictable. There is
great emphasis on local color and the language is a standard
English diction, although some of the choruses use what would
appear to be a colloquial native English featuring the absence
of syntactical connectives. It is at times a heightened poetic
prose and such lines as "The hills/ are grass-covered and
rolling, and they are lovely/ beyond any singing of it" are
beautiful and effective. The rather stock characterizations
developed without much subtlety and the rather too-easy solution suggested by the ending flaw this libretto.

Vittorio Giannini's The Taming of the Shrew, based
upon Shakespeare's comedy with text by Dorothy Fee, received its New York premiere during the Ford Foundation-
sponsored season. The plot of the Shakespearean play is essentially retained but somewhat truncated due to the demands
of sung dialogue. The basic theme--the many forms of court-
ing a woman--is retained, and the focus is on Katharina and
Petruchio and Bianca and her comic lovers. The dramatic
irony of Katharina forced to do Petruchio's bidding, and the
reversal of her submission, are the meat of this play. However, in this version far too many short cuts are taken with
the motivating action. The Katharina-Petruchio plot development is insufficient, being even more highly abbreviated than
in the play. As a result there is a lapse in the credibility:
one doubts that such a change could take place in a woman--
or that a man could change a woman in so short a time. As
might be anticipated, plot aspects of the libretto dominate the
characterization. The literary style is lifted almost intact,
but simplified, from Shakespeare. Perhaps the best job has
been achieved that is possible with the rhetoric of Shakespeare,
but what the opera lacks is due to the sketchiness of plot
structure which moves from high point to high point without
motivational scenes to prepare the climaxes.

A world premiere was the final American opera offered in this 1958 Spring Season. This was The Good Soldier
Schweik, with music by Robert Kurka and a libretto by Lewis
Allen based on the story by Jaroslav Hasek. It is the story
of a simple, good-hearted young man who, through his opti-

mistic trust in everyone, manages to be a complete misfit in
Army life. The story is a series of short scenes, in a manner reminiscent of Brecht, depicting the progress of this
young soldier. The dramatic irony and reversals that occur
are humorous commentaries on the presuppositions of regu-
lated Army life, and these acts come to their climax in
Schweik's refusal to believe the directions of a map when he
sets off independently on the battle front. Despite his good
intentions he is arrested, committed to a mental institution,
enlists in the army although he is having a bout with rheumatism, and falls in and out of favor. His straightforward logic
and lack of guile often overwhelm everyone around him. The
satiric comment on war is clearly made, although the script
is only occasionally didactic. The characterization of Schweik
is believable up to a point, but his existence seems remote,
although he is certainly consistent in his naive manner and
the results are often humorous and sometimes devastatingly
effective. The language of the libretto is a colloquial English
rendered in a spare, rhyming jingle form. Humor is always present and a light satiric touch is evident throughout
the script, which has considerable literary merit. The anti-
sentimental attitude of the libretto and the use of essentially
stock types around Schweik heighten the effectiveness of the
opera.

        A new Gian-Carlo Menotti opera, Maria Golovin, was
offered in the 1959 spring season. The story focuses on
Donato, a blind man who lives with his mother in an old
Italian villa. The central statement is concerned with the
blind man's search for love and his ultimate inability to receive it. Through his attraction to and final rejection of
Maria Golovin, Donato faces this search for love which becomes unfortunately mixed with conflicting loyalties to his
mother. Dramatic devices, as always, are effectively placed
by Menotti, who has again written his own libretto. This
time the symbolic use of the bird cages the blind man builds,
and the sub-plot of a nearby prison and its escapee, stress,
perhaps somewhat too graphically, the futile quality underlying the attempts of these characters to express their love.
Dramatic irony develops in Donato's willingness to believe
Agata's argument that Maria has other lovers and, finally,
in the ultimate irony of Donato's attempt to kill Maria, the
one person who has tried to give him a mature affection.
He is thrown back to even greater dependence upon his mother by the end of the opera--is, indeed, completely emascu-
lated. It is a touching portrait of a man with countless odds
against him and who is unsuccessful in conquering them--or

himself. Characterizations develop believably and the story
is fairly engrossing. However, a somewhat sentimental
treatment, both in language and in action, results in a disappointing lack of freshness. Symbolism seems too obvious
and poetic reflection tends toward the cliché.

        During this second spring season sponsored by the
Ford Foundation in 1959, which featured eight American operas, the second opera presented was Street Scene, with music by Kurt Weill, book by Elmer Rice and lyrics by Langston Hughes. This is a "slice-of-life" treatment of tenement
life in New York City in the 1930's. The cast is a large one
with chorus and main characters playing essentially similar
roles. The focus is on the Maurrant family: Anna, the unhappy wife; Frank, her domineering husband; and Rose, their
daughter who is in love with a college student, Sam Kaplan.
Tragedy results for everyone involved; Frank's discovery of
Anna's affair with the milkman ultimately leads to Rose's
leaving with her younger brother, Willie, for a better life.
The atmosphere of New York tenement life has verisimilitude
in this script, and the comings and goings of the neighborhood are naturalistically portrayed. Reversal is used in the
story in the daughter's refusal to marry after seeing the unhappiness of her parents. The dramatic discovery of the in-
fidelity of the wife leads to the death of Anna, Frank, and
the milkman. The characters have an earthy believability
and a consistency inherent in Rice's Pulitzer Prize play on
which the opera is based. The language is pungent and colloquial prose, interspersed with several beautiful poetic lyrics. It is a libretto with honest feeling for the milieu of the
story and its characters. The plot is believable and unsenti-
mental, and it does not glamorize essentially gritty, marginal
living conditions.

        A double bill offered in the Spring 1959 Season con-
sisted of two one-act operas, The Scarf and The Devil and
Daniel Webster, both studies of rural New England life. The
music for The Scarf was composed by Lee Hoiby and the libretto was written by Harry Duncan, centering on a frustrated
farm wife, Miriam. Her husband is a taciturn Yankee who,
early in the opera, accuses her of unnatural abilities including the casting of evil spells. To this she is non-committal,
as she is to the charge that she has had affairs with a number of traveling men who have spent the night. From this
tense situation grows the dramatic irony of the wife's murder
of her husband rather than her own death at his hands. A
third character, a mailman, stops in the house to protect

himself from the storm, and Miriam tries to seduce him.
The tone of the opera is one of mystery and impending doom
objectified by the various magic spells the wife casts to help
her to attain the mailman and, then, the murder of her husband. It is a story weighted towards a characterization of
Miriam with somewhat less emphasis on the two men. The
writing is prose mixed with poetic reflection and with some
attempt at a New England dialect. The weakness appears to
lie in lack of full character development in a rather one-di-
mensional treatment lacking variety.

The Devil and Daniel Webster, with music by Douglas
Moore and libretto by Stephen Vincent Benet, is also concerned with other-worldly doings in matter-of-fact New England. It is a story from the 1840's which focuses on Daniel
Webster, the statesman, and his neighborly help to a newly
married couple. The central statement emphasizes man's
unconquerable spirit and ability to prevail against the forces
of evil and darkness. Frankly fantastic, the magical devices
of the arrival of the Devil and the eventual trial between the
Devil and Webster before a jury of the Devil's own choosing,
provides exciting and stimulating theatre. The jury of damned
souls and Judge Hathorne, the hanging judge of Salem witchcraft trials, provide Webster's most challenging audience.
After winning his case, Webster and the neighbors celebrate
with "pie for breakfast." The ending is gay and light-hearted
and the community feeling of the piece is underlined. Although suspension of belief is required for this story, the
points made are humane and important. Colloquial New England speech is used with a rhymed poetry for the love exchanges. The style is direct and, all in all, this is a lively
piece with considerable invention and verve.

Carlisle Floyd's second opera produced at the New
York City Opera in 1959 was Wuthering Heights, derived from
Emily Brontë's novel with his own working of the libretto.
It is a theatrical story filled with dramatic reversals and
changes of fortune, straining believability but making for exciting theatre. The central statement that thwarted love can
lead to a life of unhappiness is amply expressed in the principal characters, Cathy and Heathcliff. The form of this
story is that of a flash-back, with opening and closing scenes
taking place in the present and the opera proper serving as
background. The main plot of the novel is used in the opera
to emphasize the dramatic irony that Cathy and Heathcliff
each marry the person they most hate. There is irony and
reversal in Heathcliff's eventual ownership of Thrushcross

Grange and Henley's complete reversal of position. These
moments are melodramatic and in the development, or lack
of it, they lack conviction. Cathy is too compassionate in
the opening of the opera as compared to her ruthlessness in
the latter portion. Henley's reversals appear too complete
to believe, as do Heathcliff's. How this cowering, unloved,
brutish man could become a smooth and polished gentleman
seems an almost impossible task. The plot covers several
years and the characterizations are highly developed with
many explosive elements. Despite its cardboard qualities,
the opera offers many exciting moments. Prose and poetry
are both used and the language is generally effective and utilitarian without being particularly memorable.

Another opera based on a literary work is He Who
Gets Slapped, from Andreyev's play with music by Robert
Ward and libretto by Bernard Stambler; it was performed in
the 1959 Spring Season. Like I Pagliacci, it is a behind-
the-scenes story of theatrical circus life with a development
of the irony of the tensions of involvements of performers as
people and their duty to go on with the show. Pantaloon, a
gentleman turned clown, is the central focus and through his
actions one is given to understand that when the truth is revealed to people they often react negatively. Pantaloon tra-
ditionally gets slapped, as happens several times during the
opera in real life situations. Pantaloon sums up, "No man
can do much to help others and less to help himself." The
plot has been reworked, for Pantaloon and Consuelo no longer
take poison. In the opera, after helping to "right" the situation between the performers, Pantaloon takes off his costume
and quietly leaves through the street door. He is not without
his own difficulties as he has a fantasy life which often cre-
ates trouble. But the situation is believable enough and the
dramatic devices of irony and discovery are used effectively.
However, the sentiments expressed in the language are in
rather conventionally written prose. The idea of the sad-
happy clown is not a new one and the play-within-a-play idea
has often been used. In reading, the libretto appears quite
complicated, but possibly it may play in a more direct manner.
From the appearance of the libretto, then, the opera does
not seem to achieve a life of its own sufficient to hold the
interest of the audience, but the striking visual elements in
the story could, possibly, reverse this opinion.

A New York State premiere was given in the 1959
Spring Season to Norman Dello Joio's The Triumph of St.
Joan. Both the music and libretto of this one-act opera in

five scenes are written by the composer. Implied in this
familiar story of Joan of Arc is the moral question surrounding a man's right to judge another. The focus is clearly on
Joan and her imprisonment, trial and execution. The dramatic irony is that such a straightforward, simple and devout
peasant girl, as Joan apparently is, is executed for her heret-
ical religious views. The opera is short and does not allow
for a full treatment nor for adequate characterization of Joan.
She is portrayed in sympathetic terms and there are no undue complications in the plot to distinguish the story from
what is already known of this incident in history. The story
here is cast as a series of brief tableaux which depict Joan's
last hours. The prose used throughout the opera is rather
formal and academic.

A world premiere was given during this season to Six
Characters in Search of an Author, an opera based on the
Pirandello play with music by Hugo Weisgall and a libretto
by Denis Johnston. The opera preserves the basic central
statement of the play which poses the problem of what is
reality and what is illusion. This is shown through the six
characters searching for an author and the actors who are
rehearsing. The devices of this story are frankly theatrical:
Who are these six people who appear, apparently out of no-
where? Is their problem reality or illusion? Can we take
them seriously? These problems in the play are carried
over effectively in the opera and the impact of "Who am I?"
still remains at the end. It is a consistent script and the
tension and question remain throughout the opera. The believability of the characters is acceptable and the language
is prose except for poetic reflections by the six characters.
A strong point of the script is the avoidance of undue philoso-
phizing about the situation at hand. This is not a pretentious
use of the reality-illusion theme, but a presentation of a situation in which such elements are present. As a result, it
possibly improves upon the original play. The demands of
a tighter libretto, requiring less dialogue, adds to the treatment of this subject.

In the following season, 1960, only one American work
new to the Opera Company repertoire was presented: The
Cradle Will Rock, with music and libretto by Marc Blitzstein.
Written under the Federal Theatre Project in the late 1930's,
it focuses on the poor conditions of the workers in "Steeltown, U.S.A." The little people of Steeltown are dependent
on the Mister family who control the economics of the town
and are unsympathetic to unions. The irony of this situation

is made all too apparent with flashback scenes into the lives
of people appearing in night court under false arrest and
their none-too-subtle coercion by Mr. Mister and his forces.
The artists of the town finally bow to his demands and only
through a general peoples' rising at the end of the opera is
Mr. Mister faced with meeting their demands and a reversal
of his position.   It is a polemical libretto.   Without conventional development of characterization or plot, a series of
vignettes are presented to explain the deplorable conditions
in a capitalist controlled town.   Character types are predict-
able--the street-walker, the compromised editor, the neighborly druggist, the compliant minister--and the plot's ultimate
reversal of the workers gaining their rights takes place off
stage.   The language is colloquial and tongue-in-cheek: its
strong, satiric edge is reminiscent of Brecht.   Although this
rather sassy, doggerel rhyming, Broadway-inspired script is
trite today, its message was more important for its own
time.

     Douglas Moore's new opera The Wings of the Dove,
based on the novel by Henry James, was given its world
premiere during the Fall Season of 1961.   The libretto by
Ethan Ayer treats the James story in the necessarily abbreviated form that opera requires, with the main psychological
conflicts of the triangle situation presented with considerable
conviction.   The period setting, in the wealthy London and
Venice of 1900, offers ample opportunity for impressive sets
and costumes.   Beneath this surface elegance lie the tensions
of a triangle relationship of a man and two women.   Milly is
dying and Kate urges Miles to marry Milly to gain her inheritance when she dies.   Thereafter, Kate reasons, Miles
will be eligible for her own hand.   Miles is shocked by this
proposal but finally agrees to it.   When Milly learns of the
scheme, she is stricken with a final illness.   But after her
death, Miles tells Kate he will not take Milly's money and
marry Kate too, and he confesses, upon her insistence, that
he does not love her.   The story is ironic for everyone concerned and confirms the theme of the story, which appears
to be that to be honest in love is the only attitude that really
counts.   Reversals in the women's situations are the strong
and moving scenes of the story.   It is also a story of characterization, and audience psychological involvement with the
characters is engrossing.   The writing style is a mixture of
prose and poetry--rather, a poetic prose--without clichés and
so understated that the libretto succeeds in action and characterization.   Although the period and style of the setting and
people suggest a "grand" treatment, the librettist writes in a

straightforward, non-sentimental manner without period flavor.
It is, to conclude, a convincing operatic treatment of what
must have been a difficult novel to adapt.

During the same season of the premiere of Moore's
new opera, an operatic treatment of Arthur Miller's The
Crucible was first given at City Center. The music by
Robert Ward and the libretto by Bernard Stambler set essentially the same piece that Miller wrote for the theatre. The
Salem witchcraft trials of 1692 are a subject wherein Puritanism and the possibility of witchcraft offer exciting theatrical
possibilities, and they are effectively used by the composers.
The focus is on John Proctor, a dissenting farmer, and Abigail, a woman who is in love with him. It is the irony of
this story that the honesty of John Proctor is his undoing and
that it sends him to jail and death. This irony is also com-
pounded: Abigail desires John for her own, only to lose him
through her efforts at court to condemn his wife, Elizabeth.
It is a strong, emotional situation, deepened by Elizabeth's
reversal and insight into the nature of her love for John.
She changes from a coldly judicious wife through her compassion for a husband who has spoken out honestly. An early
discovery of the story is that there are witches in Salem and
that the town fathers convict people on charges of witchcraft.
The situation, given the historical context of the play, is believable. The climax of the third act and of the opera oc-
curs when hysterical girls in the court feign madness to accuse John of being the Devil's man. The opera emphasizes
plot with striking and dramatic characterizations, but not in
unconventional terms. The language is mixed prose and poetry with a slightly suggested Biblical seventeenth century
speech pattern. The libretto is dramatically effective and
provides exciting theatrical moments.

The world premiere of The Golem, with music by
Abraham Ellstein and libretto by Abraham Ellstein and Sylvia
Regan based on a work by H. Leivick, was given in the
Spring Season of 1962. Set in Prague in the year 1580, the
story is a folk tale based on ancient beliefs of the Jews. It
is a story of the supernatural and of the perils human beings
experience when they equate themselves with God. The central statement is that to meddle with the supernatural in an
attempt to be a giver of life leads to disastrous results.
The form of the opera is centered on the birth, life, and
death of the Golem, the cretin-like creation of the mystical
formulae of Rabbi Levi Bar Bezallel. The focus of this story is the effect of this creature on men. As a result, the

plot dominates characterization in the opera. The irony of
the story lies chiefly in the fact that Deborah, the daughter
of the Rabbi, is compassionately moved by the Golem and
pleads in his defense, only to be killed by the giant.   The
reversal of the story, after Deborah is killed by the Golem,
comes when the Rabbi repents of his action and accepts his
punishment.   The giant returns to the inert clay from which
he was shaped and the saddened Rabbi returns to the Synagogue for Sabbath worship.   This story, as an ancient folk
tale, is believable.   It also carries its didactic message of
man and his relation to God whose symbolic and enriching
level adds to the story.   The language of the opera is a
stilted poetic prose whose pretentious style is lacking in natural speech rhythms, truly Biblical flavor or particular eth-
nic colloquialism.   Because of the intricacy of the plot, reading is difficult and a more straightforward story line is needed to make the libretto successful.

        A revival of Porgy and Bess, with music by George
Gershwin and libretto by DuBose Hayward and Ira Gershwin,
was given during the 1962 Spring Season.   Based on a play,
Porgy, by DuBose and Dorothy Hayward, this libretto is essentially a "slice-of-life" treatment of "Catfish Row," a wa-
terfront Negro neighborhood in Charleston, South Carolina.
The plot revolves around Porgy, a cripple, and Bess, a pro-
stitute, and their troubled love affair.   This relationship is
further complicated by Crown, a local tough, to whom Bess
is strongly attracted.   The theme that emerges in this story
is "love is blind."   Bess, torn in her loyalties and affections,
in willingness to take "happy dust," consistently follows her
sensuous appetites.   Finally Porgy, with a similar abandon,
sets out for New York at the end of the opera to follow Bess.
The focus, then, is on Porgy and Bess, with Bess developing
into the more compelling and complex personality.   Porgy is
a good person--in fact, too good to be wholly believable.
The dramatic irony of the opera lies in Porgy's insistence
on following Bess although she has repeatedly proved herself
unfaithful.   In this irony is the reversal of the story: Bess
runs off to New York with Sporting Life despite Porgy's
demonstrated affectionate concern for her.   Because of the
indecision and reversals of Bess, the characterizations dominate the plot.   It is a view of a way of life which begins and
ends the opera with no apparent change despite the deep involvement of the main characters.   Again, as in so many
contemporary American operas, the language is cast in a poetic prose and here employs a colloquial speech pattern.
This pattern, although undoubtedly done with some accuracy,

is, nevertheless, a language that now reads in a rather trite
and somewhat condescending manner. A difficulty may lie in
the librettist attempting to give a "white" abstraction of the
Negro milieu which is only occasionally successful. A "shuf-
flin' darkie" attitude is what now comes across from a re-
reading. The libretto also appears somewhat simplistic thirty-
odd years after its creation, but the psychological involvement
is still strong.

        Carlisle Floyd's third opera produced at the New York
City Center was the 1962 production of The Passion of Jonathan Wade. Again Floyd provided his own libretto, this time
based on events in the South following the Civil War. The
story is of a Northern Army officer, Jonathan Wade, whose
job it is to restore order to a southern town. Here he meets
and falls in love with a local girl, Celia, and marries her
over her father's objections. Despite Wade's determination
to rule justly, his hand is forced by Enoch Pratt, head of
the Freedman's Bureau and a self-righteous New England
abolitionist, to deal severely with the townspeople. This
brings down their wrath in the form of the Ku Klux Klan,
and leads to Wade's death at the end of the opera. The central statement appears to be that social forces often defeat
the best intentioned men in their attempts to promote justice
and fair play. It is an opera with a clearly developed three-
act plot containing short sections entitled "Episodes" which
expand and deepen the perspective of the story. The focus
is on Wade and to a lesser extent on Celia and their relationship. However, the social problems of the South tend to
overshadow any subtlety in characterization. Dramatic irony
is employed in Wade's being shot in his attempt to find peace-
ful solutions to the problems. The marriage of Celia to
Wade reverses her position in the community, and at the end
of the opera she is prepared to leave the community forever.
Discovery is used in a limited way in the arrival of special
orders from Washington and the change in action that these
orders bring about. The characterizations are generally believable, but are not too fully developed. However, it is difficult to believe that Celia could reverse herself from complete hostility to adoring affection toward Wade in such a
short time. The script offers rather conventional post Civil
War figures--the proud aristocrat, the slick manipulator,
carpetbaggers, a self-righteous New England Abolitionist, and
honest and sincere Negroes. As a result the interest in social issues dominates the characterization. Prose is used
with only brief poetic passages interspersed, and the language
as a whole is not particularly memorable. However, Floyd

has avoided an attempt to be consciously "period" in his literary style and the libretto reads with colloquial ease in accepted twentieth century speech patterns. As there are no
surprises in the plot and the characters are rather standard,
there is a conventional quality to this libretto which prevents
it commanding one's attention.

An opera with an unusual format, given its world premiere in the fall of 1963, was <u>Gentlemen, Be Seated!</u> Modeled after the minstrel show and labeled by its authors,
Jerome Moross, music, and Moross and Edward Eager, libretto, "a musical entertainment," this opera attempted a
blending of traditional music hall form with that of opera.
There are two acts and a total of twenty-two scenes and eight
"dialogues." The theme of the opera is the American Civil
War in the context of the total American experience, rather
than a "taking of sides" in the conflict. It is, however, a
rather light treatment with only touches of attitudes of bitterness and cynicism towards war. Men leave their women to
go to war singing in the rhyming couplet style of the period.
Characters, however, are only briefly developed as conventional stereotypes. As a result they become symbols of a
general attitude of a class of people--the southern soldier,
the northern soldier, the farmer displaced by the war, the
women on both sides. The most believable characterizations
are the Negroes who express doubt about the whole business
of a Civil War and their place in a conflict run by whites.
Some sharp humor about Negroes and whites and attitudes
toward war are used in the "dialogue" exchanges, which give
a deepening seriousness to the story. The attempt at period
flavor results in a libretto which is only partially successful,
and the result is more often a softened and nostalgic attitude
such as one associates with Rodgers and Hammerstein's early
musicals. Small use is made of dramatic irony or reversal
implied in the immorality of war and the inconsistency of racial attitudes. The appealing Broadway musical flavor leads
one to conclude that the opera is not equal to the statement
it is attempting to make. It remains, however, an interesting use of a popular form of American musical entertainment
knit to the more serious attitudes of opera. It is an honest
attempt to try a new approach, but it results in an uneasy al-
liance of the two forms.

The one new American opera given a premiere during
the 1964 Fall Season was an adaptation of Ivan Turgenev's
play <u>A Month in the Country</u>, by William Ball with music by
Lee Hoiby. It was entitled <u>Natalia Petrovna.</u> This adaptation

is a faithful, although necessarily shortened version of the
original play. It presents the basic conflicts of the play and
maintains the original statement, which is that people often
want what realistically they can not have. The focus is on
Natalia, a self-indulgent countess, and Belaev, the young tutor
of her son. Natalia wants her own way in everything--especi-
ally love. She entertains an author, Rakitin, on a semi-per-
manent basis as a substitute for her husband. Meanwhile her
husband, Islaev, chooses to look the other way and concern
himself with his business interests. The tutor, although much
younger than the Countess, is also an object of her affections,
and she succeeds in destroying his relationship with her or-
phaned niece, Vera. One of the ironies of the story is that
Natalia loves Belaev but cannot have him, and this situation
leads to the reversal: Belaev leaves the house and thereby
abandons Vera and Natalia. The major discovery of the opera is Vera's realization of Natalia's love for Belaev. This
prompts Vera's rejection of Natalia and pushes the young girl
into maturity. The credibility of the opera is hampered by
limitations of the form, and the general consistency of the
opera is hindered by under-characterization. Broad strokes
are used where subtle character study is called for, and in
this respect the opera does not succeed--at least in the reading of the libretto. The language is a prose conversational
style when characters interact, but many solos and ensemble
numbers are in verse. This effect is generally acceptable--
a formal prose treatment--for the mid-nineteenth century setting of the story. Perhaps the greatest irony of the opera
lies in the conclusion where the principals all sing, in ensemble, of their individual unhappinesses. All are disappointed at the end of the action, and the opera closes, as it
opens, in boredom and frustration for these characters.

The Spring Season of 1965 featured three American
operas and the first produced in that season was Gian-Carlo
Menotti's The Saint of Bleecker Street. This opera, produced first on Broadway in 1954, is set in a "little Italy"
section of New York with a focus on the strong family devotion and deep religious conviction characteristic of these people. The central statement of the opera is that family devotion sometimes overrides all rational consideration for personal well being. This story is centered on Annina, who
wishes to become a nun, and her brother, Michael, who tries
vainly to protect his sister from what he feels are harmful
influences. Out of this over-protective concern ironic situations develop: Michael kills Desideria, who taunts him for
his love for his sister, and Annina's drive to become a nun

brings death and strife to her family. The reversal is implicit in this irony which is that devoted expressions of love
can bring about opposite results. If one accepts the "given"
elements of the story--the saintliness of Annina, her wish to
become a nun, her brother's blind devotion to her, and the
melodramatic elements of the story--it is effective and exciting. It is written in a nineteenth century operatic style with
what has become identified as Italianate love of passion and
intrigue in the verismo tradition. There is an over-balance
of plot in this story of strong conflicts. Characterizations
are rather conventional, but not necessarily less interesting
therefore. The language is colloquial English with a mixture
of poetic prose in aria passages. Italian and Latin are interspersed where necessary to create the realistic background
of this religious, Italian community. A good sense of contrast is developed in the language with the use of everyday
speech patterns and the formal religious expression of the
Mass. Filled with well-observed detail, its conventional dramatic structure, because of intelligent use of these devices,
makes the opera exciting.

    Lizzie Borden, an opera based on a famous murder
case in Fall River, Massachusetts, was presented by the New
York City Opera in the Spring Season of 1965. The music
was written by Jack Beeson with a libretto by Kenward Elmslie based on a scenario by Richard Plant. The action of the
opera explores the psychological family background of the
Borden family and takes the action beyond the murder. The
central statement centers on the frustrations of Lizzie--her
wish to be free of her family, her sexual inhibitions, and her
hatred of her stepmother. Contrasted to Lizzie, upon whom
the opera focuses, is her younger sister, Margaret, who
falls in love with and marries Captain Jason MacFarlane. In
part, through her sister, Lizzie realizes her own longings
for freedom. But the climax of the action is Lizzie's growing frustration and lack of coherence, which culminate in the
off-stage murder of both her parents. The action is tense
and the portrait of Lizzie compelling and believable. Dramatic irony is used chiefly at the end of the opera in the epilogue,
wherein Lizzie several years later assumes her father's role
emotionally as well as in business. She is now a spinster
living almost in seclusion and is becoming the person from
whom she most wanted to escape. By the end of the opera,
then, Lizzie dominates her surroundings in a direct reversal
of the opening. One is led into dramatic discovery when Lizzie becomes increasingly incoherent before the murder of her
parents. Thus Lizzie's motivations for murder are deep psy-

chological ones for which the audience has been fully prepared. But the parents are somewhat of a caricature--the
mother is a stereotyped fussing woman and the father the
epitome of stern New England Puritanism. However, Lizzie's
motives for murder, to be believable, would have to be based
upon strong circumstances. The plot seems predictable, and
the portrait of Lizzie dominates the opera. Colloquial English
with poetic overtones is the language of the libretto. It is
appropriate to the style of this piece. This opera has an obvious dramatic effectiveness in which a clear and direct development with tightly drawn characterizations lead to a powerful climax.

An adaptation of August Strindberg's Miss Julie is the
basis of the opera by the same name composed by Ned Rorem
with a libretto by Kenward Elmslie. It was produced in the
Fall Season of 1965 and follows closely the form and content
of the original. The main departure in the opera is to cast
the action in two acts, whereas Strindberg wrote the play to
be performed in one continuous action. There is a natural
break which makes such a treatment valid. The central
statement, that a person's wish to defy social convention for
sexual satisfaction can lead to disastrous results, is retained
in the opera. Julie, again, is the focus of the action, and
this rich psychological study ends on a note of dramatic irony
and reversal. Miss Julie, who is a well-born woman, in-
duces the valet, Jean, to seduce her, but is rejected by him
at the end of the action. Her aristocratic qualities are of
no help to her as she realizes the implications of her act.
He gives her a razor to use as a suicide weapon as the opera ends. Although Jean wants to arrive at aristocratic
means and attitudes, Miss Julie realizes by the end of the
action, as does Jean, that he cannot change. And, for that
matter, neither can she. The social gulf is still as wide as
ever. This believable action is based on the profound psychological motivations of both characters attempting to gratify
sexual-social ambitions, only to realize too late that the gulf
is too wide to be crossed successfully. The libretto develops
the action on several levels with duets and trios for characters to express divergent views and to underline the irony of
the situation. Miss Julie, the neurotic aristocrat, is effectively contrasted to Christine, Jean's fiance, the practical,
no-nonsense cook. The opening scene of Miss Julie taunting
her fiance, Niels, helps to set her character. It is a strong
and effective libretto with exciting moments of psychological
interest as well as moments of theatricality. The language
is colloquial with some poetic passages.

In the Spring 1967 Season, a new opera entitled The
Servant of Two Masters, with music by Vittorio Giannini and
a libretto by Bernard Stambler, was presented at the New
York City Opera, now in new quarters at Lincoln Center.
Based on the Carlo Goldoni play by the same name, this opera incorporates the commedia dell'arte style of the original
play. It is a libretto of artistic balances and verbal and visual wit, filled with stock commedia characters. It is a set
form with a farcical style and improvized elements. Pantalone and Truffaldino are the clever servants who eventually
guide their masters and mistresses through a maze of complications to the final chorus which states the theme, that
"Love will turn our dreams and hopes to reality." Beginning
with a bethrothal that is fouled, and ending with three mar-
riages, the plot is classically Aristotelian in its observance
of the elements of beginning, middle and end. The standard
devices of comedy form--mistaken identity and disguise--give
ample reversal and discovery elements. The characterizations, the time-honored "types" of commedia, have univer-
sality and consistency although they are all extreme in their
statement. But it is the plot that dominates the proceedings;
it is complicated but fun. Rhyming couplets as well as colloquial speech patterns are used and the comic tone and spirit
are well sustained in the language. It requires excellent diction from the cast, as there is so much verbal wit that it
would be unfortunate to lose. It is, in short, a time-proven
libretto full of comic situation and clever business. All in
all, it would be a test for singing-actors to bring off such a
lively opera.

Douglas Moore's new opera, Carry Nation, with a
libretto by William North Jayme, was presented in the Spring,
1968 Season. This opera attempts to tell the story of the
famous prohibition character from Kansas through a probing
of her early family life. The implication of the story is that
Carry was a product of a stern, nineteenth century Protestant
ethic which condemned alcoholic beverages. The theme could
be stated to the effect that excessive drinking can lead to the
wrecking of lives and relationships. The focus is clearly on
Carry and secondarily on Charles, her husband, and her
stern, religious father. Probably the greatest dramatic irony
of the opera is the masquerade of Christian "virtues" in the
stern Bible-belt Protestantism of Carry's father and its final
affect on her. Charles is cast out as a "sinner" by her father, almost from the first meeting of the two men. Psy-
chologically, the opera suggests the strong Oedipal conflicts
between father and daughter, and these provide the basis for

plot development. However, because of the rather one-di-
mensional character development and the predictable point of
view of nineteenth century mid-America, the dramatic interest
lags. The result is that the plot dominates the work. The
language, however, is colloquial and unforced and the style
appropriate for the story. It is unfortunate that the basically
good idea behind this libretto--a psychological study--does not
prove more successful. Perhaps the issue of prohibition and
its attendant conflicts fails to interest us sufficiently as a
subject for dramatic treatment.

     Hugo Weisgall returned with a new opera for the Fall
Season of 1968 entitled Nine Rivers From Jordan, with a libretto by Denis Johnston. In their former opera, Weisgall
and Johnston had the Pirandello drama, Six Characters in
Search of an Author, as a base for development. With Nine
Rivers there was no such effective dramatic base and the
mixture of war events and symbolic happenings does not hold
one's interest. The theme of this opera, "though we are all
'dirty' we are not damned, " is carried out through a series
of contrasting real and imaginary events which focus on Don
Hanwell, a British soldier. His idealism of not carrying a
weapon leads to deception and betrayal by other soldiers and
to his discovery of man's basically "dirty" nature. The characterization is most believable in terms of the language,
which is colloquial (and even four-letter Army) in style. This
is mixed with a more poetic treatment of language in the depicting of events of an imaginary nature. Finally, the stress
is upon ideas rather than action, and there is not a full
enough development of characterization to involve one's emotions. This is a "statement" about war that is too self-con-
scious and cerebral to make it possible for the audience to
care.

     Bracketting this study of forty operas presented by the
New York City Opera are works of Gian-Carlo Menotti. Two
of his operas were presented in 1948, and in 1970 and 1971
two new operas by Menotti were staged. Help, Help, The
Globolinks Are Coming! (music and libretto by Menotti), billed
as "an opera in one act for children and those who like children, " was presented in the Fall of 1970 after having premiered at the Santa Fe Opera the year before. It is a story
of children stranded in a bus on the way to school and threat-
ened by Globolinks, who are creatures from outer space. Out
of this situation the idea develops that, if the children and
teachers use traditional musical instruments, the Globolinks,
who move by electronic sounds, can be kept at a safe dis-

tance.   The theme, "traditional music will prevail," is underlined as the Globolinks are ultimately defeated by a band
of musicians consisting of the children and their teachers.
The children and their fear of the Globolinks are the main
focus of the opera.   The dramatic devices include the reversal effected by the people playing traditional instruments
to finally defeat the Globolinks, and the discovery that the
Principal is turning into a Globolink.   He is transformed in
a way that reminds one of Ionesco's The Rhinoceros.   The
opera is believable in a caricatured, rather comic manner.
The characterizations are straightforward, lacking in subtlety,
and use the traditional clichés of student and teacher types.
As a result one is interested more in "what happens next"
than in development of character.   In this sense the adventure aspect of the opera makes it a very appealing one for
children.   The literary style of the piece is in modern colloquial prose and the language serves the story quite satis-
factorily.

     The Most Important Man, with music and libretto by
Gian-Carlo Menotti, was presented in the Spring, 1971 Season.   Set in a white-dominated African republic, the opera
treats the story of a white scientist and his black assistant.
The theme of universal brotherhood is underlined with the
scientist, Dr. Arnek, accepting Toimé, his assistant, as a
son in his home.   His wife objects strongly but his daughter
falls in love with Toimé.   Upon the occasion of Toimé discovering a secret that will change the world, other scientists
and Leona, Arnek's wife, bring pressure on Dr. Arnek to
end his association with Toimé.   The destruction by Toimé
of the newly discovered formulas leads to Dr. Arnek's seeking Toimé's forgiveness only moments before the assistant--
the most important man--is shot.   Dramatic irony is inherent
in this story of brotherhood thwarted, plus a reversal that
also includes the destruction of important scientific information.   The discovery is made anew in this opera that con-
structive black-white relations are often difficult if not impossible to realize.   The language of the opera's libretto is colloquial, with some passages of poetry.   The characterizations
are uncomplicated and clear but they also lack a fresh approach.   We are not engaged in the problems of the people
in this opera, although the theme is one of contemporary
significance.   Perhaps the treatment of this idea would be
better realized in a much more particularized approach: one
in which there would be less predictability in the characters
and in the situation.

The group of forty opera librettos discussed in this chapter represent a sampling of the current work done in this medium in America.   It is difficult to give a summary statement, but one can observe that the thematic aspect of these librettos is strongly based on American subjects of both historical and current interest.   Mythology in the form of fictionalized American history or the use of Biblical themes is evident, as well as subjects of European origin. The language is usually a colloquial prose with some use of poetry, and there is also a kind of poetic-prose used in these works.   The handling of plot and characterization varies widely, and there appears to be an increased concern for subtlety of characterization.   There are not, however, radical departures in operatic form developed here.   It would appear from a study of these librettos that they represent a logical outgrowth of the nineteenth century and early twentieth century European tradition in opera.

Note

1. David Ewen, Encyclopedia of the Opera (New York: Hill and Wang, 1963), p. 314.

Chapter IV

CRITICAL APPRAISAL OF AMERICAN OPERA LIBRETTOS
AT THE NEW YORK CITY OPERA

At the conclusion of the 1948 opera season at the New
York City Center, the music critic, Olin Downes of the New
York Times, in summing up the season, praised the Opera
Company by stating:

> Another excellent feature of the Opera seasons at
> the Center Theatre is the rapid development of an
> American part of the repertory . . . It is a sys-
> tematic effort that is already beginning to bear
> fruit . . . It is a theatre which looks to the fu-
> ture; and which can be counted upon to stay . . .
> Its escape from routine, the stereotyped and the
> unimaginative in opera makes it one of the most
> interesting operatic enterprises to have been es-
> tablished in recent years.[1]

Two operas performed that season were considered an
important step in the direction of American opera: Gian-
Carlo Menotti's Old Maid and the Thief and Amelia Goes to
the Ball.   These two operas were offered as a double bill
and were given joint reviews which made the inevitable comparisons.   Virgil Thomson wrote in the New York Herald
Tribune: "Of the two Amelia is the better theatre piece.
It is excellent modern . . . opera buffa." His comment on
the libretto of the second opera was that "The Old Maid and
the Thief is of a lower order.   It is comic strip humor about
sex worked up as a radio show in fourteen short episodes
. . ."[2] Robert A. Simon in The New Yorker commented
that "Somehow Mr. Menotti managed to transfer the drama
[Old Maid] to the stage without losing any of its original pace
and smoothness." He found Amelia " . . . a thoroughly diverting piece."[3] Olin Downes also found much to praise in
these two works. He states of Old Maid and the Thief:

> This delectable and hilarious piece was done with
> a finish and esprit altogether delightful. . . .

> Here is a naturalness, a sense of text and theatre,
> a spontaneous vocal, musico-dramatic speech, which
> is original, authentic and triumphant as an artistic
> medium.[4]

Of Amelia he states that "Like the first piece, it vastly
amused the audience. But it is neither so compact nor so
mature a composition as the one which preceded it."[5]

Earlier criticism of Amelia included praise from Olin
Downes at a 1938 production: "Unity of thought and style obtain in a dexterous and diverting concoction."[6] But Lawrence
Gilman, in the New York Herald-Tribune, said of this production, "It is essentially Latin in its plot, its characters,
its psychology, its motivation . . . there is nothing in the
least 'American' about Mr. Menotti's book or music."[7]

At later dates these operas were given additional performances by the New York City Opera. Douglas Watt in the
Daily News remarked on such an occasion that Old Maid was
" . . . a somewhat lame-brained farce that grows wearisome
before it has spun out its allotted hour."[8] But in 1963
Amelia was again greeted with praise: Paul Henry Lang
wrote of Menotti that " . . . he has the true opera composer's instinct to weave text, music and action into a unity."[9]
Winthrop Sargeant noted also at this time,

> I had not seen Amelia since its first New York
> performance, at the Metropolitan Opera House
> some twenty-five years ago, and I was amazed at
> the brilliance, intricacy, and sure sense of operatic
> theatre that this old work retains.[10]

In the 1949 Spring Season one American opera was introduced, Troubled Island, with music by William Still and
libretto by Langston Hughes. Philip Hamburger, writing in
The New Yorker, comments on the libretto:

> . . . Mr. Hughes was working simultaneously on
> several planes. He had a great many fine and
> pressing things to say about freedom for the colored
> people of the earth, symbolized by Jean Jacques'
> revolt, but I could not escape the conclusions that
> what should have been ringing truths became pro-
> saic and perfunctory statements in the welter of
> plot and counterplot. The character of Dessalines
> never really had an opportunity to develop heroic

stature; there was too much else going on . . .
the stage of the City Center was crowded with a
hodge podge of quaint Haitian types.[11]

In the New York Times Olin Downes also found the opera
lacking: "There are a good many clichés of Broadway and
Hollywood in the score . . . very little is new."[12] The
New York Herald-Tribune critic, Francis D. Perkins, however, gave a generally more favorable review. He said:

> . . . Haiti and its tragic history have distinct pos-
> sibilities as subject for the lyric stage. In 'Trou-
> bled Island' these possibilities have been realized
> to some, if not to the fullest extent. The story
> has a generally straightforward presentation; Mr.
> Hughes's verse, sometimes rhymed and sometimes
> free in structure, seems usually well suited to mu-
> sical treatment . . .[13]

A second evening of Menotti was offered in the same
1949 Spring Season when The Medium was presented. An
earlier performance, reviewed in the Christian Science Monitor, gathered the following comments:

> The lurid goings-on are conducted in a properly
> Grand Guignol atmosphere. Although one would
> scarcely regard Madame Flora as a tragic figure,
> she is without doubt a genuinely theatrical one.[14]

The review also wrote of Menotti's capacity to create and
execute opera:

> . . . a man with an unusual faculty for fusing ele-
> ments of music and theatre. Mr. Menotti develops
> his story line with an expert sense of musical and
> dramatic effects [which are] . . . tightly integrated
> into the general scheme.[15]

In the Fall of 1949 Howard Taubman commented on the wide
popularity of The Medium, noting that the opera had been
performed 600 times in two years. This total included a
two-month run on Broadway, a domestic tour, and a month's
run in both London and Paris. In addition, many amateur
groups were doing the work. He also discusses the then
current controversy over the term "opera" and "drama with
music." The unfavorable and old fashioned connotations associated with "opera" made it an unattractive term and "dra-

ma with music" was used by the producers of The Medium.[16]

Subsequent revivals of The Medium at the New York City
Opera Company have gleaned generally favorable comment.
Ross Parmenter commented that The Medium is unmistakably
Menottian in its first strange chords. And it is a powerful
economical and concentrated work in which every stroke
counts.[17] But Paul Henry Lang during this 1963 revival
stated that he preferred Amelia to The Medium.[18] Winthrop
Sargeant shared the same view by stating that The Medium
"seemed something of a musical comedown afterward" (after
Amelia).[19] Miles Kastendieck complimented Menotti on his
"true feeling for the lyric theatre" in this revival and in the
Brooklyn Eagle Paul Affelder stated:

> In one listener's opinion, 'The Medium' remains
> Menotti's dramatic and musical masterpiece, a work
> that never fails to make a gripping, eerie effect.
> Its presentation Sunday was nothing short of magnifi-
> cent.[20]

At the time of the New York City Opera production,
Olin Downes commented on the American origin of the opera
and of its "genuine entertainment value." He also praised
the "remarkable talent as composer and stage craftsman of
Gian-Carlo Menotti." In conclusion, Downes pointed out that
"Enthusiasm ran high for the operas themselves and their
very spirited interpretation."[21]

In the Fall Season of 1951 The Dybbuk, with music by
David Tamkin and a libretto by Alex Tamkin, received a mixed
reception from the critics. Olin Downes found " . . . the
first act engrossing, if somewhat episodical and unconcen-
trated." But he continued, "By the evidence of the great applause, the second act, which is more concrete and obviously
more theatrically effective, was felt by the audience to be the
strongest." He thought the third act the weakest of the three,
but concluded that "The opera itself is in some respects the
most original and important of the five American works that
have figured in its repertory."[22] Virgil Thomson, an enthusiastic supporter of Ansky's play, stated that it " . . . has
one of the great plots of our century." He commented that
"Alex Tamkin's libretto derived from it is faultless." He
also praised " . . . its sophisticated treatment of the whole
world of religion and music . . . "[23]

A less favorable review was given by Douglas Watt in

The New Yorker. He stated:

> However, the obstacles a composer is likely to en-
> counter in setting a play to music have never been
> more evident, to my way of thinking. . . .   Tam-
> kin, to his credit, has treated the story with the
> utmost sobriety and respect, but nowhere in his
> score has he been able to match its awful events.
> The music continually acts as a kind of break upon
> the play, retarding the majestic progress of the
> early scenes and limiting the terror of the later
> ones.[24]

Enlarging on this same general criticism of the opera, Irving
Kolodin wrote:

> . . . but the high points of the play are carried
> by speech, not song, as in the tremendously force-
> ful dialogue between the rabbi and the deceased
> father of the Dybbuk, in which the violated agree-
> ment is revealed . . . Tamkin's abdication of re-
> sponsibility leaves the issue with Ansky, who comes
> off well enough. But so he would in the theatre
> too.[25]

In a transfer from television to the theatre, an occasion unique in opera, Menotti's Amahl and the Night Visitors
was presented in the Opera Company's Spring Season of 1952.
Again Menotti captured the critics and audience alike with an
opera that apparently spoke to everyone. In reviewing the
telecast which was given at Christmas before it was staged
in the spring, Olin Downes commented:

> Mr. Menotti has set this subject with such masterly
> simplicity, tenderness and inborn musico-dramatic
> skill that we defy any person of normal sensibility
> to watch and listen without a tightening of the
> throat . . . What ever is done is done with the
> most remarkable dramatic precision and propor-
> tion.[26]

Time magazine reported that "The story is a simple Menotti
mixture of melodrama and pathos, with more than enough invention to fill out fifty minutes." The writer concluded:
"Menotti makes his story point with dramatic directness."[27]

On the occasion of the stage version presentation by

the New York City Opera, Douglas Watt reported that "It
turned out to be a thoroughly ingratiating little piece . . .
The story is an affecting one . . . " He liked the characterizations, noting " . . . the three Kings, each a humorous
contrast to the others . . . the worn mother [played] with
becoming gentleness." He concluded that "Amahl and the
Night Visitors is a stage work of very small proportions,
but it has a wonderful glow."28

    In a later revival at the City Center Opera Winthrop
Sargeant wrote:

> I did not like it as well as some of his earlier
> operas--notably The Medium. I thought it a shade
> arch and sentimental, and it was somewhat difficult
> for me to reconcile the three wise kings' buffoonery
> with the seriousness of their sacred mission . . .
> It is, however, an unpretentious work with a few
> charming moments, and it shows throughout the
> facility for musical theatre that distinguishes Menot-
> ti's operatic output.

Sargeant completes his comments by noting that the chal-
lenges of the script are " . . . met, on the whole with
grace and fluency."29 In a later review of a subsequent
performance of the televised version of Amahl, the following
comment is informative:

> . . . the work has already become a Christmastide
> classic in its six years' career thus far . . . The
> reasons for its widespread appeal can be found in
> its musical and emotional directness . . . and the
> composer's well-known and exceptional ability to
> project and enhance a desired mood and dramatic
> situation.30

    In the Fall Season of that same year, the New York
City Opera presented the fifth of Gian-Carlo Menotti's works,
The Consul. At the opera's Broadway opening in 1950,
Brooks Atkinson offered the following comments:

> Without the music, his drama would not make a
> very profound impression in the theatre. It begins
> on a note of violent melodrama which from the lit-
> erary point of view Mr. Menotti does not sustain.
> The story is loose. It may be even maudlin and
> banal on its own terms. Although the main style

is vividly realistic, the drama several times drifts
off into dream sequences that are in an alien key
if not, indeed, in a different medium. The dream
sequences are full of obscure symbolism that might
look sophomoric in the prose theatre. 31

Offering a more enthusiastic opinion of this performance was
the reviewer in the New York Sun and Telegram who stated
that Menotti " . . . has an unparalleled instinct for the theatre. It is an instinct that touches his creation of character,
his construction of plot, his climaxes and curtains, and inevitably his imbuing all these elements with true musical
function. " 32

        Winthrop Sargeant, twelve years later, at the New
York City Opera revival, commented:

        The Consul, to my mind, is his masterpiece thus
        far; it is a work of such immediate import, such
        stunning eloquence, and such marked originality that
        in hearing it last week, for perhaps the tenth time,
        I was touched all over again, by its humanity, grace,
        and profound musical meaning . . . It is now vir-
        tually a classic. 33

At this same time Paul Henry Lang expressed a more ad-
verse opinion: " . . . the author-composer tends to over-
state a case which has a good deal of truth in it, but which
. . . may not be best served by the rawness and sophistica-
tion of his treatment. " 34   Alan Rich praised the work in
these terms: "Here is the kind of serious musical theatre
that comes across vivid and original." He concludes: "What
really matters is that it is a strong and exciting piece of musical drama. " 35   The Journal-American concurred: "It remains a powerful work, theatrically effective and emotionally
depressing. " 36   In a more negative criticism Raymond Ericson reported:

        For Menotti is a master of theatrical effects. This
        fact helps The Consul override its inadequacies, its
        embarrassingly self-conscious lines, its shoddy mu-
        sic. From the moment when the curtain goes up
        on an empty stage . . . there are devices to com-
        mand attention, even to startle. 37

Joseph Machlis, in his book entitled Introduction to Contemporary Music, refers to this opera as a "profoundly compas-

sionate drama. "38   In an interesting concluding note in the
New York Post review, the reviewer points out that "This
opera has now been given hundreds of times on Broadway and
repeatedly at the City Center and in Central Park and on
TV. "39

     The 1953 American opera offering at the New York
City Opera was Marc Blitzstein's Regina, based on Lillian
Hellman's The Little Foxes.   This opera had been given on
Broadway in 1949, and Wolcott Gibbs, noting the many dan-
gers of setting this well known play to music, concluded:
"To some extent, these misgivings were justified, but altogether I think Mr. Blitzstein has done a remarkably able
job. "   On the other hand he said: "The result is no longer
genuinely shocking, and sometimes, as when Regina's brother
carols toward the end that she is a greedy girl, it struck me
as comic in not exactly the right way. "40   John Mason
Brown stated even more strongly the case against turning
the play into an opera:

> . . . why, in the name of reason and for the well-
> being of Miss Hellman's own exceptionally exciting
> play, the attempt should ever have been made to
> turn it into a musical drama . . . For me it un-
> does the very thing Miss Hellman had done well.
> It interrupts the action, annihilates the illusion, and
> destroys the suspense.   It acts as a brake, not an
> accelerator.   Its colloquial and mundane recitatives
> struck me as down right silly. 41

Another drama critic (as opposed to music critic), Harold
Clurman, remarked upon the transference difficulties of a
drama to opera this way:

> [It is] an interesting attempt to extend the limita-
> tions and conventions of our stage beyond the flat
> statement of journalistic naturalism and the merely
> decorative theatricality of our musical comedy and
> operetta.

But he also had problems accepting this new treatment:

> The trouble with Regina, I believe, stems from
> Blitzstein's respect for its origins . . . its spirit
> is the antithesis of the musical . . . Blitzstein
> should have taken all the liberties necessary to
> make Regina entirely his own. 42

When the revival was given at City Center, Irving
Kolodin thought that "Regina does not seem to me a substan-
tially better work than it was before, but it was well deserv-
ing of the effort applied to it." He concluded that "As a
spoken drama, The Little Foxes is so action-packed that the
music tends more often to be an intrusion than an acces-
sory."[43]

Aaron Copland's The Tender Land, with a libretto by
Horace Everett, was offered in the Spring Season of 1954 on
a double bill with Amahl and the Night Visitors. Winthrop
Sargeant noted that "This little plot . . . is obviously suit-
able for opera. But, for a number of reasons . . . does
not come off." He believed Menotti's work "far better written for voices than Copland's, and far more compelling from
a dramatic standpoint. I might add that Mr. Menotti, who
writes his own librettos, is a much more skilled craftsman
in fitting words to music than the librettist of The Tender
Land."[44] Irving Kolodin concurred with this point of view:
" . . . a rather inept script. The result is far from a really good stage work, and by no stretch of the imagination
can it be called an opera."[45] Howard Taubman, who later
wrote drama criticism for the New York Times, pointed out
that "Its total effect is that of a landscape with genre figures
rather than of a drama of vivid, moving human beings." He
believed characterization one of the faults: "The glaring
weakness in The Tender Land remains in the principal role,
that of the girl, Laurie . . . Laurie is simply not realized
as a human being."[46] In the New York Herald-Tribune Alan
Rich commented that the opera " . . . is not Copland's best
piece of Americana by a long shot, but its weaknesses have
to do more with the composer's failings as a musical drama-
tist than as a landscape artist."[47] The comment by Howard
Klein concerning the libretto was that "the drama is static."[48]

Carlisle Floyd's Susannah was given its New York
State premiere at the New York City Opera in September of
1956. Howard Taubman reported of the libretto:

> He has fashioned a simple, straightforward libretto.
> It builds steadily and surely, and it holds the at-
> tention. Its failing is that it makes its case in
> extremes . . . But [in Susannah and Rev. Olin
> Blitch] Mr. Floyd has created two people of flesh
> and blood.

In specific reference to Act Two, Scene Two, Mr. Taubman

noted that "As musical theatre, it is of the first order."[49]
Irving Kolodin in referring to the score and libretto stated
that "What comes out is a better blend of word and note than
is usually the case . . . " He concluded that "For a first
effort in such a treacherous field as folk-opera it plays well,
sings reasonably well, holds the attention almost always."[50]

The next season, 1957, the work was revived and
Howard Taubman updated his comments in this way:

> His libretto, despite some conventional moments,
> has dramatic fiber and suits his musical purposes.
> He captures the spirit of the Tennessee valley set-
> ting.
> . . . .
>
> He knows how to construct a scene and how to
> build a climax; witness the pulsating second scene
> of the second act.[51]

Harriett Johnson noted that the libretto " . . . endears itself because of its directness, its sincerity and its singable
melodic texture."[52]

At the 1963 production of the work at the New York
City Opera, Louis Snyder noted that " . . . this tale of religious and psychic tension in the Tennessee mountains again
proved an effective musical theatre piece." He also praised
the "believable operatic characters" of Susannah.[53] Howard
Klein called it " . . . a second-act opera--but what an act."
He pointed out that "The first act takes too much time drawing the characters; the mood it sets gives little preparation
for the wallop to come." "From the opening," he reported,
"it looks like a nice folk story, but from the revival scene
in Act 2, the tragic elements lurch to the powerful conclusion."[54] Harriett Johnson, viewing it again, praised it as
a "great show" as well as vital drama."[55] Miles Kastendieck, in reviewing the 1965 performance, wrote: "Whatever
the weaknesses in book and score, as a first opera this sur-
vives repetition remarkably well. The grass roots quality
remains fresh; the atmosphere communicates meaning; the
drama has human appeal."[56]

When the Douglas Moore-John LaTouche opera, The
Ballad of Baby Doe opened in the Spring Season of 1958, it
was an occasion commented on in a special way. Howard
Taubman reported:

If the City Center is crowding history, it does so
with banners flying. It believes that American opera has substance now and is not merely a dream
of the future. With a $105,000 blessing from the
Ford Foundation, it set out last night to demonstrate its faith.

It is a brave and provocative adventure that the
City Center has dared to undertake. In the next
five weeks it intends to produce ten American operas, and if it had the time and money, it could
find others worth doing. There could be no more
audacious effort to dramatize our achievements in
this field.

The Ballad of Baby Doe led the way.

His comment on the libretto was: "Mr. LaTouche managed
to put together a libretto in which action could move without
awkward stretches of recitative . . . But the main lines of
the story and character are straightforward and touching."
This was not his first acquaintance with the opera. He
pointed out that " . . . to one who saw it in Colorado two
years ago it was not a let down on reacquaintance . . .
More power to the City Center." 57   At this same opening
Winthrop Sargeant wrote that " . . . a very important event
in the current history of music" had taken place. "The work
is actually a sort of declaration of independence--," he added,
"independence from all the fashionable highbrow fiddle-faddle
and mysterious technical mumbo-jombo that during the past
forty years have tended to reduce the art of opera to a feeble
caricature of itself." On the libretto he commented that "The
drama written by the late John LaTouche is a heartwarming
tale . . . and includes several quite penetrating studies of
human character, [but] does not stray far from the conventions of show business." 58   Irving Kolodin reported the operas as " . . . the work of two experienced craftsmen who
know the verbal and musical language well enough to tell their
story effectively." His reaction to the libretto was that "In
some ways, this scheme is a little too ambitious for eleven
scenes, especially overdeveloped being those of Act II, in
which Tabor's political involvements are depicted." He was
critical also of the two-act structure and felt that the first
act could have ended sooner. 59

After the opening performance of Baby Doe in the
1962 Season, Miles Kastendieck remarked that "This choice

bit of Americana wears well as both a thoroughbred product and a moving human document."[60]   Francis D. Perkins of the New York Herald-Tribune found on this revival that the opera "wears well."[61]   In the New York Times Raymond Ericson noted that "The word apparently is getting around that this opera, which is now six years old, is easy to understand and entertaining, and this is all to the good."[62]

Ross Parmenter pointed out the next year, 1963, that "Douglas Moore's The Ballad of Baby Doe and Carlisle Floyd's Susannah are the American operas with which the New York City Opera has had the greatest success . . . John LaTouche's book continues to be interesting."[63]   The New York Herald-Tribune agreed, commenting that this opera " . . . has become one of the most popular and most frequently performed of the company's American repertoire." The review concludes with the statement that "The realization of works like this is what makes the City Opera's contribution to our creative life the invaluable service that it is."[64]   The Christian Science Monitor remarked that " . . . The Ballad of Baby Doe holds its own wonderfully well. The fact that it has had fifteen performances by City Opera indicates a repertory tendency of singular importance. This is a distinctive contribution . . . "[65]

The opera was again in the repertory in 1965 and the New York Times reported that " . . . the opera has its faults . . . But because the characters change and grow, and because that growth is fully explored in the drama, it is viable theatre." The reporter concludes that the opera " . . . seems to be holding its own. It had its premiere nine years ago, and the company has frequently given it since."[66]

Two one-act operas were offered in the Ford Foundation sponsored season of 1958: Tale for a Deaf Ear, with music and libretto by Mark Bucci, and Trouble in Tahiti, with music and libretto by Leonard Bernstein. Howard Taubman reported of Mr. Bucci's opera that "His drama shuttles between violently contrasted levels and never succeeds in mediating between the two . . . Occasionally there is an amusing line . . . But he lacks Mr. Bernstein's sure-handedness for what is effective drama."[67]   Musical America reported that the opera contained an "involved libretto."[68]   At the initial performance of this opera at the Tanglewood Music Festival a year earlier, Time magazine reported that "The opera . . . almost jolted the . . . audience out of their seats, left them applauding wildly."[69]

Bernstein's opera, originally performed on television in 1952, was reviewed by Irving Kolodin at that time. He commented on the libretto in this way:

> Two emptier, duller people never lived; and if they did knock their heads together nothing would result but a muffled thud. Perhaps Bernstein meant them to come out that way; but they should have something more dimensional to serve as types rather than individuals.[70]

John Crosby termed the opera as it appeared on television "witty and provocative."[71] On the occasion of the performance by the New York City Opera, Howard Taubman wrote that "The war between husbands and wives was the subject of both operas . . . It is a theme that has been done to death . . . " Of this libretto he said, "Mr. Bernstein's book is incisive, and underneath its barbs there is a longing for peace and love . . . The fun is not in the marital battle but in the wonderfully satiric comment on our mores."[72] Musical America called this opera " . . . a somewhat frowsy pastiche that combines an amusing satire of suburbia with clever take-offs of popular music and half-hearted attempt to touch a more serious note in some passages that sound like poor-man's Copland."[73]

The New York Journal-American reported of the Kurt Weill-Maxwell Anderson Lost in the Stars at the 1958 revival, "By including it in an American opera season, the New York City Opera Company raises the question of its proper classification. It was a Broadway show eight years ago." However, the reviewer, Miles Kastendieck, did not trouble too much over the classification; he termed his experience of the evening "gripping" and wrote that the production "qualifies as one of the finest moments in the theatrical season."[74] At the earlier Broadway opening, Howard Barnes wrote:

> Anderson faced a stupendous job in translating a tale of Negroes and whites in South Africa to terms of a libretto and lyrics. He has handled it magnificently. Interlacing fragments of straight melodrama and moving drama with songs which continually add to the sense and momentum of the action, he has captured the full essence of the original in striking stage patterns. The singing ensemble acts

as a sort of Greek chorus, while individual scenes
spotted rapidly in George Jenkins flexible and imaginative settings . . . The show moves to its climax
inexorably and with a tremendous cresdendo.[75]

Brooks Atkinson commented: "The translation of Cry, the
Beloved Country into Lost in the Stars has not been easy or
altogether successful . . . Their narrative, it seems to me,
is too literal, too realistic, too unwilling to use the incanta-
tion of the imaginative theatre."[76] Wolcott Gibbs wrote, "I
was one of a small, wayward minority that found the play
somehow disappointing." Of the libretto he states "In delet-
ing some characters completely . . . Anderson may have
produced a more compact and manageable story, but he has
also discarded a lot that gave the book its unique charm.
As to the impact of the story, he writes, " . . . the tragedy
never rises above the level of a melodramatic device."[77]

At the opening of the New York City Opera revival
Howard Taubman wrote that "Maxwell Anderson's text for
Lost in the Stars inevitably cannot encompass Paton's story
and Kurt Weill's music does not even measure up to Mr.
Anderson's book."[78] Paul Henry Lang commented: "No use
of comparing Lost in the Stars with Porgy and Bess; it has
neither the good tunes of the latter nor its truly operatic
moments."[79] Irving Kolodin remarked that "Altogether there
is more of Paton's novel in Anderson's text than in Weill's
score . . . "[80] Musical America offered a more optimistic
review:

> No one could fail to be touched by the eloquent
> production of the Maxwell Anderson-Kurt Weill
> Lost in the Stars . . . and much of the impact of
> Alan Paton's novel Cry, the Beloved Country was
> preserved . . .

Mention was made in this review of the abundance of spoken
dialogue. Also " . . . trite score, shopworn tunes and
sticky sweet orchestration in the Broadway vein, [which]
really adds nothing to the work." But the artists "transcended their material."[81]

The Taming of the Shrew, with music by Vittorio
Giannini and a libretto by Dorothy Fee, was first performed
on television in 1953. Virgil Thomson wrote that "The libretto . . . is compact, expeditious, seems to have no major fault." He also commented that the " . . . dramatic

line is sustained . . . due . . . to the excellence of the
libretto."82   At the production of the opera at City Center,
Howard Taubman reported that it "makes a capital show."
He noted the "vivacity of its spirits and boisterousness of
its laughter. [There is] . . . a gay and airy book, using
only the lusty and singing lines of Shakespeare; they have
helped themselves to passages from Romeo and Juliet and
sonnets to fill out their text." He concluded that it was
" . . . a thoroughly enjoyable evening."83   Paul Henry
Lang, addressing his remarks to the libretto, stated:

> The comic element is well utilized and the play
> goes like lightning--but there is no characteriza-
> tion whatever. In order to be believable Kate must
> be downright brutal, which in turn authorizes Pe-
> trucchio to be even tougher. There is no indica-
> tion anywhere that he is in love with Kate, in fact
> he is ready to marry her even before he has set
> eyes upon her, and this in spite of her reputation
> of being completely intractable. This is animal
> taming, not a love story . . . The denouement is
> really makeshift theatre . . . its weakest part.84

In summing up this Ford Foundation season, Musical America
reported on each American opera presented. This article
stated that " . . . of all ten works in this season of American opera, Vittorio Giannini's The Taming of the Shrew most
closely follows tradition in its style and structure. Mr.
Giannini works with practical skill . . . [it is a] delightfully
entertaining work."85   A reassessment was offered by Irving
Kolodin when he remarked in his review that " . . . closer
acquaintance with Giannini's score gave it a higher rank than
when it was done on TV several years ago. For one thing,
the text . . . has been skillfully adapted from the original
. . . "86

The world premiere of The Good Soldier Schweik, with
music by Robert Kurka and libretto by Lewis Allen, was given
at the New York City Opera in the 1958 Season. Howard
Taubman reported:

> Mr. Allen's libretto reduces Schweik's adventures
> to a series of brief episodes. They ramble a bit,
> and several could be spared. His rhymes are also
> somewhat monotonous. But he has created the
> framework for a fast moving, often funny, theatre
> piece.87

Irving Kolodin wrote that " . . . Lewis Allen has made an uneven but sometimes scandalously funny libretto . . . The tale is told in a dozen and a half short scenes in a text that is mostly colloquial, sometimes coarsely so. But, as Kipling remarked some time ago, 'men in barracks don't grow into plaster saints.' "[88] Jay Harrison wrote that " . . . the tale does not really build or develop--at least as it has been gathered together by Mr. Allen . . . [It is] a series of episodes that never congeal into a continuous forward moving plot . . . dramatically contrived and verbally clumsy. "[89] Winthrop Sargeant commented that it was " . . . a curiously hybrid concoction . . . a sort of review." Extending these remarks he wrote that

> . . . if you consider it as an opera and look into its qualities as music and evocative drama, there is really not much to it.
>
> The Good Solider Schweik, to my mind, is neither American nor an opera. It is a nostalgic rehash of a theatrical era for which I, at any rate, find it very difficult to work up any genuine nostalgia.[90]

Musical America found the opera "lusty and captivating."[91]

Six years later when the opera was performed in Minneapolis at the Guthrie Theatre, Raymond Ericson reported that " . . . neither libretto or score is distinguished in itself, but they complement each other so superbly as to form a superior piece for the musical theatre."[92]

Of the premiere of Gian-Carlo Menotti's new opera, Mario Golovin, at the Brussel's World Fair, Howard Taubman wrote:

> It has been suggested that Mr. Menotti's theatrical talents are so great that he could easily turn to writing plays without music . . . Perhaps he could . . . But the librettos are not convincing evidence that he could. If they were stripped of music, they would lack the fulness and density one expects of spoken drama.
>
> Maria Golovin is shrewd theatre . . . In the spoken theatre the denouement Mr. Menotti has devised for this opera would not go down so smoothly as it does in this form.[93]

On this same production William Mann of the New York
Herald-Tribune reported that "The weakness in the score is
that Menotti writes contemporary drama and sets it to fusty,
old fashioned music." He added that he did not think the music of Menotti was equal to his drama. 94

When the opera opened on Broadway, for a brief run,
Walter Kerr commented on the " . . . close-to-garish use
of the flashier mechanics of the theatre." He also pointed
out the static nature of the central figure and the "one-note
theme." "The figures," he said "caught in an emotional
trap, express themselves well but do not grow in stature; in
time, the mechanics become larger and more emphatic than
the meaning of a somewhat limited love story." He found
the opera " . . . adventurous musical theatre, with a stub-
born bravado about it that is sometimes foolish, but more
often stimulating." 95

The New York City Opera revival gained the comment
from Paul Henry Lang: "Well, this opera does not represent
progress in Mr. Menotti's career . . . [It is] good, efficient
entertaining musical theatre." 96 Musical America reported
that the opera was "good theatre . . . thoroughly entertaining" and a "masterly pastiche." 97

When the opera was produced in Washington, D.C.,
Donald Mintz of the New York Times noted that "Despite the
changes, despite an enthusiastic audience response, the opera
remains problematic and unsatisfactory . . . Most of the
trouble stems from the libretto." In expanding his comments
on the libretto he wrote:

> The work combines sleazy, old-fashioned melo-
> drama with muddy and often all-too-obvious sym-
> bolism. Menotti handicaps himself also with too
> many words, mostly trivial, prosaic and unidiomat-
> ic but sometimes fustian . . . And the words are
> arranged so as to interfere with each other and
> the music. 98

The second American offering of the Spring 1959
Season was Street Scene, with music by Kurt Weill and libretto by Elmer Rice and Langston Hughes. As the musical
had been performed on Broadway in 1947, comparisons by
reviewers were inevitable. Howard Taubman reported that
the work was " . . . warm-hearted and powerful theatre."
In comparison to the Elmer Rice play he said that "It was a

play . . . that retained its impact in the tightened form required for music." But he noted that "Mr. Weill did not
dare to go all-out for opera," as there was no music at the
melodic highpoint of the piece.[99] Irving Kolodin noted that
" . . . the passage of a dozen years since it was new hasn't
molded its elements into a better blend than they first pos-
sessed." He also found many clichés in the story and con-
trivances in the score.[100] Musical America found the musical "colorful, fast-moving, entertaining," but the reviewer
admitted that the realism of Street Scene seemed "faded."[101]

In the 1963 season, when Street Scene was given again,
Leonard Harris quotes Weill as saying, "Not until Street
Scene did I achieve a real blending of drama and music, in
which the singing continues naturally where the speaking
stops." Harris, mentioning the libretto, states that "The
music has a fit companion in Langston Hughes' words, which
are poetic and, at the same time, effortlessly idiomatic
without condescension."[102] Miles Kastendieck reported that
Street Scene is "a natural extension of Elmer Rice's famous
play." In noting the difficulty of placing the work properly
he wrote: "Let Street Scene serve as a transitional work,
bridging the gap between the traditional lyric theatre and a
Broadway musical."[103]

A double bill of American operas during this season
presented The Scarf, with music by Lee Hoiby and libretto
by Harry Duncan, and The Devil and Daniel Webster, with
music by Douglas Moore and libretto by Stephen Vincent
Benet. Howard Taubman wrote that The Scarf contained
" . . . a tightly written libretto by Harry Duncan based on
a . . . story by Chekhov." In his estimation, "The libretto
does not offer opportunity for depth or subtlety. It is an
achievement when a young American can turn out an opera
that has so much craft and holds the audience so effectively."[104] Irving Kolodin reported that "Unfortunately a good
dramatic anecdote has been expanded into a minor epic at an
hour's length, something which Puccini . . . would never in-
dulge."[105] In comparing The Scarf with a later effort of
Hoiby--Natalia Petrovna--Kolodin reported that "As in The
Scarf . . . an hour long occasion, Hoiby's sense of propor-
tion is still at variance with theatrical interest."[106] Musical America's comment was that the subject matter used in
The Scarf was " . . . a dangerous theme for musical treatment."[107]

Douglas Moore's The Devil and Daniel Webster was

offered on Broadway in 1939. At that time Richard Watts
wrote that Benet's lyrics were "a trifle folksy."[108] Olin
Downes in his review stated that " . . . the short opera
. . . has the advantage of an interesting and imaginative libretto which really does capture some of the quality of an
American folk legend."[109] Pitts Sandborn in the New York
World-Telegram commented that "Stephen Vincent Benet has
concocted the play with skillful use of suspense and much
verbal aptness and wit."[110] George Jean Nathan, writing in
Newsweek, wrote of the libretto that "It was almost completely dramaless and never more so than when Mr. Moore peri-
odically embroidered it with his genteel and wholly respectable, if generally impotent, score."[111] Brooks Atkinson is
quoted in the following opinion:

> As a theatrical production, The Devil and Daniel
> Webster represents some of the finest and most
> painstaking work of the season. It is original,
> versatile, talented and enjoyable . . . Speech and
> lyric song follow one another in the most natural
> sequence . . . An unerring dramatic instinct and
> sense of the theatre saved Moore from the pitfall
> of setting Webster's defense to song.[112]

When the opera was done by the New York City Opera,
Irving Kolodin reported that "It is well worth considering,
however, whether a good part of the appeal of The Devil and
Daniel Webster is not inherent in the superb script of Stephen
Vincent Benet." He concludes that "It proves beyond question
that writing can be folksy without being banal, and eloquent
without being high-flown."[113] Musical America commented
on this opera's "flimsiness" and felt it inferior to Ballad of
Baby Doe although it did possess "a certain charm and New
England flavor."[114]

Wuthering Heights, with music by Carlisle Floyd and
libretto by the composer based on the novel by Emily Brontë,
opened at Santa Fe Opera in 1958. At that time Douglas
Watt reported that the " . . . composer's own remarkably
compact libretto, [is] a model of playwriting itself."[115]
Howard Taubman, at the City Center production, noted that
"The libretto unfolds with conviction."[116] In the New York
Herald-Tribune, Floyd is quoted as saying: "I employed as
much as possible the language of opera: Highly colored,
highly poetic prose within a realistic framework."[117] Irving
Kolodin wrote a fuller accounting of the libretto:

>The composer-librettist . . . has chosen to begin
>with an anti-climatic 'prologue' showing Wuthering
>Heights in full decline . . . This cinematic sug-
>gestion of the 'flashback' really doesn't work, op-
>eratically, and tends to make the ensuing action
>less compelling than it might have been otherwise.
>What follows is a reasonably straightforward story-
>telling, though neither Heathcliff nor Catherine re-
>ally clarify the impulses that make them act as
>they do.[118]

Musical America was more enthusiastic in reporting that it
was " . . . a wholly successful and deeply moving opera
[containing] hypnotic power."[119]   The reviewer also believed
the story-within-a-story unnecessary.

Pantaloon, later renamed He Who Gets Slapped, with
music by Robert Ward and libretto by Bernard Stambler
based on a play by Andreyev, was first presented by Columbia University in 1956.   When the opera was produced at
New York City Opera, Howard Taubman said that "The libretto moves and gives the composer opportunity for music."[120]
Kolodin, however, felt that the opera was "never quite brought
into focus."[121]   Musical America reported that the libretto
was "sentimental, forced, and full of clichés."[122]

The one-act opera Triumph of St. Joan, with music
and libretto by Norman Dello Joio, was presented in the
1959 season on a double bill with Menotti's The Medium.
The initial performance of the Dello Joio work was at Sarah
Lawrence College in 1950 and Virgil Thomson reported:

>. . . tension of the narrative is low.   The device
>of presenting this through memories recalled dur-
>ing the Maid's imprisonment gives the story a
>static quality.   The Maid's own meditations, more-
>over, which bind the remembered scenes together,
>consist largely of self-pity.   The whole libretto
>lacks animation and lift.[123]

Robert Bagar of the New York Sun and Telegram reported:
"Actually I thought many of the libretto's lines were out-and-
out trite . . . they were not couched in anything like poetic
language or language for music."[124]   Later, the opera appeared on television and Howard Taubman noted that " . . .
though . . . simple and straightforward, [it] lacks contrast,
and his characters [are] almost of one shade."[125]

        At the production of the opera at City Center, Howard
Taubman found no new point of view brought to the story, but
that the composer "writes with so much sincerity and dignity
that the opera holds the attention."126 Musical America
wrote that

>   The Dello Joio opera arouses respect and admira-
>   tion for its workmanship and dignity, but it touches
>   the emotions only fitfully . . . [The] libretto is
>   merely a respectful restatement . . . well worn
>   theatre. [It] seems now only a sincere, well
>   wrought work that keeps its distance too well.127

        The last new American opera to be given its world
premiere in the 1959 season was Six Characters in Search
of an Author, with music by Hugo Weisgall and libretto by
Denis Johnston adapted from the Pirandello play. Howard
Taubman reported:

>   The libretto prepared by Denis Johnston from Luigi
>   Pirandello's play is one of the most literate and
>   stimulating to come the way of any composer. But
>   its subject--what is reality and what is illusion?--
>   poses perplexing problems for a musician. Hugo
>   Weisgall's attempt to cope with them is brave, but
>   only partly successful.128

In the Musical Quarterly for July of that year, Richard
Goldman referred to the opera as an "extraordinary work"
and made the following comments about the libretto:

>   Denis Johnston's adaptation of the play is brilliantly
>   successful: a tight, witty, literate libretto, in good
>   idiomatic English, with no false note or transla-
>   tions into librettoese. He has managed to strength-
>   en and sharpen the play, taking as his license some
>   ideas written by Pirandello himself in his foreword.
>   Johnston has played down the pseudo-philosophizing
>   about illusion and reality, greatly toned up the wit
>   and satire, and left the melodrama alone. Even
>   so, the mixture is rather wild, but theatrically ex-
>   citing, and a tremendous challenge to the compos-
>   er.129

Musical America found the opera "controversial" and thought
the "Play stands head and shoulders above the opera." For
this reviewer nothing was added to the play by making it an

opera.130

Marc Blitzstein's The Cradle Will Rock, with both
music and libretto by the composer, was offered in the 1960
Spring Season. It had originally been done in 1936 and has
been characterized by Joseph Machlis as a " . . . mixture
of violence, satire, [and] tenderness and one of the memorable documents of the Depression era. (Its revival almost a
quarter century later proved that the work was strictly of its
time.)"131 At a 1947 revival Brooks Atkinson commented:
"At the moment it is impossible to recall another musical
drama so candid, so original and so fresh in stage conception."132 But John Mason Brown reported:

> The brash insularity of The Cradle Will Rock is
> one of the reasons why it now seems old-fashioned.
> There are others. Although we may sympathize
> with the anger of Mr. Blitzstein's opera, we are
> forced today to smile at its assurance. . . . We
> are both amazed and amused at its utter blindness
> to the complexities of even national life. Its very
> confidence in the truth of the sheep-and-goats divi-
> sion of its characters destroys our confidence in it
> as an adult study. It is the world that has been
> rocked and Mr. Blitzstein's opera that has stood
> still.133

Wolcott Gibbs, reviewing this revival, reported that "The
Cradle Will Rock . . . remains a fine, robust, hilarious
show." He pointed out, further:

> . . . in spite of the fact that it has lost most of
> its political bite, The Cradle Will Rock is still
> marvelously funny on the level of simple comedy,
> and in its serious moments it still pictures human
> suffering with touching eloquence, even though it
> hardly appears to be suggesting any coherent reme-
> dies.134

At the 1960 City Center production Howard Taubman stated
that "The piece, dated and corny as it is, bursts with vitali-
ty. It fills a theatre with excitement." He then adds a
wider implication to his remarks: "If the New York City
Opera were narrow-minded about its jurisdiction it would not
bother with The Cradle Will Rock. But it takes a liberal
view of its responsibilities to American opera and it properly
encompasses this free-wheeling imaginative work."135 Irving

Kolodin wrote that in "Marc Blitzstein's morality play of the
thirties . . . there are darts and shafts, tunes and turns of
the phrase that testify to Blitzstein's agile mind and musical
assimilation."136 Paul Henry Lang, commenting on the characterization, said that the people were not individuals with
personal problems but types with messages. Also "Last but
not least, the composer-librettist failed to make clear whether
his protagonists' characters are developed by circumstances
or whether he is illuminating circumstances by characters."137   The Village Voice reviewer felt the libretto an
"old tired story" and that the dialogue "shimmered with clichés."138

     The Wings of the Dove, an opera based on the Henry
James novel with music by Douglas Moore and libretto by
Ethan Ayer, was given its world premiere at the New York
City Opera in 1961.   Harold Schonberg reported that

> [The libretto is] . . . one that necessarily cut
> through James's meanderings, added a few new ele-
> ments, simplified the characters considerably and
> turned out, in the end, not too bad a work for the
> stage.
>
> The action in the six scenes of the two acts is
> tight and concentrated, though toward the end there
> do appear to be some inconsistencies and psycholog-
> ical flaws.
>
> In the novel the motivations are clear enough, but
> in the opera the sudden sorrow and conversion of
> Miles Dunster and Kate Croy are inexplicable.
>
> But the opera does not live or die by the libretto.
> The music is the important thing.139

Paul Henry Lang commented on "The skillful libretto" which
he found "much more than a story well adjusted to an opera.
[Ayer's] text has both force and insight, it has too at times
the distinction of real poetic intensity of phrase, and it was
tailor-made for Mr. Moore."140   Winthrop Sargeant was also enthusiastic over the libretto:

> I am tempted to call it the most artistically suc-
> cessful American opera thus far written and it is
> certainly one of the very few operas written any-
> where in the past half century that seem to de-

serve a permanent place in the history of the art.

> Mr. Moore's librettist, Ethan Ayer, has used the
> story with great skill and with a reverence for the
> original that preserves most of the novel's essen-
> tial values; while pruning James's convoluted writ-
> ing down to the simple dialogue of which an opera
> libretto must consist, he has lost very little of the
> vital elements of situation and character. And,
> surprisingly, a great deal of what has been lost in
> this process is restored by the evocative power of
> the music . . . to accentuate and clarify James's
> meaning in terms of a different medium. From
> the operatic point of view, and from the point of
> view of theatre in general, this is a fascinating
> feat, and its success is a great tribute to the
> craftsmanship of both Mr. Moore and Mr. Ayer.[141]

The comment of Irving Kolodin was that "It strikes me that
Ayer has followed a sound rule of reason in letting the material decree form rather than imposing a conventional formula of three acts upon it."[142]

An operatic adaptation of Arthur Miller's The Crucible
with music by Robert Ward and libretto by Bernard Stambler
was presented in the 1961 season. Paul Henry Lang commented that

> Mr. Stambler's libretto preserved the qualities of
> the play and on the whole presented the composer
> with a good text, marred only by a wordiness
> which our librettists still do not seem to be able
> to avoid. This was especially noticeable in the en-
> sembles, where every one has too much to say
> causing a density of crisscrossing vocal lines.[143]

Harold Schonberg reported that "the audience loved it," and
added that "the libretto helped. Mr. Miller's play is a
powerful work, and has been adapted virtually intact. The
action was strong enough to come right through Mr. Ward's
frequently noncommittal music."[144] Douglas Watt wrote that
"The librettist . . . has not been entirely successful in con-
densing Miller's play into a musical script. That lengthy
first scene prepares the listener for a makeshift evening of
opera. But Stambler, too, perks up when he gets down to
cases thereafter and provides Ward with spare, forceful
lines."[145] Louis Biancolli wrote, "A combination of good

theme, good text and better music makes The Crucible as
fine an opera as has ever been written by an American. "146
Irving Kolodin commented on the "generally superior libretto. "147

  The next year the opera was again presented by the
New York City Opera Company and Winthrop Sargeant reported:

> I attended its premiere last fall and was deeply
> impressed by it. Though I thought its first act
> a bit wordy. I was wrong in thinking this . . .
> At last week's performance . . . I was able to
> get a clearer idea of this opera, which is, of
> course, a study of the human conscience based on
> Arthur Miller's play . . . If a finer opera has
> been written since the days of Strauss and Puccini,
> I have not heard it. 148

  The oldest work in the series of American operas offered at the New York City Opera was George Gershwin's
Porgy and Bess, written in 1935 with libretto by DuBose
Heyward and Ira Gershwin and based on the play, Porgy.
When it was first performed, Francis D. Perkins in the New
York Herald-Tribune wrote that "The libretto closely follows
the general lines of the original play . . . The dramatic
strength of the story was one factor in the success won by
the opera tonight. "149 Virgil Thomson, in a more extended
critical analysis, stated:

> Porgy and Bess is nonetheless an interesting ex-
> ample of what can be done by talent in spite of a
> bad set-up. With a libretto that should never have
> been accepted on a subject that should never have
> been chosen, a man who should never have at-
> tempted it has written a work that is of some power
> and importance.
>
> Gershwin does not even know what an opera is; and
> yet Porgy and Bess is an opera and it has power
> and vigor. Hence it is a more important event in
> America's artistic life than anything American the
> Met has ever done.
>
> The play, for instance, and the libretto derived
> from it, are certainly not without a good part
> hokum. Folklore subjects recounted by an outsider

> are only valid as long as the folk in question is
> unable to speak for itself, which is certainly not
> true of the American negro in 1935. <u>Porgy and
> Bess</u> has about the same relationship to Negro life
> as it is really lived and sung as have 'Swannee
> River' and 'Mighty lak' a rose.'[150]

At the New York City Opera revival Howard Taubman wrote
that he "loved" the City Center revival, but Judith Crist
found it "too operatic" without enough musical comedy techniques. Also she found it contained "theatrically offensive
staging devices of opera."[151] Winthrop Sargeant reported
that

> It also has a viable drama, though this seems to
> me to involve a good many stereotypes of both plot
> and character and to present a picture of Negro
> life that is gradually becoming almost as dated as
> <u>Uncle Tom's Cabin</u>. The necessity of singing syn-
> thetic spirituals, the romanticizing of the Negro as
> either a sexually supercharged animal or an oily
> crook or a good, infinitely pitiable masochist are
> all part of this picture, and it is a picture as seen
> from Broadway, with all the Broadway clichés and
> not much depth. I cannot see it as what it is often
> called--America's great contribution to opera.[152]

Henry Beckett in the <u>New York Post</u> found that "Its appeal
remains fresh after 27 years."[153] Raymond Ericson stated
that "It was and is an important work in the American lyric
theatre, more viable than most other serious contemporary
American operas, and certainly more successful with the
public. It has survived a long time already, and should survive for a long time to come."[154] Joseph Machlis wrote in
1961 that "As time goes on, Gershwin's masterpiece more
and more takes on the character of a unique work . . . This
'folk opera' . . . goes on to new triumphs with the years,
and has been hailed the world over as an American classic."[155]

The third opera of Carlisle Floyd's to be produced by
the New York City Opera was <u>The Passion of Jonathan Wade</u>,
staged in the 1962 season. Ross Parmenter commented:
"But despite many fine moments, one felt that the 36-year-
old Mr. Floyd had bitten off more than he could chew."[156]
In discussing the libretto, Paul Henry Lang reported that
" . . . the plot is lively, the characters drawn with a cer-

tain delicacy; but both text and music suffer from professional weakness." He continued to comment on libretto writing
in general:

> Very few composers--if any--have sufficient literary
> ability to write a good libretto . . . but too often
> the singers in his scenes are the mouthpieces of
> moral and social ideas, giving the figures of the
> drama that pale semblance which in fictional char-
> acters indicates insufficient nourishment from ex-
> perience.
>
> The [dramatic] tempo of the drama is curiously un-
> even. Most of the time it is slow, there are in-
> terruptions by incidental matters . . . in . . .
> the first meeting of hero and heroine, the haughty
> Celia is defrosted by Jonathan in an incredibly
> short time.[157]

Winthrop Sargeant's remarks were:

> . . . beginning with the second part of the second
> act, it grips the audience with a strong sense of
> drama as well as with some fine music. Before
> that point, I am afraid, it is somewhat static, for
> a number of reasons. For one, the libretto, which
> Mr. Floyd has, as usual, written himself, is
> dreadfully complicated for operatic treatment . . .
> this portrayal tends to hold up the action. More-
> over, Mr. Floyd's words are often very prosy for
> his purpose, and one occasionally finds him doing
> what no opera composer should do--setting more
> talk to music.[158]

Irving Kolodin found that there were two operas: " . . .
one interesting opera of emotions, one less interesting opera
of ideas." He added that "For this, composer Floyd has one
librettist Floyd to blame." He found that the "text gets
wordy."[159]

Gentlemen, Be Seated was an American opera given
its world premiere in 1963 with music by Jerome Moross
and libretto by Edward Eager. Harold Schonberg reported
that the opera was "nothing more or less than a slick musical comedy . . . with little that lives up to the promise of
the basic situation . . . Indeed there is something flippant
about the book and its score." He concluded that "Even

within the confines of a musical comedy, there should be respect for what they [important events] represent."160 Louis
Biancolli wrote that " . . . the theme . . . is forceful as
far as it goes--the good-humored satire and reproof of old
ways and the implicit pleas for things still to be done. The
spoofing is light but telling . . . there is an air of pleasant
improvisation about the show that keeps it going." However,
his concluding remarks pointed out that "This is in many
ways a tame and superficial confection, built around an out-
moded divertissement and stereotyped but valid as a variety
show of good will and facile entertainment. Who called it an
opera?"161 Winthrop Sargeant followed this same development:

> The piece was not an opera, it was not a minstrel
> show, it was not very good music, and it was not
> even effective theatre . . . [It] lacked continuity,
> dramatic force, evocative music, and sympathetic
> characters. But its main fault was absymal taste.
> It treated its theme humorously and satirically . . .
> The Civil War is surely not one of the most hilar-
> ious episodes in history . . . [It was] not only un-
> funny but insulting.162

For Irving Kolodin "The idea has perhaps challenged the authors more than they might have welcomed, for it left them
still groping for a form, more than a little uncertain whether
what they were writing was a revue, operetta, musical come-
dy--or something of all these things." But he compliments
the New York City Opera " . . . for venturing so far from
the course so commonly associated with opera."163

Turgenev's drama A Month in the Country was adapted by
William Ball (libretto) and Lee Hoiby (music) into Natalia Petrovna, presented in the fall of 1964. Harold Schonberg wrote
that the libretto " . . . misses the point of the Turgenev play
and fails to contribute anything of its own as compensation.
[Mr. Ball makes] three-dimensional characters one-dimen-
sional."164 Alan Rich reported that the libretto was

> . . . a reasonably respectful condensation of the
> play's broad outlines, but it sacrifices a great deal
> that is crucial. The gentle but incisive irony of
> Turgenev's conception has been dispensed with by
> and large. This may have been unavoidable; irony
> is not a quality that translates very well into music.
> But its lack in this case simplifies some of the

characters almost to the point of falsification.

He also pointed out that " . . . none of the action [around
Belaev] seems very importantly motivated."165 Harriet
Johnson found " . . . a libretto that not only dilutes, confuses and distorts Turgenev but, as drama, itself, seldom
emerges from its sour bubble bath." This reviewer also
added that the librettist " . . . gives cheap speech to his
characters . . . and makes weak caricatures out of people
whom Turgenev has painfully but understandingly dramatized
through five acts." Finally, she found the inner conflicts of
the play "unoperatic."166 Irving Kolodin pointed out that
"Turgenev's drama is less a play of action than it is a play
upon words . . . subtleties and nuances that William Ball's
libretto tends to erase for broader strokes of dramatic action." He also wrote in general terms that " . . . the most
successful subjects for operatic treatment are those in which
the lines of conflict are strongly drawn and there is a minimum of confusion as to the 'why' of the happenings (the 'how'
is something else again)." He concluded that the opera
needed a "tightening of the dramatic structure."167 Winthrop
Sargeant wrote about the problems of libretto writing in his
review: "In general, success comes when little but the plot
remains, for in opera the music must dominate the proceedings." On the particular opera he continued: "It was, to
be sure, cut to manageable proportions by the librettist . . .
but it retained its main outlines, and also many psychological
intricacies of a type that music has little power to illuminate."
He concluded that "The finest passages in it are the ones in
which the formalities of opera for the moment take precedence
over the drama, and the ones dealing with broadly humorous
situations."168

        Gian-Carlo Menotti's The Saint of Bleecker Street was
performed on Broadway in 1954 before the 1965 production
given at the New York City Opera. At its premiere performance Brooks Atkinson noted that Menotti " . . . has an instinct for theatre. His operas are vivid and alive. His
characters are people." However, Atkinson also wrote that
"From the literary point of view The Saint of Bleecker Street
is undistinguished. That is to say, Mr. Menotti's English
style is perfunctory. The motivations of the characters are
incomplete; and the plot--if there is a plot--is trivial."169
Olin Downes, also attending this first performance, wrote:
"Yet this opera, as human drama, and first-rate theatre,
gives one the feeling of the masterfully integrated whole."
He called this opera " . . . verismo opera, with a dash of

modern psychology."[170]   Miles Kastendieck commented in
reference to the libretto that "He has not solved the problem
of his third acts.   They still tend toward anti-climax musically as well as dramatically."[171]   In Women's Wear Daily,
Thomas R. Dash reported that "Menotti's libretto surges with
high voltage power.   True, on occasion, there are solecisms
and banalities in some of the lyrics, and the author might
have benefited from some judicious editing by another mind.
But these are minor blemishes . . . "[172]   John McClain in
the Journal-American wrote of the libretto that " . . . I
thought Mr. Menotti's story was adequate but not great.   To
be an old meanie and dissect the plot one cannot fail to become occasionally impatient with the plight of a young man
who just doesn't want his sister to be a nun."   He concluded:
"Who am I to say so, but what's against a more plausible
plot?"[173]   Time magazine wrote that Menotti showed " . . .
an excellent hand at concocting workable dramatic episodes.
Moment by moment, he has his audience believing in his action, even if laden with stereotypes."[174]   Newsweek commented that "As a librettist, Menotti is a man of many pe-
destrian words and very little genuine poetry.   Like Tennessee Williams, he is not ashamed to use any device that sac-
rifices logic in favor of dramatic impact.   His story is a
thin one . . . "[175]   Howard Klein at the City Center revival
called the story "a complex libretto."   "Some of the situations," he pointed out, "generate strong theatre.   Others are
heart-on-sleeve attempts at drama."   He concluded that
" . . . what we get is melodrama.   Comedy relief does not
help."[176]   In the New York Herald-Tribune William Bender
wrote that "The musical drama (Mr. Menotti's term) teems
with all sorts of dramatic potential.   The only trouble is that
it is turned on and off at will.   Mr. Menotti never really
builds a scene."   He also found the theme one of "cloying
stickiness."[177]

    A second American opera given during the 1965 season
was a world premiere performance of Lizzie Borden, with
music by Jack Beeson and libretto by Kenward Elmslie.   Alan
Rich reported:

        Mr. Beeson's opera rests on a valid premise:
        that the story of the famous Fall River ax-murder-
        ers has solid operatic possibilities.   Furthermore,
        his scenarist, Richard Plant, and his librettist,
        Kenward Elmslie, had the good sense to base their
        text on the inner personality conflicts in the Borden
        household, rather than producing a penny-dreadful

bloodbath.

> Some of the libretto's language is stilted and anti-
> dramatic, although this is always a problem in deal-
> ing with homely speech in a naturalistic way. More
> important is the over-all impression of a well
> shaped and fluent play that has the substance that
> can challenge the best that is in a composer.

He concludes that the opera is " . . . an honest and earnest
piece of work."[178] Time magazine called it a "striking new
opera."[179] Irving Kolodin wrote that "To serve the needs
of their plot . . . they have perhaps strained the liberty that
goes with poetic license." He stated further that "Neat and
tidy as it is, the formulation . . . tends to beg the dramatic
question rather than answer it." Pursuing the idea of a too-
neatly made play, he concluded: "The question is, however,
whether the alignment of characters that produces three of
each sex in the principal parts serves dramatic truth as
much as it does theatrical convenience."[180] Winthrop Sargeant reported that "Mr. Elmslie has created a stage spectacle of considerable power and obvious operatic possibilities.
Lizzie Borden . . . is made . . . into a wholly believable
person caught in an intolerable situation." "To this admira-
ble libretto," he continues, "Mr. Beeson has, however, added
music so uninspired that the whole thing falls flat." He concluded that "One is left with the impression that the music
is simply an impediment to the drama."[181]

On the occasion of a television performance of the opera in 1967, Robert Sherman in the New York Times wrote:

> This is an opera of characterization rather than
> action, of recitatives rather than arias, of probing
> insight rather than surface posturing. Thus it can
> well do without the greater scope of a stage produc-
> tion, and indeed gains presence from the intimacy
> of TV, with its emphasis on close-up details.

> Kenward Elmslie's libretto, after a scenario by
> Richard Plant, is concerned not so much with the
> famous ax murders as the psychological climate
> that made them inevitable.[182]

Theodore Strongin reported at a revival of the opera
at City Center in 1967 that "The libretto . . . is beautifully
constructed drama." He found this a paradox because of the

"eclectic music" and the fact that there were "no real thrill-
ing moments." Still he found it a "thoroughly absorbing and
enjoyable" evening.[183]

A world premiere was given Miss Julie, an opera with
music by Ned Rorem and libretto by Kenward Elmslie based
on Strindberg's play, in the Fall of 1965 at City Center.
Variety reported:

> It is too much to expect that Kenward Elmslie's
> libretto would strengthen the illogical behavior of
> Strindberg's pair, the shallow characterization of
> the girl and the abrupt changes of the man and
> while it is faithful to the original in the main,
> there is an agonizing and distasteful quarter of an
> hour at the finale where the man, in the worst op-
> era tradition, repeatedly urges the girl to kill her-
> self. It is a 15 minute singing suicide razor com-
> mercial which tries audience patience to the point
> where only the downcoming curtain brings welcome
> relief. Strindberg did it in seven speeches, one
> minute.[184]

Irving Kolodin found that it " . . . came off mostly as a
mismatch." He wrote that " . . . the libretto . . . has
possibilities for musical treatment . . . But strong is just
what Rorem's treatment is not."[185] Winthrop Sargeant
wrote that it " . . . must be written off as just another good
try." He concluded that "In any case, Miss Julie is not an
effective opera."[186]

The first American opera to receive a world premiere
by the New York City Opera in the Lincoln Center New York
State Theatre, where the Opera Company moved in 1966, was
The Servant of Two Masters, with music by Vittorio Giannini
and libretto by Bernard Stambler. Servant was the final opera of Giannini, whose Taming of the Shrew was produced by
New York City Opera in 1958.

Harold Schonberg's comment on the March 10, 1967,
premiere was:

> The Servant of Two Masters comes out a fun op-
> era . . . What they [Stambler and Giannini] aimed
> for was fast action backed by a certain degree of
> characterization. The music runs when it does not
> sprint, and there are only a few spots where there

is a pause for long breathed phrases.

He concludes that Servant is " . . . a good, lightweight opera, composed along traditional lines with skill and integ-
rity."187

The comments on the libretto, based on Goldoni's
eighteenth century play, were mixed. Irving Kolodin reported that the libretto was "adroitly done" and that

> It is an additional evidence that Stambler's good
> work on behalf of Robert Ward (in making singable
> texts from Andreyev's He Who Gets Slapped and
> Arthur Miller's The Crucible) qualifies him as a
> specialist in that rarest of skills, operatic libret-
> tists.188

Opera News found that "Bernard Stambler's libretto was only
fitfully intelligible"189 and Hi-Fi/Musical America commented
that the evening "didn't quite happen" but "admired the play-
into-libretto adaptation of Bernard Stambler."190 Winthrop
Sargeant called it " . . . a highly respectable opera. It is
a genuine opera buffa . . . " He concludes that "The total
effect, however, was entertaining, melodious, and visually
pleasing."191

In the 1968 Spring Season the New York City Opera
presented Douglas Moore's new opera Carry Nation with a
libretto by William North Jayme. This opera had been first
performed in April 1966 in Lawrence, Kansas, where it had
been commissioned for the University's one-hundredth anniversary. The reaction to the libretto was generally unfavorable. Irving Kolodin remarked on " . . . a narrowness of
mood and futility of purpose."192 Harold Schonberg found
" . . . the basic conception of the opera, lacked point and
variety. Too much psychology and not enough action: that's
what's wrong with the libretto of Carry Nation . . . "193
In Hi-Fi/Musical America the opinion was that

> The libretto by William North Jayme, proceeds
> from a basis of kindergarten psychology by which
> a good girl turns into a virago tinged with madness
> through a concatenation of circumstances; a hard-
> shell father (who secretly loves her), a mother de-
> generating into insanity, and a husband, her One
> True Love, who is an alcoholic (because of the
> Horrors of War). Swollen with clichés both as to

language and situation, the opera can never compel
any sort of belief . . . [194]

Winthrop Sargeant stated that " . . . the trouble is
in its libretto, which is pretty thin in action, ambiguous in
point of view, and short of strong characters except for
Carry herself." He continues by pointing out that "One of
the troubles with this libretto is that both principal male
characters are so weak, and think that they are so dependent
for survival on Carry, that neither of them makes a figure
of much interest." He concludes that " . . . the main dramatic impulse of the serious part is an attempt to give up
drink--not the most absorbing of problems for an opera."[195]

Nine Rivers From Jordan, with music by Hugo Weisgall and a libretto by Denis Johnston, was a new work performed in the Fall Season of 1968. A mixed reception
greeted the libretto. Irving Kolodin remarked that the opera
was " . . . hampered more than a little by an over-elaborate,
wordy text . . . "[196] However Opera News reported that
" . . . the librettist, an Irish poet named Denis Johnston,
has . . . an ear for the way men speak."[197] Harold Schonberg wrote this opinion:

> But the basic message is clear enough, cloudy as
> some details may be. 'I'm told we're all dirty,
> but it seems we're not all damned,' the Christ-
> figure says. So, we come back to original sin and
> free will, a concept that is of scant consolation to
> billions of anxious people in the world today.[198]

Winthrop Sargeant noted that " . . . the libretto, though its
philosophy is ambiguous and its symbolism often incompre-
hensible, has a certain amount of theatrical flair . . . "
He finally states that "I applaud the New York City Opera's
interest in new works, but not in works of this kind."[199]
In the Village Voice Leighton Kerner wrote this of the libretto:

> Much of this libretto is strongly written, complete
> with appropriately used four-letter words certainly
> not new to the spoken stage but quite new to opera.
> However, another much of the libretto is very badly
> written and saddles some otherwise realistically
> drawn soldiers with pretentious, Maxwell Anderson
> politics.

He concludes that "Three scenes, few as they are, deserve
the gratitude of opera audiences in search of a contemporary
work that neither insults their intelligence nor starves their
need for a worthwhile experience of contemporary music-
drama."200

   In the Spring Season of 1969 two American operas
were revived--The Ballad of Baby Doe and The Crucible.
Comments were again made on seeing these operas after a
lapse of time following their premiere seasons. In the New
York Times the comment on the libretto of Baby Doe was
that

> Based on real people in real situations drawn from
> Colorado's mining boom in the last decades of the
> nineteenth century, the libretto by John LaTouche,
> tells a fascinating story--swiftly but thoroughly--
> through the actions of vividly drawn characters. 201

Winthrop Sargeant offered this opinion on another viewing of
The Crucible:

> When Robert Ward's opera The Crucible was first
> performed, some seven years ago, I had a good
> many enthusiastic things to say about it, and I ap-
> proached its revival by the New York City Opera
> at the New York State Theatre on Friday night just
> a little apprehensively. Would it turn out to be
> really as good as I said it was? The answer
> proved to be 'Every bit.' In fact, to me, it is
> one of the two or three best American operas so
> far written--which to be sure, is not an overwhelm-
> ing statement. It has a strong plot drawn from the
> Arthur Miller play and well tailored for operatic
> purposes by Bernard Stambler. . . . One gets
> deeply involved in the problems of John Proctor,
> and his Puritan neighbors, and a great deal of this
> involvement is evoked by Mr. Ward's robust
> score. 202

   Gian-Carlo Menotti presented another opera with the
New York Opera Company in the Fall Season of 1969. This
time he had written the music and libretto to the one-act
Help, Help, The Globolinks Are Coming! and the opera was
premiered the summer of 1969 at the Santa Fe Opera. On
this occasion Harold Schonberg wrote " . . . Menotti has set
out to create a light weight work and hit his goal dead cen-

ter," and added that "It is the best thing Menotti has done in
years. . . ."203 On the opening of the opera in New York,
Schonberg noted that the opera had "created much favorable
notice. Last night's New York premiere did nothing to change
that impression."204 In Life magazine Herbert Kupferberg
wrote that Menotti " . . . has written another remarkable
children's opera, a satiric yet tender space-age masterpiece
. . . It is one of the most enjoyable and provocative musical
works of the last decade."205

> Winthrop Sargeant gave the following opinion:

> > Nobody else living knows how to write an opera
> > with such skill--that is to say, nobody else has
> > such a keen theatrical instinct for the sort of libret-
> > to that is suitable to the operatic form, or for
> > dealing with the problem of where and how to or-
> > ganize arias and ensembles for the greatest effect.
> > It is just possible that Menotti is one of the few
> > composers of the twentieth century who is going to
> > be remembered in the twenty-first.

He also remarks of the libretto that "The idea is a bit cute,
but it enables Menotti to show about as much virtuosity with
electronic music as he shows with conventional type . . .
and it's lots of fun." He concludes that "It is not a great
opera, but it is an amusing show."206 But Paul Zimmerman
in Newsweek thought differently: "It is astounding how little
Menotti has changed in eighteen years." He termed the opera a " . . . militantly traditional, sentimental vision of the
world."207

> The ninth opera of Gian-Carlo Menotti to be presented
at the New York City Opera was The Most Important Man,
in the Spring Season of 1971. Again Menotti provided his
own libretto. Miles Kastendieck wrote this opinion:

> > As frequently happens in contemporary operas, the
> > libretto lacked strength. An inept third act did not
> > help, but latent weaknesses had become evident
> > earlier. Perhaps sociological problems do not
> > make good operas. The confrontation of blacks
> > and whites at the core of this story took precedence
> > over the personal problem of the black scientist
> > whose discovery made him the most important man
> > in the world. Thus the emotional dimension behind
> > the situation became diffused. Even the love affair

with his mentor's daughter did not intensify any
feeling of urgency supposedly motivating the scientific project from the start. 208

Harriet Johnson wrote that this opera " . . . is first rate
musical theatre." Also she commented that Menotti " . . .
has created an opera of compelling emotional impact. "209
However, Irving Kolodin's opinion was that "What he [Menotti]
has thought to do with racial prejudice in The Most Important
Man is not only skimpy playwriting, but insufficiently pro-
ductive of musical impulse. "210   Schonberg also wrote a
negative opinion: "It is an opera with noble aspirations, but
most of it is more soap opera than opera. With all the good
will in the world, Mr. Menotti has not been able to escape
cliché and stereotype, both in his libretto and his music. "211

     In his review, Winthrop Sargeant expressed a much
more positive view of the opera:

> There are good reasons that Gian-Carlo Menotti is
> the most successful and noteworthy of contemporary
> opera composers. He has an infallible sense of
> theatre, he knows how to write effectively for the
> human voice, and his scores employ the traditional
> language of music as it has been understood by
> generations of operagoers.

He concluded that "The motives in this story are plain, and
the characters well drawn. "212   Time, noting that "None of
the characters are very believable, even by opera standards, "
also offered the statistical information that "Upwards of a
thousand performances of his [Menotti's] thirteen operas are
given every year. "213   Perhaps that is a fitting conclusion
to the controversy.

     Critical reaction to the American opera librettos in
this study is generally one of creative concern. All the reviewers appear to approach their responsibility with a view
to remaining constructively critical rather than negative.
They appear to recognize that American opera is a new form
in need of encouragement. However, the attitude of critical
forgiveness is rarely carried too far. Also the critical remarks are generally musical in nature first, with remarks
concerning the dramatic elements second.

     By such an intense production of American opera in
so short a period, the critics were able to observe a wide

selection of the genre and made valuable observations based
on revivals and additional performances and productions of
these works.

Notes

1. Olin Downes, New York Times, May 2, 1948.

2. Virgil Thomson, New York Herald-Tribune, April 9,
   1948.

3. Robert A. Simon, The New Yorker, April 17, 1948.

4. Downes, New York Times, April 9, 1948.

5. Ibid.

6. Downes, New York Times, March 4, 1938.

7. Lawrence Gilman, New York Herald-Tribune, April 4,
   1938.

8. Douglas Watt, New York Daily News, April 19, 1962.

9. Paul Henry Lang, New York Herald-Tribune, May 6,
   1963.

10. Winthrop Sargeant, The New Yorker, May 18, 1963.

11. Philip Hamburger, The New Yorker, April 9, 1949.

12. Downes, New York Times, April 1, 1949.

13. Francis D. Perkins, New York Herald-Tribune, April
    1, 1949.

14. John Beaufort, The Christian Science Monitor, April 1,
    1949.

15. Ibid.

16. Howard Taubman, New York Times, October 2, 1949.

17. Ross Parmenter, New York Times, October 2, 1949.

18. Lang, New York Herald-Tribune, May 6, 1963.

19. Sargeant, The New Yorker, May 18, 1963.

20. Paul Affelder, Brooklyn Eagle, May 7, 1963.

21. Downes, New York Times, April 8, 1949.

22. Downes, New York Times, October 5, 1951.

23. Thomson, New York Herald-Tribune, October 5, 1951.

24. Douglas Watt, The New Yorker, October 13, 1951.

25. Irving Kolodin, The Saturday Review, October 20, 1951.

26. Downes, New York Times, December 31, 1951.

27. Time, December 31, 1951.

28. Watt, The New Yorker, April 19, 1952.

29. Sargeant, The New Yorker, April 10, 1954.

30. Perkins, New York Herald-Tribune, December 31, 1957.

31. Brooks Atkinson, New York Times, March 27, 1950.

32. New York Sun and Telegram, May 6, 1950.

33. Sargeant, The New Yorker, April 7, 1962.

34. Lang, New York Herald-Tribune, April 29, 1962.

35. Alan Rich, New York Times, March 29, 1962.

36. New York Journal-American, March 29, 1962.

37. Raymond Ericson, New York Times, March 18, 1966.

38. Joseph Machlis, Introduction to Contemporary Music (New York: W. W. Norton & Co., 1961), p. 572.

39. Henry Beckett, New York Post, March 29, 1962.

40. Wolcott Gibbs, The New Yorker, November 12, 1949.

41. John Mason Brown, Saturday Review, November 19, 1949.

42. Harold Clurman, New Republic, December 5, 1949.

43. Kolodin, Saturday Review, April 18, 1953.

44. Sargeant, The New Yorker, April 10, 1954.

45. Kolodin, Saturday Review, April 12, 1954.

46. Taubman, New York Times, April 8, 1954.

47. Alan Rich, New York Herald-Tribune, July 29, 1965.

48. Howard Klein, New York Times, July 29, 1965.

49. Taubman, New York Times, July 29, 1965.

50. Kolodin, Saturday Review, October 13, 1956.

51. Taubman, New York Times, October 11, 1957.

52. Harriett Johnson, New York Post, October 11, 1957.

53. Louis Snyder, New York Herald-Tribune, May 4, 1963.

54. Klein, New York Times, May 4, 1963.

55. Johnson, New York Post, May 5, 1963.

56. Miles Kastendieck, New York Journal-American, March 29, 1965.

57. Taubman, New York Times, April 4, 1958.

58. Sargeant, The New Yorker, May 10, 1958.

59. Kolodin, Saturday Review, April 19, 1958.

60. Kastendieck, New York Journal-American, March 24, 1962.

61. Perkins, New York Herald-Tribune, March 24, 1962.

62. Ericson, New York Times, March 24, 1962.

63. Parmenter, New York Times, April 29, 1963.

64. New York Herald-Tribune, April 29, 1963.

65. Christian Science Monitor, April 30, 1963.

66. New York Times, March 8, 1965.

67. Taubman, New York Times, April 7, 1958.

68. Musical America, May 1958.

69. Time, August 19, 1957.

70. Kolodin, Saturday Review, November 29, 1952.

71. John Crosby, New York Times, November 17, 1952.

72. Taubman, New York Times, April 7, 1958.

73. Musical America, May, 1958.

74. Kastendieck, New York Journal-American, April 11, 1958.

75. Howard Barnes, New York Herald-Tribune, October 31, 1949.

76. Atkinson, New York Times, November 6, 1949.

77. Gibbs, The New Yorker, November 12, 1949.

78. Taubman, New York Times, April 11, 1958.

79. Lang, New York Herald-Tribune, April 11, 1958.

80. Kolodin, Saturday Review, April 26, 1958.

81. Musical America, May 1958.

82. Thomson, New York Herald-Tribune, February 2, 1953.

83. Taubman, New York Times, April 14, 1958.

84. Lang, New York Herald-Tribune, April 14, 1958.

85. Musical America, May 1958.

86. Kolodin, Saturday Review, April 26, 1958.

87. Taubman, New York Times, April 26, 1958.

88. Kolodin, Saturday Review, May 10, 1958.

89. Jay Harrison, New York Herald-Tribune, April 24,
     1958.

90. Sargeant, The New Yorker, May 31, 1958.

91. Musical America, May 1958.

92. Ericson, New York Times, February 12, 1966.

93. Taubman, New York Times, August 31, 1958.

94. William Mann, New York Herald-Tribune, September
     3, 1958.

95. Walter Kerr, New York Herald-Tribune, November 6,
     1958.

96. Lang, New York Herald-Tribune, March 25, 1959.

97. Musical America, May 1959.

98. Donald Mintz, New York Times, January 25, 1965.

99. Taubman, New York Times, April 3, 1959.

100. Kolodin, Saturday Review, April 18, 1959.

101. Musical America, May 1959.

102. Leonard Harris, New York World-Telegram and Sun,
     April 27, 1963.

103. Kastendieck, New York Journal-American, April 27,
     1963.

104. Taubman, New York Times, April 6, 1959.

105. Kolodin, Saturday Review, April 18, 1959.

106. Kolodin, Saturday Review, October 24, 1964.

107. Musical America, May 1959.

108. Richard Watts, Jr., New York Herald-Tribune, May
     19, 1939.

109. Downes, New York Times, May 19, 1939.

110. Pitts Sandborn, New York World-Telegram, May 19, 1939.

111. George Jean Nathan, Newsweek, June 5, 1939.

112. Atkinson, New York Times, May 21, 1939.

113. Kolodin, Saturday Review, April 18, 1959.

114. Musical America, May 1959.

115. Watt, New York Daily News, July 18, 1958.

116. Taubman, New York Times, April 10, 1959.

117. Herald-Tribune, March 22, 1959.

118. Kolodin, Saturday Review, April 25, 1959.

119. Musical America, May 1959.

120. Taubman, New York Times, May 18, 1956.

121. Kolodin, Saturday Review, April 25, 1959.

122. Musical America, May 1959.

123. Thomson, New York Herald-Tribune, May 11, 1950.

124. Robert Bagar, New York Sun and Telegram, May 13, 1950.

125. Taubman, New York Times, April 9, 1956.

126. Taubman, New York Times, April 17, 1959.

127. Musical America, May 1959.

128. Taubman, New York Times, February 19, 1960.

129. Richard Franko Goldman, Musical Quarterly, July 1959.

130. Musical America, May 1959.

131. Machlis, op. cit., p. 568.

132. Atkinson, New York Times, December 28, 1947.

133. Brown, Saturday Review of Literature, January 17, 1948.

134. Gibbs, The New Yorker, January 10, 1948.

135. Taubman, New York Times, February 12, 1960.

136. Kolodin, Saturday Review, February 27, 1960.

137. Lang, New York Herald-Tribune, February 12, 1960.

138. Nancy K. Siff, The Village Voice, April 27, 1960.

139. Schonberg, New York Times, October 13, 1961.

140. Lang, New York Herald-Tribune, October 13, 1961.

141. Sargeant, The New Yorker, October 21, 1961.

142. Kolodin, Saturday Review, October 28, 1961.

143. Lang, New York Herald-Tribune, October 27, 1961.

144. Schonberg, New York Times, October 27, 1961.

145. Watt, New York Daily News, October 27, 1961.

146. Louis Biancolli, New York World-Telegram, October 27, 1961.

147. Kolodin, Saturday Review, November 11, 1961.

148. Sargeant, The New Yorker, April 7, 1962.

149. Perkins, New York Herald-Tribune, October 1, 1935.

150. Virgil Thomson, Modern Music, Nov.-Dec., 1935, pp. 13-19.

151. Judith Crist, New York Herald-Tribune, May 18, 1962.

152. Sargeant, The New Yorker, April 14, 1962.

153. Henry Beckett, New York Post, April 2, 1962.

154. Ericson, New York Times, April 2, 1962.

155. Machlis, op. cit., pp. 564-5.

156. Parmenter, New York Times, October 12, 1962.

157. Lang, New York Herald-Tribune, October 12, 1962.

158. Sargeant, The New Yorker, October 20, 1962.

159. Kolodin, Saturday Review, October 27, 1962.

160. Schonberg, New York Times, October 11, 1963.

161. Biancolli, New York World-Telegram, October 11, 1963.

162. Sargeant, The New Yorker, October 19, 1963.

163. Kolodin, Saturday Review, October 26, 1963.

164. Schonberg, New York Times, October 9, 1964.

165. Alan Rich, New York Times, October 9, 1964.

166. Johnson, New York Post, October 9, 1964.

167. Kolodin, Saturday Review, October 24, 1964.

168. Sargeant, The New Yorker, October 16, 1964.

169. Atkinson, New York Times, December 28, 1954.

170. Downes, New York Times, December 28, 1954.

171. Kastendieck, New York Journal-American, December 28, 1954.

172. Thomas R. Dash, Women's Wear Daily, December 28, 1954.

173. John McClain, New York Journal-American, December 28, 1954.

174. Time, January 10, 1955.

175.   Newsweek, January 10, 1955.

176.   Howard Klein, New York Times, March 19, 1965.

177.   William Bender, New York Herald-Tribune, March 19, 1965.

178.   Rich, New York Times, March 26, 1965.

179.   Time, April 2, 1965.

180.   Kolodin, Saturday Review, April 10, 1965.

181.   Sargeant, The New Yorker, April 3, 1965.

182.   Robert Sherman, New York Times, January 26, 1967.

183.   Theodore Strongin, New York Times, October 27, 1967.

184.   Variety, October 27, 1965.

185.   Kolodin, Saturday Review, November 20, 1965.

186.   Sargeant, The New Yorker, November 13, 1965.

187.   Schonberg, New York Times, March 10, 1967.

188.   Kolodin, Saturday Review, March 25, 1967.

189.   Opera News, April 15, 1967.

190.   Osborne, Conrad L., Hi-Fi/Musical America, June 1967.

191.   Sargeant, The New Yorker, March 18, 1967.

192.   Kolodin, Saturday Review, April 13, 1968.

193.   Schonberg, New York Times, March 29, 1968.

194.   Hi-Fi/Musical America, June 1968.

195.   Sargeant, The New Yorker, April 6, 1968.

196.   Kolodin, Saturday Review, October 26, 1968.

197.   Opera News, November 23, 1968.

198. Schonberg, New York Times, October 10, 1968.

199. Sargeant, The New Yorker, October 19, 1968.

200. Kerner, Leighton, The Village Voice, October 17, 1968.

201. New York Times, March 8, 1969.

202. Sargeant, The New Yorker, March 16, 1969.

203. Schonberg, New York Times, August 24, 1969.

204. Schonberg, New York Times, December 21, 1969.

205. Kupferberg, Herbert, Life, December 19, 1969.

206. Sargeant, The New Yorker, January 3, 1970.

207. Zimmerman, Paul, Newsweek, January 5, 1970.

208. Kastendieck, Miles, Christian Science Monitor, March
      15, 1971.

209. Johnson, Harriet, New York Post, March 13, 1971.

210. Kolodin, Saturday Review, March 27, 1971.

211. Schonberg, New York Times, March 14, 1971.

212. Sargeant, The New Yorker, March 20, 1971.

213. Time, March 22, 1971.

Chapter V

SUMMARY AND CONCLUSIONS

During the history of the New York City Opera, the critics have maintained a constant interest in its developing repertoire, and reviewers often reflect upon the Company's total impact. Winthrop Sargeant noted in 1959 that

> It has given the musical public countless perform-
> ances of works that have been too experimental or
> controversial to fit into the more ponderous and ex-
> pensive repertoire of the Metropolitan--most nota-
> bly, perhaps, in its spring seasons of American
> opera. And it has made the City Center the place
> where opera lovers go in search of novelty, stimu-
> lating contention, and the excitement attending pre-
> mieres of contemporary works.[1]

At the conclusion of the Spring Season of 1963, Harold Schonberg, after noting the operas performed, commented: "All of which emphasized the fact that the New York City Opera is a lively organization, more enterprising and daring not only than any opera group in America--that would not be much praise--but quite possibly in the world."[2]

Despite this excellent record of the production of new operatic works, choosing and performing these operas entailed great risk both financial and artistic. As Virgil Thomson pointed out: "In the long run, of course, everything is up to the composer--if he has a libretto." He added "A decent literary text for theatre music is very rare."[3] And, apparently, he is right. One of the problems in this study has been that of discovering from reviewers just what constitutes a good libretto. The approach used by many critics is to state what they do not like but not necessarily what is acceptable. It is an understandable approach although it does not often lead to added insights into libretto construction. Librettos do not, of course, "happen" and neither, by the same token, is there a simple formula for their creation. Usually those reviewers who review drama are often most

137

conscious of the dramatic elements in opera, while critics
of opera are, in general, reviewers whose main interest is
music, and who, as a result, concentrate on musical elements.   Again, for both there is the problem of space and
time since many reviews are not sufficiently lengthy to treat
the dramatic elements of opera.   Music is treated first, and
usually in some detail, and thereafter the libretto is considered in much more summary form.   The reviews of opening
night necessarily consider the high points of music and story,
and it is only longer reviews found in magazines or in special follow-up reviews in daily papers that take the time to
consider opera elements in detail.   As a result, revivals of
a particular work are valuable for the opportunity they give
reviewers to reassess the work at hand.   The responsibilities
of the opera critic, then, are often an individual matter, with
each critic bringing out what he can best offer to the experience.   Usually this means extensive musical background and
a more limited one in drama.   For this reason alone, a
study such as this can provide a valuable opportunity to correct this imbalance.

However, it is regrettable that more drama critics
do not attend opera performances and comment on them.   It
would undoubtedly point up the need for a greater concern on
the part of opera artists to enhance sound dramatic values.
True, much of the audience attends opera for the music, but
many times they find lacking the dramatic values with which
opera must legitimately concern itself.   Winthrop Sargeant
and Harold Schonberg provided the most comprehensive opera
criticism among the reviewers noted in this study.   Howard
Taubman, also, proved valuable in his constant encouragement of the principle of production of American opera and
its cultural importance.   These three critics gave sufficient
space many times to comment fully on all the elements of
the production.   Their concern was constantly the larger one
of the context of the opera in the tradition of the art, as
well as the individual merits of the particular work in question.

Of the forty librettos considered in this study, one
may point out librettos fulfilling most completely the qualities
that make successful librettos as well as those that do not.
The dramatic elements that were discussed in Chapters II
and III are the elements that must combine if a libretto is to
achieve distinction: elements of theme, characterization,
plot, dramatic devices of irony, reversal, and discovery,
and an appropriate literary style.

These librettos may be rated, in terms of their effectiveness as works for the theatre, in three groupings. In the first group fall the following librettos: The Consul, The Medium, The Ballad of Baby Doe, The Wings of the Dove, The Devil and Daniel Webster, Susannah, The Crucible, Six Characters in Search of an Author, Lizzie Borden, Miss Julie, The Good Soldier Schweik, and Street Scene. These librettos, in the opinion of the author, are the most successful.

The second group includes the following librettos: Old Maid and the Thief, Amelia Goes to the Ball, The Saint of Bleecker Street, Amahl and the Night Visitors, Help, Help, The Globolinks Are Coming!, The Dybbuk, Regina, Lost in the Stars, Wuthering Heights, The Servant of Two Masters, and Porgy and Bess. These works, while achieving many fine theatrical moments, do not, in my opinion, deserve a status of the first rank.

A third group in this study, the remaining librettos, generally lack dramatic distinction. These librettos are: Troubled Island, The Tender Land, Tale for a Deaf Ear, Trouble in Tahiti, The Taming of the Shrew, Maria Golovin, The Scarf, He Who Gets Slapped, The Triumph of St. Joan, The Cradle Will Rock, Gentlemen, Be Seated, Natalia Petrovna, The Golem, Nine Rivers to Jordan, Carry Nation, The Most Important Man, and The Passion of Jonathan Wade.

The first group is distinguished in several ways. Five of the librettos are based on dramas which have been adapted for operatic use here (The Crucible, Six Characters, Miss Julie, Good Soldier, Street Scene). Three are adaptations of stories or novels (Wings of the Dove, Devil and Daniel Webster, Susannah) and two librettos are based on actual events (Baby Doe and Lizzie). All possess eminently a combination of dramatic elements necessary in a successful libretto. Menotti's two operas, The Consul and The Medium, are most theatrically effective in that both stories contain elements of great suspense. These two operas, however, are not only plot-centered but also have effective, fully developed portraits of the main characters. Magda Sorel in The Consul and Madame Flora in The Medium are distinctive and believable figures moving through complex events to tragic and gripping climaxes. Both librettos effectively use dramatic devices-- especially dramatic irony and reversal. Spine-chilling moments in both operas have held audiences most effectively. The weakness of these two librettos is their undistinguished use of language. While not inappropriate, it lacks literary merit and at times verges on the sentimental and trite.

The three Douglas Moore operas (Baby Doe, Wings of the Dove, and Devil and Daniel Webster) contain three uncommonly good librettos. Each has a literary merit which impressed immediately on reading or hearing. Probably Ethan Ayer's adaptation of Henry James' novel is one of the most outstanding librettos from a literary point of view considered in this study. The language is fresh and does not become hackneyed at any point, and advances the action in meaningful terms without verbosity. The libretto of Baby Doe, by John LaTouche, is notable in that it uses many devices of the period (turn of the nineteenth century) without sacrificing a language that is both colloquial and natural. The period is suggested through action, but the language remains straightforward and modern without "poetic" or forced diction. This same use of natural speech patterns prevails in Carlisle Floyd's Susannah, which achieves several lyric heights, giving the language a particular distinction. Characterizations are strong, almost stereotyped, but there is a dramatic thrust to the action which effectively holds the interest of the audience.

Understandably, the operas in this group, derived from dramas previously produced, provide some of the most theatrically effective writing in this group. The success of these dramas with audiences had been firmly established already, and it is to the credit of the librettists that such values were preserved. Of course, success in one area does not guarantee a success in another, as appears in the last group. However, The Crucible and Six Characters are both dramas that succeeded well as librettos for opera. Six Characters, as has been conceded by critics, is an improvement in its operatic version. In the necessary reduction of the length of the script, essential drama was preserved and sharpened through a concise treatment. Kenward Elmslie's Miss Julie is likewise most successful. The drama of these two lovers is intense as conceived by Strindberg, and it was transferred almost intact to the operatic stage. However, the problem in this opera, according to critics, was the mismatch of Rorem's music to the play, for his essentially lyric gift was not appropriate to the play's strong dramatic forces. It is, then, seriously flawed in this respect, but the libretto remains strong and compelling. Street Scene also proves quite successful in operatic treatment, and the episodic form of the play is used effectively in the operatic form. Dramatic force and color are maintained and expanded in

the opera in a libretto written jointly by Elmer Rice, the
original author, and the Negro poet, Langston Hughes.

The Good Soldier Schweik, another episodic story, is
successful as a libretto through its clever use of language.
In a satiric situation the language, in almost doggerel verse
form, complements the author's caustic view of Army life.
Moreover, the comic nature of the action is underscored by
this light ironic tone, and the characterization, even though
somewhat marred by clichés, is filled with broad and telling
strokes. The realization of Schweik is, however, delightful,
pathetic and unhackneyed. The language moves at once on
two planes of humor and serious comment, and quite successfully.

With the exception of Miss Julie, not a successful
fusion of music and libretto, all of this first group of operas are successful works containing dramatically effective
treatments of their subjects. From a view of these twelve
librettos, it appears that effectively written librettos must
contain a language which can develop characterization, create
mood, and sustain a consistent style. The most successful
librettos are apparently those which respect natural speech
rhythms without becoming mere talk set to music. Even in
Good Soldier Schweik, with its deliberate sing-song verse
style, the libretto is nevertheless appropriate to the spirit
and intent of the piece.

The second group of operas is comprised of several
works which have enjoyed the acclaim of critics and public
alike. Certainly four of Menotti's operas (Old Maid, Amelia,
Saint, and Amahl) have been widely performed over a number
of years, as Gershwin's Porgy and Bess has been. However,
these works and the other works in the group are dated in
terms of language, style, and dramatic impact. Although
we can go back to Aristotle for advice on what good drama
is, we can also see certain works fade in effectiveness over
a period of years even though they employ sound dramatic
values. In the case of Menotti's works, the language, although colloquial and idiomatic, contains a sentimental style
and point of view which mar its total effectiveness. It appears that Menotti's dramatic pertinence, considerable as it
is, finally rests on the effect rather than the inherent drama
of the event. His use of the medium achieves effects that
dazzle but often do not convince. With Porgy and Bess the
language of the libretto is particularly dated in light of the
rapid social change of the twentieth century. The attitude of

the libretto is one of paternalism toward the "problem" of
the Negro in America. Engaging as the opera as a whole is,
characterizations are too obvious, lacking both subtlety and
conviction. The marks of the commercial Broadway show
are too clearly impressed on this work but, despite objections,
this opera continues to command great popular attention.

So, too, Lost in the Stars is dated in its point of view
toward racial conflicts. The denouement of this opera now
appears simplistic, and its characterizations too broadly
sketched to remain believable. There are genuine lyric high-
lights, but these are all that seem to survive.

Regina, based on The Little Foxes; Wuthering Heights,
based on the Bronte novel; and The Dybbuk, based on Ansky's
play, are all worthwhile librettos. In each opera dramatic
elements are deftly handled with a strong sense of theatrical
values correctly employed. Still, strong reservations must
be stated in terms of weak characterization in all three operas, poor plot development in Wuthering Heights and language weakness in The Dybbuk. In this group the works all
offer over-simplified characterization (more so than is obviously necessary in opera) and short cuts in plot development. Necessary scenes are too often cut short or left out
of the action and the plausibility of the events suffers. In
The Dybbuk the emphasis on theatrical values of mystical
religious expression leaves only brief outlines of characterization. Again, the language is formal and stiff in its attempt
to reflect a kind of universal peasant vocabularly through a
poetic treatment which lacks literary distinction.

The Servant of Two Masters, one of the comedies of
this list, suffers from a libretto that is too rich in language,
action and general demands on the performers. Performing
in commedia style is difficult enough without adding operatic
conventions. Help, Help, while not a major work of Menotti,
does have a simple, straightforward plot that is clear and
dramatic. As a children's opera it succeeds very well.

Of the seventeen operas listed in the final grouping,
The Cradle Will Rock has enjoyed the largest public success.
Unfortunately, the specific point of view taken in the opera,
as well as the changing circumstances around the subject of
labor-management disputes, dates this opera. It was hailed
at its advent, produced at great hardship, but burning issues
of 1936 have ceased to have great import in the 1960's. The
opera now takes on a rather quaint period charm as a result.

Another opera, in the very mixed bag of works in this group, is <u>Taming of the Shrew</u>, based on Shakespeare's play. The comedy is played up fully and many times to good effect, but the severely truncated plot harms its libretto. Character development is almost unbelievable and plausibility is replaced by broad farce, all to the detriment of the piece.

<u>Natalia Petrovna</u>, based on the Turgenev play, <u>A Month in the Country</u>, while offering sensitive moments and following the intent of the original play, does not handle the subtleties of characterization closely enough to provide for satisfactory dramatic development. Also lacking in strong characterization are <u>The Golem</u> and <u>The Tender Land</u>. Neither opera offers satisfying theatrical moments, since the first is too concerned with plot development, and the second seems to be more a lyrical exercise than a dramatic effort.

Both Menotti and Floyd's operas, <u>Maria Golovin</u>, <u>The Most Important Man</u>, and <u>The Passion of Jonathan Wade</u>, represent distinctly second-rate efforts of noted composers. Each has written his own librettos and each seems bent on providing a "theatrical" evening without the organic development of plot necessary for credibility. Undoubtedly each is a knowledgeable theatre artist, but here technique shows, conviction is missing, and ideas often dominate characterization.

Of the four one-acts in this group, Leonard Bernstein's <u>Trouble in Tahiti</u> is by far the most engaging. It is, however, more a clever exercise than a serious effort. There are original touches, but it needs a deepening enrichment to bring it into serious focus as opera.

The other operas do not hold the attention because of various problems--poor literary quality, lack of dramatic force, hackneyed points of view, and generally dated ideas.

In retrospect, the librettists who stand out are Gian-Carlo Menotti, Carlisle Floyd (both double-threat men), Kenward Elmslie, Lewis Allen, John LaTouche, and Ethan Ayer. There is probably no one outstanding librettist, but Menotti, to name one, although deficient in strength of language, compensates in theatrical skill. So too, in general, does Floyd. Probably the most talented of the group are Allen, LaTouche and Ayer, for their librettos have true literary distinction. It is rare that all qualities exist in one librettist, but this list of artists does offer strong qualifications for what one envisions as the ideal.

Artistic growth represented by the operas in this
study is to be considered on an individual basis as well as
on an overall basis. As one can speak of the progress of
individual composers and librettists, so one can speak of a
total representation. Raymond Ericson, in reviewing the
1959 season in Opera magazine, noted that " . . . the basic
criterion for selection seems to have been theatrical effectiveness and avoidance of the musical esoteric." He added
that the " . . . choice of repertory was remarkably shrewd
[and that] the musical values were decidedly mixed . . . but
far from negligible and sometimes encouraging."[4] Perhaps
this note of cautious optimism is the best way to view these
operas with their decided high points and decided failures.
Also, the most important contribution may be that the works
were done. An opera company actually made the commit-
ment (and continues to do so) to select and perform what the
management considered significant American works of opera.
Enthusiasm generated through these productions has led to
additional performances in other opera houses, and encouragement has produced in turn more opera from the composers
and librettists involved. The New York City Opera has carried several composers by performing subsequent works as
they are written: certainly an ideal situation for the creative
artist. Douglas Moore and Carlisle Floyd are two such composers whose new works have been given productions through
their association with the Opera Company. Gian-Carlo Menotti's operas represent another type of situation: the composer's works were all performed outside the New York City
Opera and then were brought into the repertoire. After the
Ford Foundation seasons of 1958-59, an additional amount of
money from the Foundation was given the Opera Company to
produce ten new American works. These works have been
commissioned and a number have been performed, to the obvious advantage of American opera composers and librettists.

Thematically this group of operas indicates an interest
in distinctly "American" subjects. These are generally stories drawn from American novels, plays, short stories and
actual events. Of course, there are exceptions, but the
themes, if not distinctly American, have thematic qualities
with universal application. The treatment of these themes
is, for the most part, emphasis on psychological exploration
as opposed to more episodic treatment or emphasis on plot.
The ideal is perfect balance of characterization and plot, and
in some cases this balance is maintained to a fair degree.

These operas, too, represent a fairly traditional approach to opera writing. There is some influence of the colloquial style of the Broadway musical in some of the works (in language and theme), but most are logical outgrowths of nineteenth century operatic and dramatic tradition. Avant-garde ideas of Virgil Thomson and Gertrude Stein or George Antheil are not continued in the works represented in this study. Situation and character development proceed along the accepted lines of Aristotle and refinements of his theories. Still, opera has usually been a conservative art form using the more traditional dramatic and musical techniques. In part because of the great expense of opera production, as well as the amount of expert technical and theatrical skills involved, opera does not often move toward startling new forms. New ideas are most often expressed in terms of theme, language and characterization, not in terms of basic format.

Again, on the question of artistic growth, it is this author's opinion that, compared with the American operas studied in the first half of the twentieth century in Chapter I, these operas represent an attempt to provide a more honest reflection of twentieth century America and less a panoramic view of American history. Folk opera themes, contemporary dramas, historical American incidents, and themes of social concern dominate these operas. In this respect the operas are an attempt to achieve an organic basis in American culture. They attempt to show American life as it has been lived or is being lived at the present time, and discard romantic historical subjects of the nineteenth century operatic tradition. Artistic growth appears in the sophisticated psychological approach of many of the works. Often these operas demonstrate a sensitive and subtle concern for character growth and development in the course of the action that is lacking in earlier American operas. Black and white portrayals of characters are generally avoided for a more mature point of view. Language, as a result, is more colloquial and informal. Attempts at "poetic" language are generally avoided in favor of everyday speech patterns. These operas show a concern for better communication with the contemporary audience, a desire to make a strong and lasting impact and to develop an audience that will take opera as a contemporary form concerned with contemporary problems. Many times there is new wine in old bottles. These operas do not strike out in new directions as to form, but content often has a rewarding freshness and contemporary concern. There is increased awareness of dramatic values

among the librettists of this group of operas and the writers
attempt to incorporate a strong sense of theatre in the telling
of the story. As American culture matures, there is a
greater sense of effective use of theatre techniques in opera
production. The mere idea of writing an American opera
fifty years ago seemed odd. Opera, obviously, was a European product and Americans could not be expected to create
this form. However, partially through the development of
the popular American musical theatre, there have developed
artists seeking to create more serious works for the lyric
stage. So American opera, as studied here, reflects this
growing concern to "dust off" the operatic form and infuse it
with an American life.

Through the encouragement of the critics, the determination of the New York City Opera management, the Ford
Foundation, and last but not at all least, the growing audience
support for opera in America, American opera is maturing.
It has achieved a considerable degree of artistic sophistica-
tion, although it still lacks a strong and distinctive voice.
Important groundwork has been laid by the New York City
Opera to focus the attention of Americans on a viable operatic
form indigenous to our time and place. It is to be hoped that
the tradition now established may grow and encourage an even
greater achievement by artists of an opera native to America.

Notes

1. Winthrop Sargeant, The New Yorker, October 17, 1959.

2. Harold Schonberg, New York Times, May 19, 1963.

3. Virgil Thomson, Hi-Fi/Stereo Review, February, 1962.

4. Raymond Ericson, Opera, June 1958.

SELECTED BIBLIOGRAPHY

Operas

Beeson, Jack, and Elmslie, Kenward. Lizzie. New York:
    Boosey and Hawkes, 1966.

Bernstein, Leonard. Trouble in Tahiti. New York: G.
    Schirmer, 1953.

Blitzstein, Marc. The Cradle Will Rock. New York: Tams-
    Witmark Music Library, 1936.

_____. Regina. Unpublished score, New York City Opera
    Company.

Bucci, Mark. Tale for a Deaf Ear. New York: Frank
    Music Corp., 1958.

Copland, Aaron, and Everett, Horace. The Tender Land.
    New York: Boosey and Hawkes, 1956.

Dello Joio, Norman. The Trial at Rouen. Unpublished score,
    New York City Opera Company.

Ellstein, Abraham, and Regan, Sylvia. The Golem. Unpub-
    lished score, New York City Opera Company, in two vol-
    umes.

Floyd, Carlisle. The Passion of Jonathan Wade. Unpublished
    score, Boosey and Hawkes.

_____. Susannah. New York: Boosey and Hawkes, 1957.

_____. Wuthering Heights. New York: Boosey and
    Hawkes, 1959.

Gershwin, George; Heyward, Dubose; and Gershwin, Ira.
    Porgy and Bess. New York: Gershwin Publishing Corp.,
    n. d.

Giannini, Vittorio, and Stambler, Bernard. The Servant of
Two Masters. New York: Franco Colombo, Inc., 1967.

_____, and Fee, D. The Taming of the Shrew. New
York: Ricordi, 1953.

Hoiby, Lee, and Ball, William. Natalia Petrovna. Unpublished manuscript, New York City Opera Company.

_____, and Duncan, Harry. The Scarf. New York: G.
Schirmer, n.d.

Kurka, Robert, and Allen, Lewis. The Good Soldier Schweik.
New York: Program Publishing Co., 1958.

Menotti, Gian-Carlo. Amahl and the Night Visitors. New
York: G. Schirmer, Inc., 1951.

_____. Amelia al Ballo. Italy: Ricordi, n.d.

_____. The Consul. New York: G. Schirmer, Inc.,
1950.

_____. Help, Help, The Globolinks Are Coming! New
York: G. Schirmer, Inc., 1969.

_____. Maria Golovin. Unpublished score in two volumes,
New York City Opera Company.

_____. The Medium. New York: G. Schirmer, Inc.,
1947.

_____. The Most Important Man. Unpublished score,
New York City Opera.

_____. The Old Maid and the Thief. New York: Franco
Colombo Inc., 1943.

_____. The Saint of Bleecker Street. New York: G.
Schirmer, Inc., n.d.

Moore, Douglas, and LaTouche, John. The Ballad of Baby
Doe. New York: Chappell and Co., Inc., n.d.

_____, and North, William Jame. Carry Nation. Unpub-
lished score, New York City Opera.

_____, and Benet, Stephen Vincent. The Devil and Daniel Webster. New York: Boosey and Hawkes, n. d.

_____, and Ayer, Ethan. The Wings of the Dove. New York: G. Schirmer, 1961.

Moross, Jerome, and Eager, Edward. Gentlemen, Be Seated. Unpublished score, New York City Opera Company.

Rorem, Ned, and Elmslie, Kenward. Miss Julie. Unpublished score, New York City Opera Company.

Still, William, and Hughes, Langston. Troubled Island. Unpublished score, New York City Opera Company.

Tamkin, David, and Tamkin, A. The Dybbuk. Unpublished score, New York City Opera Company.

Ward, Robert, and Stambler, Bernard. The Crucible. Unpublished manuscript, New York City Opera Company.

_____ _____. Pantaloon. New York: Highgate Press, n. d.

Weill, Kurt, and Anderson, Maxwell. Lost In the Stars. New York: Chappell and Co., 1950.

_____, and Rice, Elmer, and Hughes, Langston. Street Scene. New York: Chappell and Co., n. d.

Weisgall, Hugo, and Johnston, Dennis. Nine Rivers From Jordan. Bryn Mawr, Penna.: Theodore Presser Company, 1969.

_____ _____. Six Characters in Search of an Author. Bryn Mawr, Penna.: Merion Music, Inc., n. d.

Books

Armitage, Merle. George Gershwin: Man and Legend. New York: Duell, Sloan and Pearce, 1958.

Auden, W. H. The Dyer's Hand. New York: Random House, 1962.

Baker, George Pierce. Dramatic Technique. Cambridge: The Riverside Press, 1919.

Bekker, Paul. The Changing Opera. Mendel, Arthur (trans.). New York: W. W. Norton & Co., 1935.

Bentley, Eric. The Playwright as Thinker. New York: Reynal and Hitchcock, 1946.

_____. The Life of the Drama. New York: Atheneum, 1964.

Brockway, Wallace & Weinstock, Herbert. The World of Opera. New York: Pantheon Books, 1962.

Brooks, Cleanth and Heilman, Robert B. Understanding Drama. New York: Holt, Rinehart & Winston, 1964.

Butcher, Samuel H. Aristotle's Theory of Poetry and Fine Art. Fourth ed. New York: Dover Publications, Inc., 1951.

Chase, Gilbert. America's Music from the Pilgrims to the Present. New York: McGraw-Hill Co., 1955.

Chotzinoff, Samuel. A Little Nightmusic. New York: Harper & Rowe, Publishers, 1964.

Clark, Barrett H. European Theories of the Drama. New York: Crown Publishers, 1945.

Cole, Toby and Chinoy, Helen. Directing the Play. New York: Crown Publishers, 1945.

Cone, John F. Oscar Hammerstein's Manhattan Opera Company. Norman, Okla.: University of Oklahoma Press, 1966.

Copland, Aaron. Our New Music. New York: Whittlesey, 1941.

Corrigan, Robert W. (ed.). Tragedy: Vision and Form. San Francisco, Calif.: Chandler Publishing Co., 1965.

Cowell, Henry (ed.). American Composers on American Music. New York: Frederick Ungar Publishing Co., 1961.

Damrosch, Walter. My Musical Life. New York: Scribner, 1923.

Dorsch, T. S. Classical Literary Criticism. Baltimore, Md.: Penguin Books, Inc., 1964.

Downes, Olin. Olin Downes on Music, Irene Downes (ed.). New York: Simon and Schuster, 1957.

Dunlap, William. A History of the American Theatre. New York: J. and J. Harper, 1832.

Eaton, Quaintance (ed.). Musical U.S.A. New York: Towne and Heath, Inc., 1945.

Ellis-Fermor, Una. The Frontiers of Drama. London: Oxford University Press, 1946.

Ewen, David. The Complete Book of Twentieth Century Music. Englewood Cliffs, N.J.: Prentice-Hall, Inc., 1959.

_____. American Composers Today. New York: H. W. Wilson Co., 1949.

_____. Encyclopedia of the Opera. New York: Hill & Wang, 1963.

_____. David Ewen Introduces Modern Music. Philadelphia: Chilton Co., 1962.

Gassner, John and Allen, Ralph G. (eds.). Theatre and Drama in the Making. Boston: Houghton Mifflin Company, 1964.

Gilbert, Allan H. Literary Criticism: Plato to Dryden. Detroit, Mich.: Wayne State University Press, 1962.

Graf, Herbert. Opera and Its Future in America. New York: W. W. Norton & Company, 1941.

_____. Producing Opera for America. New York: Atlantis Books, 1961.

Grout, Donald Jay. A Short History of Opera, 2 vols. New York: Columbia University Press, 1965.

Grove, Sir George. Dictionary of Music and Musicians.
    Edited by Eric Blom. London: Macmillan, 1954. Fifth
    ed. 9 vols. Supplementary Volume. New York: St.
    Martin's Press, 1961.

Himelstein, Morgan Y. Drama Was a Weapon. New Bruns-
    wick: Rutgers University Press, 1963.

Hipsher, Edward Ellsworth. American Opera and Its Com-
    posers. Philadelphia: Theodore Presser Company, 1927.

Howard, John Tasker. Our American Music. New York:
    Thomas Y. Crowell Co., 1954.

_____, and Mendel, Arthur. Our Contemporary Com-
    posers. New York: Thomas Y. Crowell Co., 1941.

Huber, Louis. Producing Opera in the College. New York:
    Bureau of Publications, Teachers College, Columbia Uni-
    versity, 1956.

Hyman, Stanley Edgar. The Armed Vision. New York:
    Vintage Books, 1955.

Ireland, J. N. Records of the New York Stage, from 1750
    to 1860. New York: T. H. Marell, 1866-67.

Istel, Edgar. The Art of Writing Opera Librettos. Trans.
    Dr. Th. Baker. New Yorker: G. Schirmer, Inc., 1922.

Johnson, H. Earle. Operas on American Subjects. Boston:
    Coleman-Ross Co., Inc., 1963.

Kerman, Joseph. Opera as Drama. New York: Vintage
    Books, 1959.

Kolodin, Irving. The Story of the Metropolitan Opera, 1883-
    1950. A Candid History. New York: Alfred A. Knopf,
    Inc., 1953.

Kouwenhoven, John A. Made in America. Newton Center,
    Mass.: Charles T. Branford Co., 1957.

Krehbiel, Henry E. Chapters of Opera. New York: Henry
    Holt and Company, 1909.

_____. More Chapters of Opera. New York: Henry
Holt and Company, 1919.

Krutch, Joseph Wood.   Modernism in Modern Drama.   New
York: Russell and Russell, 1962.

Lawson, John Howard.   Theory and Technique of Playwriting
and Screenwriting.   New York: G. P. Putnam's Sons,
1949.

Lerner, Laurence.   Shakespeare's Tragedies, an Anthology
of Modern Criticism.   Baltimore, Md.:   Penguin Books,
1963.

Lucas, F. L.   Tragedy: Serious Drama in Relation to Aristotle's Poetics.   New York: Collier Books, 1962.

McGaw, Charles.   Acting Is Believing.   New York: Rinehart
& Company, Inc., 1955.

Machlis, Joseph.   American Composers of Our Time.   New
York: Thomas Y. Crowell Co., 1963.

_____. Introduction to Contemporary Music.   New York:
W. W. Norton and Co., Inc., 1961.

Mates, Julian.   The American Musical Stage Before 1800.
New Brunswick: Rutgers University Press, 1962.

Mattfield, Julius.   A Hundred Years of Grand Opera in New
York (1825-1925).   New York: New York Public Library,
1927.

_____. A Handbook of American Operatic Premieres
1731-1962.   Detroit: Information Service, Inc., 1963.

Mellers, Wilfrid.   Music in a New Found Land.   London:
Barrie and Rockliff, 1964.

Newman, Ernest.   Gluck and the Opera.   London: Bertram
Dobell, 1895.

Nicoll, Allardyce.   World Drama.   New York: Harcourt,
Brace and Company, 1949.

Peyser, Ethel and Bauer, Marion.   How Opera Grew.   New
York: G. P. Putnam's Sons, 1956.

Ritter, Frederic Louis. Music in America. New York:
Scribner, 1883.

Shaw, G. B. Major Critical Essays. London: Constable
and Company, 1932.

Smith, Julia Frances. Aaron Copland, His Work and Contribution to American Music. New York: E. P. Dutton,
1955.

Sonneck, O. G. Early Opera in America. New York: G.
Schirmer, Inc., 1915.

Stanizlavsky, Constantin. An Actor Prepares. Elizabeth
Hapgood (trans.). New York: Theatre Arts Books, 1948.

Stein, Gertrude. Last Operas and Plays. New York: Rinehart and Company, Inc., 1948.

Stravinsky, Igor. Poetics of Music. New York: Vintage
Books, 1956.

Thompson, Alan R. The Anatomy of Drama. Berkeley,
Calif.: University of California Press, 1946.

Thomson, Virgil. The Musical Scene. New York: Alfred
A. Knopf, 1945.

_____. The State of Music. New York: W. Morrow,
1939.

_____. Virgil Thomson. New York: Rinehart & Com-
pany, Inc., 1967.

Thrall, William F.; Hibbard, Addison and Holman, C. Hugh.
A Handbook to Literature. New York: The Odyssey
Press, 1960.

Toffler, Alvin. The Culture Consumers. New York: St.
Martin's Press, 1964.

Watson, George. The Literary Critics. Baltimore, Md.:
Penguin Books, 1962.

Weales, Gerald. American Drama Since World War II.
New York: Harcourt Brace & World, Inc., 1962.

Weisstein, Ulrich (ed.). The Essence of Opera. Glencoe,
Ill.: The Free Press of Glencoe, 1964.

Wellesz, Egon. Essays on Opera. Patricia Kean (trans.).
New York: Roy Publishers, 1950.

Articles

Affelder, Paul. Brooklyn Eagle, May 7, 1963.

Antheil, George. "Opera--a Way Out, " Modern Music, XI,
No. 2 (January-February, 1934), pp. 89-94.

_____. "Wanted--Opera by and for Americans, " Modern
Music, VII, No. 4 (June-July, 1930), pp. 11-16.

Atkinson, Brooks. New York Times, May 21, 1939; November 6, 1949; December 28, 1947; March 27, 1950; December 28, 1954.

Bagar, Robert. New York Sun and Telegram, May 13, 1950.

Barlow, Samuel. "Blitzstein's Answer, " Modern Music,
XVIII, No. 2 (January-February, 1941), pp. 81-83.

Barnes, Howard. New York Herald-Tribune, October 31,
1949.

Beaufort, John. The Christian Science Monitor, April 1,
1949.

Beckett, Henry. New York Post, March 29, 1962; April 2,
1962.

Bender, William. New York Herald-Tribune, March 19,
1965.

Berger, Arthur. "On First Hearing Copland's The Tender
Land, " Center, I (May, 1954), pp. 6-8.

Biancolli, Louis. New York World-Telegram, October 27,
1961; October 11, 1963.

Blitzstein, Marc. "On Writing Music for the Theatre, "
Modern Music, XV (January-February, 1938), pp. 81-85.

Brown, John Mason. Saturday Review of Literature, January 17, 1948; November 19, 1949.

Bryant, Henry. "Marc Blitzstein," Modern Music, XXIII (Summer 1946), pp. 170-175.

Chase, William B. "15th Native Opera in Gatti's Regime," New York Times, February 11, 1934.

The Christian Science Monitor, December 11, 1926; April 30, 1963.

Clurman, Harold. The New Republic, December 5, 1949.

Copland, Aaron. "In Memory of Marc Blitzstein," Perspectives of Modern Music. II (Spring-Summer, 1965), pp. 6-7.

Crist, Judith. New York Herald-Tribune, May 18, 1962.

Crosby, John. New York Times, November 17, 1952.

Current Opinion, February, 1918.

Dash, Thomas R. Women's Wear Daily, December 28, 1954.

Downes, Olin. New York Times, February 20, 1927; February 22, 1931; February 11, 1934; February 25, 1934; May 12, 1937; March 4, 1936; May 19, 1939; April 9, 1948; May 2, 1948; April 1, 1949; April 8, 1949; October 5, 1951; December 31, 1951; December 28, 1954.

Ericson, Raymond. "Festival of American Opera," Opera, 9:415-421, 1958.

_____. New York Times, March 24, 1962; April 2, 1962; February 12, 1966; March 18, 1966.

Everett, Horace. "Note on The Tender Land," Tempo, No. 51 (Spring, 1954), pp. 13-16.

_____. "Scheme for an Opera: The Sources and Construction of The Tender Land," Center, I (April, 1954), pp. 14-16.

Eyer, Ronald. "Carlisle Floyd's Susannah," Tempo, No. 42 (Winter, 1956-7), pp. 7-11.

Floyd, Carlisle. "The Composer as Librettist," Opera News, XXVII (November 10, 1962), pp. 8-12.

Gibbs, Wolcott. The New Yorker, January 10, 1948; November 12, 1949.

Gilman, Lawrence. New York Herald-Tribune, May 12, 1937; April 4, 1938.

Goldman, Richard F. "Six Characters in Search of an Author," The Musical Quarterly, XLV, No. 3, July, 1959.

Guthrie, Tyrone. "Out of Touch," Opera News, Vol. 31, No. 16, February 11, 1967, p. 11.

Hamburger, Philip. The New Yorker, April 9, 1949.

Hanson, Howard. "Twenty Years Growth in American Music," Modern Music, XX (November-December, 1942), pp. 95-101.

Harper's Weekly, March 4, 1911, p. 1.

Harris, Leonard. New York World-Telegram and Sun, April 27, 1963.

Harrison, Jay. New York Herald-Tribune, April 24, 1958.

Hayes, Richard. "The Making of Americans," Commonweal, LXIV (September 28, 1956), pp. 634-35.

Heinsheimer, H. W. "Opera for the Valleys," Educational Music Magazine, XXVIII (March-April, 1950), pp. 54-56.

_____. "Opera in America Today," Musical Quarterly, 37:316-22, July, 1951.

Hinton, James, Jr. "The Saint of Bleecker Street," Opera Annual 1955-56, II, p. 133-140.

Johnson, Harriett. New York Post, October 11, 1957.

Kastendieck, Miles. New York Journal-American, December 28, 1954; April 11, 1958; March 24, 1962; April 27, 1963; March 29, 1965.

Kerr, Walter. New York Herald-Tribune, September 3, 1958.

158 American Opera Librettos

Kirstein, Lincoln. "The Future of American Opera, " The Atlantic Monthly, CIC (March, 1957), pp. 50-55.

_____. "Menotti: The Giants in Bleecker Street, " Center, I (December, 1954), pp. 3-9.

Klein, Howard. New York Times, May 4, 1963; March 19, 1965; July 29, 1965.

Kolodin, Irving. Saturday Review, October 20, 1951; November 29, 1952; April 18, 1953; April 12, 1954; October 13, 1956; April 19, 1958; April 26, 1958; May 10, 1958; April 18, 1959; April 25, 1959; February 27, 1960; October 28, 1961; November 11, 1961; October 27, 1962; October 26, 1963; October 24, 1964; April 10, 1965; November 20, 1965.

Kramer, A. Walter. "Louis Gruenberg, " Modern Music, November-December, 1930.

Krehbiel, Henry. New York Tribune, February 27, 1913.

Krenek, Ernst. "Opera Between the Wars, " Modern Music, XX, No. 2 (January-February, 1943), pp. 102-111.

Krauss, Clemens. Capriccio (New York: Boosey and Hawkes, 1959), p. 21.

Laderman, Ezra. New York Times, June 16, 1968.

Lang, Paul Henry. New York Herald-Tribune, April 11, 1956; April 14, 1958; March 25, 1959; February 12, 1960; October 13, 1961; October 27, 1961; April 29, 1962; October 12, 1962; May 6, 1963.

_____. "The Future of Opera, " reprinted from the Columbia University Quarterly, March, 1938.

Latouche, John. "About the Ballad of Baby Doe, " Theatre Arts, XL (July, 1956), pp. 80-83.

Literary Digest, March 18, 1911.

McClain, John. New York Journal-American, December 28, 1954.

Mann, William. New York Herald-Tribune, September 3, 1958.

Meltzer, Charles Henry. Arts and Decorations, February, 1920.

Menotti, Gian-Carlo. "Notes on Opera as Basic Theatre," New York Times Magazine, January 2, 1955.

Mintz, Donald. New York Times, January 25, 1965.

Moore, Douglas. "Our Lyric Theatre," Modern Music, 18:3-7, November-December, 1940.

Musical America, May, 1958; May, 1959.

Musical Courier, March 22, 1911; March 28, 1918; February 5, 1920.

Nathan, George Jean. Newsweek, June 5, 1939.

Newsweek. January 20, 1955.

New York Evening Post. February 28, 1913.

New York Herald-Tribune. February 11, 1934; March 22, 1959; April 29, 1963.

New York Journal-American. March 29, 1962.

New York Sun-Herald. February 1, 1920.

New York Sun and Telegram. May 6, 1950.

New York Times. January 31, 1920; December 26, 1926; March 8, 1965.

New York World. January 31, 1920.

Parmenter, Ross. New York Times, July 23, 1960; October 12, 1962; April 29, 1963; May 6, 1963.

Patterson, Frank. "Fifty Years of Opera in America," Proceedings of the Music Teachers National Association, XXIII (1928), pp. 176-85.

Perkins, Francis D. New York Herald-Tribune, October 1,
    1935; April 1, 1949; December 31, 1957; May 24, 1962.

Philadelphia Public Ledger. February 26, 1911.

Pizzetti, Ildebrando. "Music and Drama," Musical Quarterly,
    17:419-426, October, 1931.

Rich, Alan. New York Times, March 29, 1962; October 10,
    1964; March 26, 1965; July 29, 1965.

Rochberg, George. "Hugo Weisgall," American Composers
    Alliance Bulletin, VII, No. 2 (1958), pp. 2-7.

Rogers, Francis. "America's First Grand Opera Season,"
    Music Quarterly, I (1915), pp. 93-101.

Sabin, Robert. "Carlisle Floyd's Wuthering Heights," Tempo,
    No. 59 (Autumn, 1961), pp. 23-26.

Sandborn, Pitts. New York Telegram, February 18, 1937.

_____. New York World-Telegram, May 19, 1939.

Sargeant, Winthrop. The New Yorker, April 10, 1954; May
    10, 1958; May 31, 1958; October 17, 1959; February 20,
    1920; October 21, 1961; April 7, 1962; April 14, 1962;
    October 20, 1962; May 18, 1963; October 19, 1963; Octo-
    ber 16, 1964; April 3, 1965; November 13, 1965.

Saunders, William. "The American Opera: Has it Arrived?"
    Music and Letters, XIII (July, 1932), pp. 147-155.

_____. "National Opera, Comparatively Considered,"
    Music Quarterly, XIII (1927), pp. 72-84.

Schonberg, Harold. New York Times, October 13, 1960;
    October 27, 1961; May 19, 1963; October 11, 1963; Octo-
    ber 9, 1964.

Sherman, Robert. New York Times, January 26, 1967.

Siff, Nancy D. The Village Voice, April 27, 1960.

Simon, Robert A. The New Yorker, April 17, 1948.

Skilton, Charles Sanford. "American Opera," Proceedings of the Music Teachers National Association, XX (1925), pp. 112-18.

Snyder, Louis. New York Herald-Tribune, May 4, 1963.

Steigman, B. M. "The Great American Opera," Music and Letters, VI (1925), pp. 359-67.

Stevenson, Robert. "Opera Beginnings in the New World," Music Quarterly, XLV (1959), pp. 8-25.

Strongin, Theodore. New York Times, October 27, 1967.

Taylor, Deems. "What is an American Opera?" Opera News, 25:9-11, December 17, 1960.

Taubman, Howard. "American Opera on the Upbeat," New York Times Magazine, January 12, 1958.

_____. "Proving Opera Can Be Modern," New York Times Magazine, March 19, 1950.

_____. New York Times, October 2, 1949; April 9, 1954; April 9, 1956; May 18, 1956; September 29, 1956; October 11, 1957; April 4, 1958; April 7, 1958; April 11, 1958; April 14, 1958; April 24, 1958; May 4, 1958; August 31, 1958; April 3, 1959; April 6, 1959; April 10, 1959; April 17, 1959; February 12, 1960; February 19, 1960.

Thomson, Virgil. "From Regina to Juno," Saturday Review, XLII (May 15, 1959), pp. 82-83.

_____. "George Gershwin," Modern Music, XIII (November-December, 1935), pp. 13-19.

_____. "In the Theatre," Modern Music, XV (January-February, 1938), pp. 112-114.

_____. New York Times, June 16, 1968.

_____. New York Herald-Tribune, April 9, 1948; October 5, 1951; February 2, 1953.

_____. "Opera: It Is Everywhere in America," New York Times Magazine, September 23, 1962, pp. 16-20.

162   American Opera Librettos

_____. "The Rocky Road of American Opera, " Hi-Fi/
Stereo Review, VIII (February, 1962), pp. 49-52.

Time. December 31, 1951; January 10, 1955; August 19,
1957; April 2, 1965.

Variety. October 27, 1965.

Watt, Douglas. New York Daily News, October 13, 1951;
July 18, 1958; October 27, 1961; April 19, 1962.

_____. The New Yorker, April 19, 1952.

Watts, Richard, Jr. New York Herald-Tribune, May 19,
1939.

Weill, Kurt. "The Future of Opera in America, " Modern
Music, 14:183-87, May-June, 1937.

Unpublished Material

Aufdemberge, Leon Maurice. "Analysis of the Dramatic
Construction of American Operas on American Themes,
1896-1958. " Unpublished Ph.D. dissertation, Northwestern University, Evanston, Ill., 1965.

Casmus, Mary. "Gian-Carlo Menotti: His Dramatic Technique." Unpublished Ph.D. dissertation, Columbia University, New York, N.Y., 1962.

Crooker, Earle T. "The American Musical Play." Unpublished Ph.D. dissertation, University of Pennsylvania,
1957.

Davis, Ronald Leroy. "A History of Resident Opera in the
American West." Unpublished Ph.D. dissertation, University of Texas, 1961.

Katz, Ruth Torgovnik. "The Origins of Opera: The Relevance of Social and Cultural Factors to the Establishment
of a Musical Institution." Unpublished Ph.D. dissertation,
Columbia University, New York, N.Y., 1963.

Appendix A

Complete New York City Opera
Repertoire, 1948-1971[1]

OPERA	COMPOSER	1st PERF.	LANGUAGE
1. TOSCA	Puccini	2/21/44	Italian
2. MARTHA	Flotow	2/22/44	English
3. CARMEN	Bizet	2/24/44	French
4. BOHEME	Puccini	5/ 4/44	Italian
5. CAVALLERIA	Mascagni	5/ 5/44	Italian
6. PAGLIACCI	Leoncavallo	5/ 5/44	Italian
7. TRAVIATA	Verdi	5/ 8/44	Italian
8. MANON LESCAUT	Puccini	11/ 9/44	Italian
9. GYPSY BARON	J. Strauss	11/13/44	English
10. FLYING DUTCHMAN	Wagner	4/12/45	German
11. FAUST	Gounod	4/16/45	French
12. BARTERED BRIDE	Smetana	10/ 3/45	English
13. RIGOLETTO	Verdi	5/ 9/46	Italian
14. PIRATES OF PENZANCE	Gilbert & Sullivan	5/11/46	English
15. MADAME BUTTERFLY	Puccini	5/15/46	Italian
16. ARIADNE AUF NAXOS (AP)	R. Strauss	10/10/46	German
17. EUGENE ONEGIN	Tchaikovsky	11/14/46	Russian
18. ANDREA CHENIER	Giordano	4/ 9/47	Italian
19. SALOME	R. Strauss	4/16/47	German
20. WERTHER	Massenet	10/ 2/47	French
21. BARBER OF SEVILLE	Rossini	10/ 5/47	Italian
22. DON GIOVANNI	Mozart	10/23/47	Italian
23. PELLEAS ET MELISANDE	Debussy	3/25/48	French
24. OLD MAID AND THE THIEF (NYSP)	Menotti	4/ 8/48	English
25. AMELIA GOES TO THE BALL	Menotti	4/ 8/48	English
26. MARRIAGE OF FIGARO	Mozart	10/14/48	English
27. AIDA	Verdi	10/28/48	Italian
28. TROUBLED ISLAND (WP)	Still	3/31/49	English
29. TALES OF HOFFMAN	Offenbach	4/ 6/49	French
30. THE MEDIUM	Menotti	4/ 8/49	English
31. ROSENKAVALIER	R. Strauss	10/ 6/49	German
32. LOVE FOR THREE ORANGES (NYP)	Prokofiev	11/ 1/49	English
33. TURANDOT	Puccini	4/ 6/50	Italian
34. MEISTERSINGER	Wagner	10/13/50	German
35. MANON	Massenet	3/ 2/51	French
36. THE DYBBUK (WP)	Tamkin	10/ 4/51	English
37. FOUR RUFFIANS (AP)	Wolf-Ferrari	10/18/51	English

---

1. List taken from files of the New York City Opera Company.

OPERA	COMPOSER	1st PERF.	LANGUAGE
38. WOZZECK (NYP)	Berg	4/ 3/52	English
39. AMAHL AND THE NIGHT VISITORS (NYSP)	Menotti	4/ 9/52	English
40. BLUEBEARD'S CASTLE (ASP)	Bartok	10/ 2/52	English
41. L'HEURE ESPAGNOLE	Ravel	10/ 2/52	English
42. THE CONSUL	Menotti	10/ 8/52	English
43. LA CENERENTOLA	Rossini	3/26/53	Italian
44. REGINA	Blitzstein	4/ 2/53	English
45. DIE FLEDERMAUS	J. Strauss	4/ 8/53	English
46. HANSEL & GRETEL	Humperdinck	10/14/53	English
47. THE TRIAL (AP)	Von Einem	10/22/53	English
48. THE TENDER LAND (WP)	Copland	4/ 1/54	English
49. SHOW BOAT	Kern	4/ 8/54	English
50. FALSTAFF	Verdi	4/15/54	English
51. DON PASQUALE	Donizetti	3/24/55	Italian
52. MERRY WIVES	Nicolai	3/31/55	English
53. THE GOLDEN SLIPPERS (NYP)	Tchaikovsky	10/13/55	English
54. TROILUS & CRESSIDA (NYP)	Walton	10/20/55	English
55. TROVATORE	Verdi	4/ 4/56	Italian
56. SCHOOL FOR WIVES (NYP)	Liebermann	4/15/56	English
57. IMPRESARIO	Mozart	4/15/56	English
58. ORPHEUS IN THE UNDER-WORLD	Offenbach	9/20/56	English
59. MIGNON	Thomas	9/25/56	French
60. SUSANNAH (NYP)	Floyd	9/27/56	English
61. THE TEMPEST (AP)	Martin	10/11/56	English
62. THE MOON (AP)	Orff	10/16/56	English
63. L'HISTOIRE DU SOLDAT	Stravinsky	10/16/56	English
64. VIDA BREVE/AMOR BRUJO (ballet)	De Falla	10/16/57	Spanish
65. MACBETH (NYP)	Verdi	10/24/57	Italian
66. MERRY WIDOW	Lehar	10/27/57	English
67. ABDUCTION FROM THE SERAGLIO	Mozart	10/30/57	English
68. BALLAD OF BABY DOE (NYP)	Moore	4/ 3/58	English
69. TALE FOR A DEAF EAR (NYP)	Bucci	4/ 6/58	English
70. TROUBLE IN TAHITI	Bernstein	4/ 6/58	English
71. LOST IN THE STARS	Weill	4/10/58	English
72. TAMING OF THE SHREW (NYP)	Giannini	4/13/58	English
73. GOOD SOLDIER SCHWEIK (WP)	Kurka	4/23/58	English
74. SILENT WOMAN (AP)	R. Strauss	10/ 7/58	English
75. RAPE OF LUCRETIA	Britten	10/23/58	English
76. MARIA GOLOVIN	Menotti	3/30/59	English
77. STREET SCENE	Weill	4/ 2/59	English
78. THE SCARF (AP)	Hoiby	4/ 5/59	English
79. THE DEVIL & DANIEL WEBSTER	Moore	4/ 5/59	English
80. WUTHERING HEIGHTS (NYP)	Floyd	4/ 9/59	English
81. HE WHO GETS SLAPPED	Ward	4/12/59	English
82. THE TRIUMPH OF ST. JOAN (NYSP)	Dello Joio	4/16/59	English

OPERA	COMPOSER	1st PERF.	LANGUAGE
83. 6 CHARACTERS IN SEARCH OF AN AUTHOR (WP)	Weisgall	4/26/59	English
84. OEDIPUS REX	Stravinsky	9/24/59	Latin
85. CARMINA BURANA (NYSP)	Orff	9/24/59	Latin
86. THE MIKADO	Gilbert & Sullivan	10/ 1/59	English
87. COSI FAN TUTTE	Mozart	10/ 8/59	English
88. THE CRADLE WILL ROCK (NYSP)	Blitzstein	2/11/60	English
89. THE PRISONER	Dallapiccola	9/29/60	English
90. ORFEO (NYSP)	Monteverdi	9/29/60	Italian
91. THE INSPECTOR GENERAL (AP)	Egk	10/19/60	English
92. IL TABARRO	Puccini	10/ 5/61	Italian
93. SUOR ANGELICA	Puccini	10/ 5/61	Italian
94. GIANNI SCHICCHI	Puccini	10/ 5/61	Italian
95. THE WINGS OF THE DOVE (WP)	Moore	10/12/61	English
96. H.M.S. PINAFORE	Gilbert & Sullivan	10/18/61	English
97. THE CRUCIBLE (WP)	Ward	10/26/61	English
98. THE GOLEM (WP)	Ellstein	3/22/62	English
99. TURN OF THE SCREW	Britten	3/25/62	English
100. PORGY AND BESS	Gershwin	3/31/62	English
101. LOUISE	Charpentier	10/ 4/62	French
102. PASSION OF JONATHAN WADE (WP)	Floyd	10/11/62	English
103. MIDSUMMER NIGHT'S DREAM (NYP)	Britten	4/25/63	English
104. THE NIGHTINGALE (NYP)	Stravinsky	10/ 3/63	Russian
105. JEANNE D'ARC AU BUCHER (NYSP)	Honegger	10/ 3/63	English
106. GENTLEMEN, BE SEATED (WP)	Moross	10/10/63	English
107. BORIS GODUNOV	Moussorgsky	10/ 1/64	English
108. NATALIA PETROVNA (WP)	Hoiby	10/ 8/64	English
109. KATERINA ISMAILOVA (NYP)	Shostakovich	3/ 4/65	English
110. DIE DREIGROSCHENOPER (NYP in German)	Weill	3/11/65	German
111. SAINT OF BLEECKER STREET	Menotti	3/18/65	English
112. LIZZIE BORDEN (WP)	Beeson	3/25/65	English
113. FLAMING ANGEL (AP)	Prokofiev	9/22/65	English
114. CAPRICCIO	R. Strauss	10/27/65	English
115. MISS JULIE (WP)	Rorem	11/ 4/65	English
116. DON RODRIGO (NAP)	Ginastera	2/22/66	Spanish
117. DIALOGUES OF THE CARMELITES (NYSP)	Poulenc	3/ 3/66	English
118. DANTON'S DEATH (AP)	Von Einem	3/ 9/66	English
119. GIULIO CESARE (NYSP)	Handel	9/27/66	Italian
120. THE MAGIC FLUTE	Mozart	10/13/66	English
121. THE SERVANT OF TWO MASTERS (WP)	Giannini	3/ 9/67	English
122. LE COQ D'OR	Rimski-Korsakov	9/21/67	English
123. BOMARZO (NYP)	Ginastera	3/14/68	Spanish

American Opera Librettos

OPERA	COMPOSER	1st PERF.	LANGUAGE
124. CARRY NATION (NYP)	Moore	3/28/68	English
125. NINE RIVERS FROM JORDAN (WP)	Weisgall	10/ 9/68	English
126. PRINCE IGOR	Borodin	2/27/69	English
127. MEFISTOFELE	Boito	9/21/69	Italian
128. LUCIA DI LAMMERMOOR	Donizetti	10/ 9/69	Italian
129. SONGS OF CATULLIUS (NYP)	Orff	10/30/69	Latin
130. ROBERTO DEVEREUX	Donizetti	10/15/70	Italian
131. THE MAKROPOULOS AFFAIR	Janacek	11/ 1/70	English
132. HELP, HELP, THE GLOBOLINKS ARE COMING!	Menotti	11/28/70	English
133. THE MOST IMPORTANT MAN IN THE WORLD (WP)	Menotti	3/ 7/71	English
134. UN BALLO IN MASCHERA	Verdi	3/21/71	Italian
135. ALBERT HERRING	Britten	9/12/71	English

WP	World Premiere	NYP	New York Premiere
AP	American Premiere	NYSP	New York Stage Premiere
ASP	American Stage Premiere	NAP	North American Premiere

Appendix B

Synopses of Opera Librettos

(arranged in chronological order by date
of first performance by the New York City Opera)

The Old Maid and the Thief*

Scene I: Miss Todd's parlor. Late afternoon.

Miss Todd and Miss Pinkerton exchange gossip over their tea cups. Each discloses that, years ago, a man wrecked her life. Knocks are heard at the back door. Laetitia announces a man to see Miss Todd. Miss Pinkerton leaves. The man proves to be a tramp, yet such an attractive one that he is invited to stay overnight.

Scene II: The kitchen of Miss Todd's house. Next morning.

Miss Todd and Laetitia cannot bear the thought of Bob's leaving. They decide to ask him to remain a week. To the neighbors it can be explained that he is Miss Todd's cousin. But how to persuade him to stay? Laetitia suggests that a good breakfast will be the most convincing argument possible.

Scene III: Bob's bedroom. A few minutes later.

Laetitia arrives with breakfast. Bob agrees to stay, but warns her that he will be a cousin --nothing more--since he hates women.

Scene IV: The street. Later in the morning.

Miss Pinkerton excitedly informs Miss Todd that a notorious desperado has escaped from the county jail of Timberville, and has been seen in the neighborhood. She describes him as "tall and burly, black hair and curly, light complexion, Southern inflection, and altogether handsome. "

Scene V: Miss Todd's parlor. A few minutes later.

Miss Todd relays the news to Laetitia. Both women

---

*Menotti, Gian-Carlo, music and libretto, The Old Maid and the Thief, (New York: Franco Colombo, Inc. Used by permission of Belwin-Mills Pub. Corp.), n. p. g.

are convinced that Bob is the escaped criminal. Goodness
gracious! He might rob and murder them in their beds.
Yet ... he has such lovely eyes. They decide to let him
stay. But for his contentment (and their safety) they must
keep him liberally supplied with money. There being no al-
ternative, they decide to rob the neighbors.

Scene VI: The kitchen. A week later.

For days, remarks Laetitia, Miss Todd has been
committing robberies in Bob's behalf, and has been making
languid eyes at him. Bob accepts the money with entrancing
smiles, yet shows no affection for her. Laetitia reveals
that she, too, has lost her heart to him.

Scene VII: The porch of Miss Todd's house. Later in the
    day.

According to Miss Pinkerton, the thief is still hiding
in the neighborhood. Many houses have been mysteriously
robbed. The town must ask for police protection.

Scene VIII: Bob's bedroom. A few days later.

Bob voices his philosophy that "a man born in a house
is a bird born in a cage." Laetitia discovers him packing,
begs him to stay, and learns that he longs for "just something to drink." (The next scene follows without pause.)

Scene IX: The parlor. Immediately afterwards.

Laetitia and Miss Todd confer. How to avert the
imminent catastrophe? Miss Todd, a leader in a temperance
movement, cannot buy liquor publicly. Laetitia suggests that
they rob the liquor store, and rationalizes such conduct by
pointing out that "sinning against a sin can be no sin."

Scene X: In front of the liquor store. That same night.

The two women break through a window, fill their
basket with gin bottles (so noisily that they rouse the store-
keeper from his sleep upstairs), and flee helter-skelter
through the town.

Scene XI: Miss Todd's parlor. The next morning.

Miss Pinkerton reports that last night's robbery in

the liquor store has thrown the town into an uproar.   A famous detective has been hired.   Every house will be searched.
As Miss Todd struggles to conceal her alarm, Bob's voice,
wavering in a drunken song, floats down from upstairs,
arousing Miss Pinkerton's suspicions.   When Miss Pinkerton
leaves, Laetitia and Miss Todd decide that Bob must be
warned.

Scene XII: Bob's bedroom.   Immediately afterwards.

     The two women rouse Bob from a drunken stupor to
warn him that the police are closing in.   His puzzlement
leads to the disclosure that he is not a hunted criminal--just
an honest beggar, a "lost-wind-tossed leaf." Miss Todd ro-
mantically urges him to flee to France with her.   He prosa-
ically refuses.   Infuriated, she declares she will call the police, accuse him of heinous crimes and see him sent to prison.   (The next scene follows without pause.)

Scene XIII: The same.   Immediately afterwards.

     Laetitia sees her opportunity for romance.   She per-
suades Bob that Miss Todd has unlimited influence with the
local authorities, and that "it would be a pity for one so
young to be electrocuted." His only hope of freedom lies in
flight ... and it might as well be with her, in Miss Todd's
car.   Bob is forced to agree.   But since he must assume
the role of thief, he may as well really become one.   So he
and the unscrupulous Laetitia plunder the house of all its
valuables before taking flight.

Scene XIV: Miss Todd's house.   A few moments later.

     A brief picture of Miss Todd's tragi-comic return to
her empty house.

Amelia Goes to the Ball*

The curtain rises on Amelia's frenzied preparations for the first ball of the season. Her husband enters and reveals that he has intercepted a letter sent by Amelia's lover. He upbraids her, and declares he will shoot the lover. Amelia is upset by these threats, not because she fears for her lover, but because she is afraid she will be prevented from going to the ball.

Her husband demands the lover's name; Amelia agrees to tell him if he will promise to take her to the ball. She reveals that her lover lives on the floor above. The husband rushes out, threatening to shoot him at sight.

Left alone, Amelia fears that a serious quarrel between the men will endanger her chances of attending the ball, and going out on the balcony, calls to her lover. She warns him to escape. The lover immediately slides down a rope ladder to Amelia's balcony. He proposes that they elope. Amelia refuses, having her heart set on the ball, and asks him to return later with his proposal. Before she can convince the amazed and unfortunate lover, her husband is heard returning. Amelia conceals her lover. The husband, unsuccessful in his search, agrees that he will take her to the ball, but tells her that if he had caught the lover he would have had his revenge.

Suddenly he spies the lover, who comes out of hiding to demand satisfaction for the husband's bitter words. The husband, confronted by a young, vigorous man, many years his junior, abandons the idea of killing him. He urges reason instead, and tries to mend matters by discussing love and the rights of marraige. Amelia, bored and impatient, reminds her husband he is to take her to the ball.

Interested in their discussion, both husband and lover

---

*Menotti, Gian-Carlo, music and libretto, Amelia Goes to the Ball, (New York: G. Ricordi and Co., 1938. Used by permission of Belwin-Mills Music Pub. Corp.), n.p.g.

remain indifferent to Amelia's pleadings. When her husband
rudely tells her to be quiet, she becomes desperate and
breaks a vase over his head, knocking him unconscious.
For a moment Amelia is at a loss. Then she calls loudly
for help as the lover seeks to revive the husband.

The police and neighbors rush into the room. Amelia
accuses her lover of being a burglar, declaring that he entered the apartment and attacked her husband. Amazed by
this deceit, the lover appeals to her, but Amelia says she
has never seen the man before. The police hustle the lover
out and take the unconscious husband to an ambulance.

At this Amelia bursts into tears. The Chief of Police
is touched, and remains to console her. He tells her that
she still has her pearls and her money, and that her husband's condition is not serious.

But Amelia tells him the reason she is crying is that
her heart is set on going to the ball. Now what can she do?
She cannot go alone. The gallant Chief of Police proposes
that if she will not think him presumptuous, he will be
charmed to escort her. This is all Amelia could wish for.
Joyfully she accepts, and they hasten out, arm in arm.

The moral of the story with which the Chorus concludes the opera is, "If Woman Sets Her Heart Upon a Ball,
The Ball is Where She'll Go."

Troubled Island*

Led by Jean Jacques Dessalines, the Haitian slaves revolt against their French masters of the Napoleonic era. Azelia, Dessalines' wife, stands by his side in all his dangerous enterprises. As Haiti's new Emperor, Dessalines lives in splendor with the lovely mulatto Empress, Claire. Azelia is cast off, though she comes to warn him of his danger when she finds that he is resented by those who wish to supplant him: those whom he forces to work for the good of the nation. These people plot against him, assisted by his mistress, Empress Claire, who secretly loves the traitor, Vuval. The sumptuous banquet of state, with entertainment by the court ballet is interrupted by the throbbing of voodoo drums; insistent throbbing that presages ill for Dessalines. Dessalines goes to quell the uprising against him. In a distant marketplace he meets his traitorous general, Stenio, and is at the point of winning a duel with him when Vuval shoots him in the back. His body is left in the square to be robbed by ragamuffins and wept over by Azelia who, now crazed by her harrowing experiences, alone remains faithful to her husband, that broken Dessalines who once had all Haiti at his feet; who once cast her aside for the unfaithful Claire.

---

*Still, William, music; Hughes, Langston, libretto, Troubled Island (unpublished material from New York City Opera Company Files).

The Medium*

ACT I

    In Madame Flora's cluttered apartment the mute Toby
plays in an old trunk, dressing up in odd bits of clothing.
Monica, who is combing her hair, joins him, warning him
of her mother's anger. Soon Baba, Monica's mother, does
appear to scold them and urge them to prepare for the seance.

    When the doorbell rings, Toby and Monica disappear
to play their parts in the seance and the clients enter. Baba
moans during the seance and Monica, hidden, imitates a
small child's voice and speaks to the visitors who are parents of a dead girl. Suddenly Baba feels something in the
dark. She turns on the lights and, frightened, asks the clients to leave. Monica tries to comfort her but she still
hears the child's voice. Toby goes downstairs to investigate
but no one is there. Baba is still disturbed as Monica repeats a comforting ballad.

ACT II

    Several days later Toby and Monica are playing and
exchanging loving moments together. Baba, who has been
drinking, interrupts them. She cannot forget the incident
during the seance of a hand touching her. She bribes and
later threatens Toby into indicating it was he who touched
her, but he will not respond. Finally she grabs a whip in
a fit of temper and uses it on him.

    When the parents of the dead child return, Baba tries
to discourage them, stating there will be no more seances.
The visitors refuse to believe that it is all a fraud, even
after the gimmicks of the seance are pointed out. She throws
their money on the table, and they are pushed out the door,
still willing to believe in the seance. Now Baba clears Toby

*Menotti, Gian-Carlo, music and libretto; The Medium, (New
York: G. Schirmer, Inc., 1947).

out of the house despite Monica's pleas, and she locks
Monica in her room. Baba then sings of her fear of the
voices and finally falls into a drunken sleep.

As she sleeps, Toby returns quietly to look in the
trunk. When he finishes, the lid falls noisily and he jumps
behind the puppet theatre curtains. Baba awakes, terrified.
She calls out, "Who's there?" and notices the curtains moving. She fires into them and Toby falls forward into the
room, tangled in the curtains. She unlocks Monica's door
and then kneels over Toby's body with Monica, wondering if
the hand in the dark was his.

The Dybbuk*

ACT I

Channon, an impoverished Talmudic student, loves
Leah, who returns his love. But her father, the rich Sender,
plans a match for her with the son of a wealthy man. To
win the riches that would make him eligible in Sender's eyes,
Channon studies the Kabala and masters the power to call upon the Evil One but the knowledge costs him his life.

ACT II

The day of Leah's wedding to the bridegroom chosen
by her father. According to custom, the beggars of the town
are given a feast and insist upon dancing with the bride. She
visits the grave of her mother to ask her to stand with her
under the wedding canopy, and, seeing the grave of Channon,
her dead love, mourns for him and shrinks from the thought
of the loveless marriage that lies ahead of her. As the
bridegroom places the veil over her face, the spirit of Channon takes possession of her body, to find fulfilment through
her. This is the Dybbuk.

ACT III

Leah's distracted father, Sender, takes her to Azrael,
a "wonder-working" rabbi who summons the spirit of Channon's father and learns from him that Sender had pledged
him, when they both were young, that their children should
be married when they reached maturity. Sender has broken
the pledge. He is judged and accepts the penalty imposed
upon him. Thereupon Azrael, on threat of excommunication,
exorcises the Dybbuk from the body of Leah and orders her
father to prepare the marriage. But Leah, calling upon
Channon, dies and is united with her lover.

---

*Tamkin, David, music; Tamkin, Alex, libretto, The Dybbuk
(reprinted by permission of the New York City Opera Company, 1951), n. p. g.

Amahl and the Night Visitors*

Somewhere in the world lives a crippled little shepherd called Amahl, with his mother, an impoverished widow. Nothing is left to them of the little they ever had, and they are now faced with hunger and cold in their empty house.

Three Wise Men, on their way to Bethlehem, stop at the hut and ask to be taken in for the night. Amahl and his mother welcome them as well as they can, and are much astonished at the splendor of their robes and the wealth of gifts they are carrying with them. When Amahl's mother realizes that the Three Kings are looking for a newborn babe and that the expensive gifts are all destined for him, she becomes bitter and envious. She cannot understand why at least some of these gifts are not to be bestowed upon her own child, who is so poor and sickly.

Under cover of darkness, while the Three Kings are asleep, she steals some of the gold from them ... and is caught red-handed. When she explains to the Three Kings that she needs this gold to feed her starving child, she is readily forgiven. With great tenderness they try to explain to her who this newborn child is and how much he needs the love of every human being to build his coming kingdom. Touched by their words, the poor widow not only gives back the stolen gold, but wishes she could add a gift of her own. Little Amahl comes to her rescue. He impulsively hands to the Three Kings his wooden crutch, his most precious possession, and in doing so he is miraculously cured of his lameness.

As dawn appears in the sky, the Three Kings make ready to resume their journey. Amahl begs his mother to let him join them, and he is finally allowed to follow the Kings to Bethlehem to adore and give thanks to the Christ Child.

---

*Menotti, Gian-Carlo, music and libretto; Amahl and the Night Visitors (RCA Records, copyright, 1952). Reprinted by permission.

The Consul*

The Consul is a tragedy of the meek who, far from
inheriting the earth, live desperately beneath the burden of
man's inhumanity to man. Set in a nameless European country, the drama tells the story of men and women caught in
the red tape and official papers of a Consulate which bars
their escape to freedom. Primarily, the action centers
about the lives of John and Magda Sorel, their child, and
John's mother, when circumstances force them to depend
upon the refuge of the Consulate.

As the curtain rises on the Home, John Sorel stum-
bles through the door, calling for his wife. A member of
the underground, John has been wounded in a raid and is
still being pursued. He barely has time to hide when the
Secret Police Agent enters with his two henchmen. After a
violent search and questioning, they leave, threatening that
they will return. John comes out of hiding, advises Magda
to seek help at the Consulate, and reluctantly leaves his
family.

Magda goes to the Consulate. There she is confronted by a meticulously efficient Secretary who rules in a
kingdom of applications, request forms, and endless documents. With the other applicants--Mr. Kofner, a Foreign
Woman, Magadoff the Magician, and two other women--Magda
submits her case to the unyielding Secretary and meets with
failure and delay.

As the second act opens, the days of waiting have
lengthened into months. Magda watches helplessly as the
Mother tries to comfort the sick child. In a moment of
nightmare, Magda sees both her husband and the child threat-
ened by death. A few moments later a visit from the Secret
Police Agent coincides with the first message from John,
brought by Assan the glasscutter. Knowing the police are

---

*Menotti, Gian-Carlo, music and libretto, The Consul (New
York: copyright 1950 by G. Schirmer, Inc.). Used by permission. n. p. g.

becoming impatient and learning that John threatens to return
to help her, Magda decides to return to the Consulate.

At the Consulate, the stage is held by Nika Magadoff,
the Magician, who attempts to win a visa with feats of pres-
tidigitation and hypnotism.   When Magda can at last appeal
to the Secretary, her request is denied.   Finally defiant,
Magda cries out against the senseless chains of paper that
bind all the hopeless who come to the Consulate.   Relenting,
the Secretary offers to see the Consul.   But this last hope
is destroyed a moment later.

At the opening of the last act, Magda sits alone in
the Consulate.   Ignoring the Secretary's insistence that she
is wasting her time, Magda watches one fortunate woman receive her papers and visa.   Then Assan hurries in to tell
her that John will return unless she can find a way to stop
him.   Knowing what she must do, Magda writes a note to
John and sends Assan to deliver it.   In a moment she too
leaves the Consulate.

Left alone, the Secretary has a frightening vision of
the myriad names and faces which pass in endless procession
before her.   Suddenly John Sorel enters, begs for news of
his wife and for help.   Almost immediately, the Secret Police
enter and force John to go with them, but not before the Secretary, moved for the first time, promises to call his wife.

Magda enters her home an instant too late for the
call.   In hopeless resignation, she shrouds the windows and
the door and turns on the gas.   As she dies, she sees again
John, his mother, and the people she has watched in the Consulate.   She hears them urging her to join them but struggles
futilely, unable to move.   At last the Magician appears and
with great compassion leads her once more to her place at
the stove.

The ringing of the phone shatters the dream.   Magda
makes one more effort to answer.   But death has freed her.
The curtain falls.

Regina*

PROLOGUE:

Outside the Giddens house. It is a lovely Spring
morning. Addie and Zan come out to clap and dance when
the Angel Jazz Band passes the house. Regina interrupts
the happy scene and calls raspingly from the window, re-
minding them that there will be company for dinner and work
must be done.

ACT I:

Living room of the Giddens house, the same evening.
Regina and her brothers are entertaining William Marshall,
hoping to persuade him to put some Northern capital into
their cotton mill. Horace Giddens is away from home, in a
hospital in Baltimore, recovering from a heart attack.   The
Hubbards and their guest drift into the living room after dinner. Birdie comes first, slightly tipsy, and sings of how
she loves music. Oscar Hubbard chides her roughly for
talking too much to Mr. Marshall, but then Mr. Marshall,
after many compliments to Regina's beauty and her Southern
hospitality, agrees to become their partner. When he has
gone, the Hubbards tell in turn what they will do with their
new riches. Birdie sings touchingly of Lionnet, her girlhood
home, which she would like to see restored as it used to be.
Oscar suddenly reminds Regina that her third of the Hubbard
capital will have to come from Horace. She retorts by trying to blackmail her Hubbard brothers into promising her
half instead of a third of the profits. "You must take what
you want" is the burden of the aria she sings when they have
left her. Ruthlessly, she orders Zan to go to Baltimore
next day and bring Zan's father home from the hospital, sick
or well. Zan reluctantly assents. Birdie and Zan have a

---

*Blitzstein, Marc, libretto and music; based on play The
Little Foxes by Lillian Hellman, Regina. Reprinted from
Stories of 100 Operas by Helen L. Kaufmann. Copyright
1960 by Helen L. Kaufmann. Published by Grosset and
Dunlap, Inc., p. 244-47.

final scene, in which Birdie warns Zan not to marry Leo, as
the family wish her to do. Birdie sings feelingly of her own
unhappy life. Zan has no intention of marrying Leo. She
dreams of true love. "What will it be for me?" she wonders in song. Oscar overhears Birdie's warning, and when
Zan's back is turned, he slaps his wife's face. She muffles
her scream, and Zan goes slowly and uneasily upstairs.

ACT II:

       The Giddens living room, a week later. Oscar men-
tions to his son Leo, who works in Horace's bank, that it
might be a good thing for him to "borrow" the stocks and
bonds from Horace's safe deposit box, since Horace is not
yet home, and Mr. Marshall is coming to a party that evening to clinch the deal. Leo plays dumb, and dances out
singing a foolish jingle in anticipation of the party. When
they have gone, Zan and Horace enter. He is exhausted
from the trip, but Regina gives him no rest. For her it is
now or never. She wheedles, flatters, then quarrels out-
rageously with him when he refuses to invest in the Marshall
venture. Ben enters to add his arguments to Regina's, but
Horace refuses him too.

       The scene shifts to the ball-room and veranda. It is
evening, and the party is in full swing. There is a lively
chorus of guests, with an undertone of criticism of the Hubbard family's business methods. Horace, an unwilling guest
in a wheelchair, orders his safe deposit box brought from
the bank the next day, for he wishes to change his will. To
soothe Birdie, again rebuked by Oscar, Addie sings a blues
song, "Night could be time to sleep." In "Chinky-pin,"
Jazz expresses his scorn of white people. Now the Hubbards, all smiles, come in with Marshall. Ben Hubbard
has Horace's bonds, stolen by Leo. He smugly announces
that everything is settled and they drink a toast to the new
partnership. Regina is dumbfounded. When the men have
gone, she turns furiously on Horace showering reproaches
on him as Zan and Birdie try to restrain her. "I'll be
waiting for you to die," she shrieks rather than sings, and
as she goes upstairs, adds menacingly "I'll be waiting."

ACT III:

       The Giddens living-room, the next afternoon. The
"good people"--Zan, Birdie, Horace and Addie--are there
together. Horace's safe deposit box is on the table beside

his wheelchair. "Make a quiet day," sings Zan in a charming madrigal, in which the others join. Birdie sings her
big aria "Mamma used to say" and bursts into tears of
homesickness at the refrain "Lionnet, Lionnet." She has
had too much currant wine, and Zan escorts her home.
Horace seizes the opportunity to make Addie promise to take
Zan away from her mother after his death. Regina enters,
and Horace shows her the empty safe deposit box. She
knows at once who has taken the securities, and again they
have a furious quarrel over her insistence on blackmailing
her brothers and his refusal to do so. The excitement
brings on a severe heart attack. As Horace reaches for the
life-saving medicine beside him, he accidentally knocks it
over. The bottle is shattered, the contents spilled. He
gasps painfully that Regina should quickly bring him another
bottle from upstairs. She does not move, but sits coldly
watching him suffer. He struggles to his feet, gets halfway
up the stairs, and collapses on the landing. She calls for
help, and Cal carries him to the bedroom. A few minutes
later, the Hubbard brothers come in, and Regina coldly demands 75% of the profits as her share, or the exposure of
the theft of the securities. "What a greedy girl!" sings Ben
uneasily, in an obvious understatement. At this point, Zan
comes from her father's bedside. "What was papa doing on
the staircase, Mamma?" she asks accusingly. Ben repeats
the question, and ere-long he is accusing Regina of murdering Horace. Zan sings a final aria, "All in one day" summing up her grief and disillusionment. She tells Regina that
she is going away, and Regina beseeches her to sleep with
her that night. "What's the matter, mamma, are you
afraid?" asks Zan. And the curtain falls on the sound of
a spiritual sung by the servants mourning the master, one
of many expressive melodies packed into the score.

The Tender Land*

ACT I

     The day before graduation, late afternoon, on a farm
in the midwest in the early 1930's in early June, Beth Moss,
ten years old, is playing in the yard and her mother, Ma
Moss, is sitting on the porch rocker, sewing. The mailman
arrives with a package which contains the graduation dress
for Laurie Moss, Beth's older 17-year-old sister, who ends
her high school career tomorrow. They are planning a party
to celebrate the event that evening and the postman is invited
to come and bring his wife and violin. Laurie arrives home
from school filled with the emotion of graduation and maturity.
She is impatient to be free. Top and Martin, two drifters,
enter, looking for work and food. When Grandpa Moss, Laurie's father, returns from the fields, he talks to them, and
though he is suspicious of strangers, he needs the help for
the field work and agrees to let them stay.

ACT II

     That evening everyone is just finishing eating at the
party. Dancing is suggested and finally couples begin to
move to the music. Martin dances with Laurie and before
very long they are showing a great interest in each other.
But Grandpa discovers them kissing and orders the two drifters off the place by morning. Laurie is crushed and the
neighbors all say good night.

ACT III

     Later that night Martin calls softly for Laurie and she
comes to him. They plan to run away together at dawn.
However, Top, Martin's companion, points out that their life
is no life for a girl like Laurie and convinces him to leave
immediately and not take Laurie.

---

*Copland, Aaron, music; Everett, Horace, libretto, The
Tender Land, (New York: Boosey and Hawkes, 1956), no
synopsis given.

At dawn, Laurie emerges from the house ready to leave, but discovers that the two men have left. She is heartbroken, but her sister and mother comfort her. Then she resolves to leave her home anyway to find her own life, and she strikes off down the road as her mother and little sister watch.

Susannah*

ACT I

The yard of the New Hope church. The young people
are square dancing while their mothers watch and gossip.
Susannah, by virtue of her beauty, high spirits and brightly
colored dress is outstanding. Some spiteful remarks are
made about the motherless girl and her drunken brother,
Sam. But she is happily oblivious. The dancing stops for
a moment when the traveling preacher arrives, announcing
in song "I am the Reverend Olin Blitch." When it resumes,
he at once notices Susannah, asks who she is, and joins the
dance with her as his partner.

We next see Susannah on the porch of the dilapidated
house she and her brother call home. Little Bat McLean
comes to see her, first making sure that she is alone because he says that he is afraid of her brother. She sings a
contented aria, "Ain't it a pretty night," and Sam, coming
in, echoes the refrain. There is a loving scene between
brother and sister. She begs him to sing the ballad with
which he lulled her to sleep when she was a child, "Jay-bird
sittin' on a hick'ry limb," and they go quietly into the house.

The next morning, Susannah runs lightly into the
woods, singing as she goes. The four Elders arrive. They
are looking for a creek in which the Evangelist may baptize
repentant sinners. Susannah's voice is heard in the distance.
They follow the sound, and spy her bathing in the creek.
They watch her in silence, lasciviously, then burst out in
self-righteous condemnation of her shameless nakedness--
watching all the while, however. They go off, with many a
backward glance, as they sing that she shall be punished.

In the yard of the church, that evening, the four wives

---

*Floyd, Carlisle, music and libretto, Susannah. Reprinted
from Stories of 100 Operas by Helen L. Kaufmann, c. 1960
by Helen L. Kaufmann. Published by Grosset and Dunlap,
Inc., p. 293-96.

of the four elders discuss Susannah's immodesty, while they
prepare a church supper. When she appears with a covered
dish, friendly and smiling as always, she gets the cold shoulder. Mrs. McLean sings "You ain't welcome here," and
Susannah, bewildered and hurt, goes home. As she sits on
her porch wondering, Little Bat McLean again comes. He
tells her that the elders are threatening to run her out of the
Valley for her sinful behavior. She defends herself until he
admits that he has been forced to confess falsely that she allowed him to "love her up." Infuriated, she chases him off
the place, crying "Lyin varmint." She sobs out her story in
Sam's arms, begging "Sing me the jay-bird song agin."

ACT II

        Susannah's porch. It is Friday morning. Sam tells
her that he must leave her overnight, to collect the meat
from his traps. She beseeches him to stay with her, and he
promises to return the next day by sundown. He tells her
to go to the meeting that night, so that she will not be alone,
and also to prove to the elders that she is not afraid of them.
Unwillingly, she agrees.

        The scene shifts to the interior of the church, that
same evening. There is all the bustle of a revival meeting--
a collection is being taken, hymns are being sung. Susannah
sits quiet and alone on the last bench. Blitch delivers a
"hell-fire" sermon. A few sinners kneel at the altar. Then
he addresses Susannah directly, exhorting her to save her
soul. Almost hypnotized, she slowly approaches Blitch at
the altar. At sight of the smile of triumph on his face, she
screams, "No!" and rushes away.

        An hour later, on her porch, she sings a ballad to
comfort herself, "The trees on the mountain are cold and
bare." Blitch comes to pray with her, and dramatically she
defends her innocence. It is his turn to break down. He
asks her to pity him as a lonely man, a homeless wanderer,
and finally, in doubt and utter weariness of body and spirit,
she allows him to lead her into the house, her head on his
shoulder.

        The next morning, within the church, the guilty Blitch
prays with agonized intensity. Susannah seats herself without
a word to him. When the elders come, Blitch tells them
that Susannah is innocent, that they have been unjust. They
refuse to believe him and he does not confess his own sin.

Susannah laughs hysterically as they all go to the baptism.
When her brother returns, she tells him the whole story.
In a rage, he seizes his shotgun and runs out, when her
back is turned. Susannah sees the gun gone, and listens
with dread. At the sound of the shot, she falls to her knees,
shrilling "Oh Lord, I never meant him to do it." Little Bat
comes to warn her that the people are threatening to hang
Sam and to run her out of the valley. Chanting implacably,
"Out'n the valley, Susannah, git out, git out tonight," the
mob approaches. She stands them off with her shotgun. In
a last bitter revenge, she invites Little Bat to kiss her, and
slaps him violently when he comes close. As the curtain
falls, she stands alone, shotgun in hand, defending her home
and her honor.

The Ballad of Baby Doe*

ACT I, SCENE 1

Outside the Tabor Opera House, Leadville, 1880, Tabor and his cronies escape the concert, and mix with the girls from the next-door saloon. Augusta and her friends come in search of their husbands. Baby Doe arrives on the scene from Central City.

SCENE 2

Outside the Clarendon Hotel, later that evening. The Tabors return from the concert. Augusta retires but Tabor lingers outside, and a romantic meeting with Baby Doe awakens their passion.

SCENE 3

The Tabor apartment, several months later. Augusta discovers evidence of Tabor's affair with Baby Doe. She is determined to destroy the relationship.

SCENE 4

The lobby of the Clarendon Hotel, shortly thereafter. Baby Doe is about to leave Tabor, and writes her mother to explain why. Augusta enters, and Baby Doe tells her the innocent adventure has ended, but begs understanding for Tabor. Augusta reacts derisively to her young rival's idealization of her husband; her stinging exit makes Baby Doe decide she will remain with Tabor after all.

SCENE 5

Augusta's parlor in Denver, a year later. Augusta's friends bring her news that Tabor is divorcing her. They

*Moore, Douglas, music; Latouche, John, libretto, The Ballad of Baby Doe (New York: Program Publishing Co.) p. 6-7.

goad her into revenge.

SCENE 6

A suite in the Willard Hotel, Washington, D.C., 1883.
Tabor, during his thirty-day senatorship in the capitol, marries Baby Doe. At the reception, the bride's family chat
with young dandies from the State Department as they await
the couple. Only the wives of the foreign ambassadors are
present; the Washington women have refused to attend. When
the Tabors arrive, the fact that they are both divorced is
revealed. The priest who married them stalks out, scandal-
ized. The exodus of the other guests is prevented by the
timely arrival of President Arthur.

ACT II, SCENE 1

The Windsor Hotel, Denver, 1893. At the Governor's
Ball, Augusta's friends snub Baby Doe, despite their husbands' protests. Baby Doe, inured to this treatment during
the past ten years, is startled by the unexpected arrival of
Augusta Tabor. She has conquered her pride in order to
warn her successor about the impending collapse of the silver
standard. Tabor must sell out or be ruined. Tabor, enter-
ing, misunderstands Augusta's meaning and orders her out.
He asks Baby Doe to promise, no matter what happens, never
to sell the Matchless Mine.

SCENE 2

Two years later. Tabor, whose fortune is involved
in the collapse of silver, appeals to his former cronies for
financial help. When he tells of William Jennings Bryan,
who is a candidate for President on a free silver platform,
they greet him with derision. Tabor angrily replies that
they have betrayed the source of their wealth.

SCENE 3

The Matchless Mine, Summer 1896. Bryan addresses
the voters and rouses them to a high pitch of optimism.

SCENE 4

Augusta's parlor. November, 1896. Newsboys announce Bryan's defeat. Augusta is visited by Mama McCourt
who asks her to help Tabor in his hour of defeat. But

Augusta's hurt is too deep; she can do nothing.

SCENE 5

     The stage of the Tabor Grand Theatre, April 1899.
Tabor, old and ill, returns unrecognized to the stage of the
theatre he built. In his dying thoughts, he relives the night
it was dedicated: a politician presents him with a gold
watch-fob that recreates scenes from his life. Augusta
moves through these scenes like a prophetic figure, as his
realization of failure grows. Adrift in time, he sees how
even his beloved little Silver Dollar will end up in tragic
degradation. He cries out desperately for one thing which
has not failed him, and Baby Doe appears, real among the
images to despair. As she sings a lullaby to her dying husband, the song grows into a celebration of their love. The
lights dim ... years flow past, and a white-haired old woman
moves toward the Matchless Mine, and snow falls on her
quietly as her melody draws to a close.

Tale For A Deaf Ear*

Laura and Tracy Gates are sitting in their home on Sunday, reading the papers, and he gets a drink, which begins an argument about alcoholism. In the heat of the discussion, Tracy falls to the floor, apparently dead. An unseen chorus tells of Old Hypraemius the Mariner who gave back life to repentant souls and a new scene reveals a Florentine noblewoman of 1500 asking for her child in her arms to be given back life. It is given this life, and the scene changes to show a 15-year-old Scottish girl asking for her cow that has been killed by lightning to be revived--and it is. Another scene shows a soldier grieving his brother's premature death on the battlefield and the brother is finally revived. The scene again shifts to the living room of Laura and Tracy, and Tracy revives. Laura is thankful and tender, but Tracy again begins the argument. Finally the fight reaches the point of physical violence it had reached the first time and again Tracy falls down, apparently dead. The doctor arrives, pronounces death due to a coronary thrombosis, and to Laura's apparently incoherent words, the doctor responds by giving her a sedative. The chorus again sings the opening lines of the "death of love."

---

*Bucci, Mark, music and libretto, Tale For a Deaf Ear, (New York: Frank Music Corp., 1957), no synopsis given.

Trouble in Tahiti*

The scene is an American suburban home of the
1950's where a cheerful singing television commercial ac-
companies Dinah and Sam who are at breakfast. It is not a
happy scene as the two squabble with each other although
they long to have a greater understanding. At the end of
the scene Sam goes to his work.

In his office, Sam is unhappy about his marriage, but
when the phone rings, he proceeds to handle a business deal
with strength and knowledge--quite unlike his manner at home.

Meanwhile Dinah visits her psychiatrist and the audience sees contrasting views of Dinah and Sam in their day's
activities. At lunch-time the couple bump into each other
but escape with many excuses, and both sing of the wish for
happiness. The TV commercial chorus ironically comments
further on the pleasures of suburbia.

That afternoon Sam is at the handball court, where he
is a great success, and Dinah visits a women's clothes shop,
where she tells of seeing a movie, "Trouble in Tahiti." She
becomes more and more involved in telling the story, only
to realize to her embarrassment that it serves as a fill-up
for her own frustration. She rushes out and hurries home
to prepare dinner for Sam.

After dinner, as they sit by the fireplace with coffee,
Sam and Dinah recount their loneliness and inability to establish meaningful contact. Interpolated with this sad scene
is the television chorus singing of the "Island Magic" of the
movie Dinah has seen earlier.

---

*Bernstein, Leonard, music and libretto, Trouble in Tahiti
(New York: G. Schirmer, 1953).

Lost in the Stars*

ACT I

Reverend Stephen Kumala, a black preacher in a small town in South Africa, worries about his son, Absalom, who is working in the mines to earn money for his education. It has been a year since the minister and his wife have heard from Absalom and they fear he is in trouble.

Stephen agrees with his wife to go looking for Absalom and sets out for Johannesburg. At the train station Stephen meets Arthur Jarvis, a white landowner, who puzzles with Stephen over his own son's friendship for blacks.

In Johannesburg Stephen is unable to find Absalom but agrees to return to his village with his sister's son, Alex, to live with him.

Meanwhile Absalom sits in a Shantytown nightclub listening to Linda, the singer, and trying to decide on a course of action. He is considering joining a group of robbers to provide for Irina and their unborn child. He joins the robbing group, but in the complications that develop, Absalom fires a gun, killing a white man. The chorus at this point comments on the fears of the strong white minority and the weak black majority.

ACT II

Now Stephen faces a dilemma--he knows of his son's action, but the legal action has not been taken. Alone, he argues with himself and prays. Irina also prays for Absalom and vows to stay by him regardless of the consequences.

In a scene in the courtroom the other members of the gang lie, but Absalom tells the truth. He is sentenced to hang and the rest go free. The chorus sings of the broken

---

*Weill, Kurt, music; Anderson, Maxwell, libretto, Lost in the Stars, (New York: Chappell and Co., n.d.).

past of these people in the number, "Cry The Beloved Country."

Back at the village of Rev. Kumalo's congregation, the little boy, Alex, plays by himself while Stephen calls the congregation together to pray in this sad time.

As the time for Absalom's execution arrives, Jarvis, the father of the man who was killed, visits Stephen. He comes to the realization that the sorrow he is experiencing is a universal one that transcends skin color. Stephen responding to this gesture exclaims, "I have a friend."

The Taming of the Shrew*

ACT ONE

     On a street in Padua, Lucentio, his servant, and Tranio, discuss Lucentio's arrival in the city and his determination to pursue knowledge. Katharina, Bianca, their father, Baptista, and suitors Gremio and Hortensio to Bianca discuss the possibilities of marriage. Baptista is determined to have Katharina married first, but her willful nature makes this difficult. Lucentio and Tranio decide that the way to attract Bianca is to serve as her tutor, so they exchange clothes and then tell Biondello, Lucentio's other servant, the plan. Petruchio enters to visit his "dearest friend Hortensio." He announces that his father has died and left him wealthy and he wishes to marry. Grumio and Hortensio tell him of Katharina and he is interested. They all present themselves to Baptista--Petruchio for Katharina, Gremio presenting Lucentio as a young scholar to tutor Bianca, and Hortensio disguised as a musician come to tutor her also. The father states the dowry he will leave to Katharina, and Petruchio urges that the marriage contract be drawn. Tranio and Gremio vie with each other to out-offer their hand to Bianca, but the father remains undecided. They are interrupted by Katharina running Hortensio out of the house with a broken lute around his neck. Petruchio is curious to meet Katharina and Baptista goes into the house to bring her out. They immediately spar verbally for advantage but, despite her protestations, Petruchio is determined to marry her and Baptista gives them his blessing.

ACT TWO, SCENE ONE

     In the garden of Baptista's house, the afternoon before the wedding, Hortensio and Lucentio are arguing over who should give Bianca her lesson first--music or Latin. Petruchio enters, garbed in ragged clothes, and asks to see

---

*Giannini, Vittorio, music; Fee, Dorothy, libretto, The Taming of the Shrew, (New York: Ricordi, 1953), no synopsis given.

Kate. She is disgusted with his outfit and declares she will
not marry him. Her father, however, says that she will
and when they exit, Lucentio tells Bianca of his love for her
and wants to plot a quick marriage.

SCENE TWO

The following morning in the garden Katharina is
heard making wedding preparations. Bianca and Lucentio
come into the garden and disappear lovingly in a nook. It
is discovered that Petruchio is late for the wedding, but a
letter is produced explaining that he had business that de-
tained him. He asks to meet Katharina at the church and
after much hesitation on Baptista's part everyone goes to the
church.

ACT THREE

In Petruchio's house a few days after the marriage,
the servants speak of the mad-house atmosphere. They
agree that Petruchio is more of a shrew than she. The
newlyweds enter and Petruchio finds fault with the work of
the tailor on Katharina's hat and dress, and demands they
be redone. She, however, likes them, but he will have none
of it. When the food is brought in, he won't let her eat it
and says it is unfit to be consumed. She is famished and
wishes to eat anything. Lucentio and Bianca arrive and announce their secret marriage; on their heels are both fathers.
After a series of mistaken identities are cleared up, all is
forgiven and Katharina declares her happiness with Petruchio
and he with her.

The Good Soldier Schweik*

ACT I

Joseph Schweik hears about the assassination of Arch-
duke Ferdinand at Sarajevo from his cleaning woman, Mrs.
Muller, and receives the news with characteristic good-natured calm. He goes, as usual, to "The Flagon," a tavern
occupied at the moment by Palivec, the landlord, and Bretschneider, a plain-clothes policeman on secret service who
is hoping to pick up some anti-Austrian expressions of opinion
on the heels of the assassination. He draws the conversation
into political channels and arrests Schweik and Bretschneider
for some harmless remarks.

Schweik is taken to police headquarters where he is
interrogated and thrown into a cell among other innocent vic-
tims of the war hysteria, including Palivec. Schweik, always the optimist, points out how much better off they are
than in the days of medieval torture. As he is expounding
his ideas, he is dragged out to be examined by a commission
of medical authorities consisting of three psychiatrists of divergent schools of thought. His bland good nature convinces
them that he is an idiot and they commit Schweik to a mental
institution.

In contrast to the world outside, Schweik enjoys the
advantages of a public institution. He is examined again by
two other doctors who become convinced that he is feigning
the role of a happy simpleton and is in reality a malingerer
seeking to escape military service. They have him thrown
out of the asylum despite his resentful and vigorous protests.

Back home again, in bed with a chronic attack of
rheumatism, Schweik informs Mrs. Muller that he has received his draft call and patriotism impels him to report for
induction immediately. His excited behavior and feverish enthusiasm alarm Mrs. Muller but she obeys his wishes and

---

*Kurka, Robert, music; Allen, Lewis, The Good Soldier
Schweik, (New York: Program Publishing Co., 1958), p. 4-5.

tearfully pushes Schweik along the street in a wheelchair
while he brandishes his crutches and shouts enthusiastically,
"On to Belgrade!" followed by an appreciatively gleeful crowd.

ACT II

Schweik and a group of other suspected malingerers,
including Palivec, are confined to a hut used as an infirmary,
where an army doctor tries to convince them by various un-
orthodox methods that serving the Emperor is preferable to
malingering. As he is engaged in this practical group thera-
py, the sergeant ushers in Baroness Von Botzenheim, followed by her retinue bearing hampers of food and gifts. She
has come to see Joseph Schweik whose patriotic gesture in
reporting for the draft in a wheelchair and with crutches has
captured the columns of the newspapers. Schweik and his
companions devour the food with ravenous appetites. When
the Baroness and her retinue have gone, the furious doctor
has them all thrown into the guardhouse.

There, they attend a sermon conducted by the Army
Chaplain, who storms at them for their enslavement to carnal
appetites at the expense of the spirit. Schweik breaks into
tears and sobs audibly. The Chaplain appoints him as his
orderly. Shortly after, the Chaplain loses Schweik to Lieutenant Henry Lukash during a spirited game of poker.

In his first day of service, the good-natured Schweik
amiably complicates Lieutenant Lukash's life. He lets the
canary out of its cage to become friends with the cat, where-
upon the cat gobbles up the bird. Annoyed at the cat's un-
friendly disposition, he chases him out of the house. In order
to replace the cat, he steals a monstrous dog. At the same
time, Mrs. Katy Wendler, one of the Lieutenant's paramours,
arrives bag and baggage. Schweik puts her up in the Lieutenant's bedroom and to facilitate her early departure notifies
her husband. When Lieutenant Lukash arrives home, he is
caught in the center of a vortex involving the dog, Katy Wendler, Colonel Kraus Von Zillergut, owner of the stolen dog,
Katy's husband, Mr. Wendler and, of course, Schweik. As
a result, the furious Colonel orders Lieutenant Lukash and
Schweik sent off immediately to the front.

On the Prague-Budejovice express, enroute to their
destination, Schweik gets the Lieutenant into further difficulties with a bald-headed General Von Schwarzburg, whom he
mistakes for a bald-headed Mr. Purkabek. The Lieutenant

gives Schweik a wrathful dressing down for the mistaken identity, at the conclusion of which Schweik accidentally pulls the
emergency brake, bringing the train to a sudden stop. Schweik
is arrested and taken off the train, to the great relief of
Lieutenant Lukash who now sees a tranquil future ahead of
him, even though at the front.

During the final stopover in Budejovice before moving
into the front lines, the Lieutenant tries to establish a romance between himself and a Madame Kakonyi. While he is
writing a letter to the lady to arrange for a meeting, Schweik
unexpectedly arrives to report for duty again. Overwhelmed
by the fate which pursues him in the person of Schweik, Lieutenant Lukash accepts the inevitable and sends his orderly to
deliver the letter to Madame Kakonyi personally.

On the way Schweik meets Voditchka, an old pal, and
they celebrate at a tavern. Schweik finally remembers his
unfulfilled mission and the pals leave, somewhat unsteadily,
to complete it. In attempting to deliver the letter to the
lady, they become embroiled in an argument with her husband, Mr. Kakonyi, out of which develops a street brawl involving the local police, Czech soldiers and German military
police. To protect Lieutenant Lukash, Schweik swallows the
letter.

Lieutenant Lukash and Schweik finally reach the front,
a scene of vast devastation. The Lieutenant sends Schweik
and a sergeant on advance patrol. They set out together but
later differ as to the correct direction to continue. Even
though the sergeant's memory and the map seem to prove
him right, Schweik insists that maps may be wrong. Schweik
and the sergeant part company, the sergeant following the
map and Schweik following his inclination. He takes another
road and disappears.

Maria Golovin*

ACT I, SCENE 1

Donato, a man who is blind, lives with his wealthy
Mother in an old villa. It is after a world war. Agata, in
love with Donato, and other servants share these quarters.
Maria Golovin and her son, Trottolo, a young boy, also live
here. Maria's husband is a prisoner of war and she expects
him to return soon; in the meantime she has taken quarters
in this mansion which Donato's mother has rented to her.
The mother comments on the sadness of these old surroundings for a child, but Maria feels it will be pleasant anyway.
She meets Donato and is shown the bird cages he builds, as
he is unable to fulfill his ambition to be an architect. Maria
tells him of her painting and promises to keep him company.

SCENE 2

Donato is eager to get Agata and his mother off to
church in order to be alone with Maria. They have a tender
scene together, even though Agata has spoken out against her
to Donato and predicts his ultimate disappointment. Maria
tells him of her affectionate relationship with a young man
the past summer and Donato feels that she toyed with him the
same way she toys with Donato. She, however, declares her
undying love for Donato.

ACT II, SCENE 1

At a prison at the bottom of the hill the alarm has
been sounded. Agata and Donato speak of the possibility of
a prisoner having escaped. The prisoner enters and Agata
gives him a place to hide. She also tells him that a letter
has come to Maria from Aldo (the young friend of the summer before). She points out to Donato that Maria has other
admirers. He is worried and finally convinced that Maria

---

*Menotti, Gian-Carlo, music and libretto, Maria Golovin
(unpublished score in two volumes, New York City Opera),
no synopsis given.

is unfaithful to him.   A scene between Donato and his mother
underlines the mutual dependence of the two upon each other.
The act ends with Agata, Maria, the mother, and Donato
singing together of their loneliness and their wish to recap-
ture their youths.   Donato foresees trouble and compares the
three women to the three fates.

SCENE 2

The little boy, Trottolo, is sent off to a costume party next door and Maria and Donato talk.   He tells her his
love for her is over.   Finally the reasons are revealed and
Maria has Agata come in and read the letter aloud.   Maria
admits to lying about who the letter was from, but only to
protect Donato.   He forgives her and begs her never to leave
him.   The prisoner enters and is about to leave, telling
Donato that he has overheard the conversation and doesn't
feel sorry for him any longer.   He then defends himself by
saying that reason has nothing to do with the human heart.
The prisoner then runs off to escape the searchers and gives
Donato a gun.

ACT III, SCENE 1

The mother and Zuckertanz are reading through some
old music and Maria joins them to sing too.   Maria then receives word of the release of her husband.   In a scene between Maria and Donato he asks her if she will now tell her
husband how things are between them.

SCENE 2

We hear the prisoners singing down the hill.   The
mother and Maria talk of a small welcoming home party for
relatives and her husband.   When will she be leaving?   She
is not sure, but the mother thinks she should leave soon.
But neither of the women wish to tell Donato this and finally
the mother asks her forgiveness for being so rude.   Donato
and Maria see each other and she assures him she'll return
to him right after the party.

SCENE 3

It is late at night and the Mother urges Donato to go
to bed but he waits for Maria and he asks to be left alone.
He listens to the party music.   When Maria arrives he is
bitter and accuses her of not thinking of him.   She argues

with him and finally tells him that this is goodbye. He refuses to let her go and calls for his Mother to help him. She comes and helps him point the gun at a blank wall and fire it. He thinks he has killed Maria and goes to place a flower on her body. The mother leads him off, telling him they will leave and never come back to this house, and Maria picks up the flower and goes upstairs as she is called.

Street Scene*

The plot concerns Mrs. Anna Maurrant, hungry for
love, which she does not get from her domineering husband
Frank, so she carries on an affair with the milk collector.
Love also complicates the life of their daughter, Rose, and
her neighbor, the college student, Sam Kaplan. Sam is only
too willing to give up his studies to marry Rose, but she is
reluctant to have him make this sacrifice. When Frank returns home unexpectedly one day to find his wife with the
milkman, he shoots them and is captured by the police. This
tragedy convinces Rose that she must not destroy Sam's life
by marrying him before he has made his way in the world.
She goes off with her younger brother, Willie, to find a new
life elsewhere.

As Street Scene opens it is a hot June evening in
front of a New York tenement; Isadore Kaplan, Greta and
Lippo Fiorentino, Emma Jones, and the janitor's wife, Mrs.
Olsen, are talking. When Mrs. Maurrant disappears after
giving her son Willie ice cream cone money, we learn that
she is tempting fate by carrying on with Sankey, the milk
collector. The subject is changed when Mrs. Maurrant appears, saying that she would have gone to the park concert,
but her husband doesn't care for anything like that. From a
third-story window, Mr. Buchanan is calling, keeping a vigil
for his expectant wife. Frank Maurrant, a "tall, powerfully-
built man of 45, with a rugged, grim face," enters and comments peevishly that he will have to go to Stamford tomorrow
for a tryout (he's a stagehand), an announcement that interests Mrs. Maurrant.

He is anxious about his daughter and berates his wife
for not keeping track of her. As he storms upstairs, and
as Mrs. Maurrant is explaining she thinks it's a shame people can't make allowances for a lot of things, Steve Sankey
appears, a flashily dressed man in his early thirties.

---

*Weill, Kurt, music; Rice, Elmer, libretto, Street Scene
(New York: Program Publishing Company), n.p.g.

He goes off to the drug store, and Mrs. Maurrant also goes off in the same direction, ostensibly to look for Willie. The ladies gossip about the rather flagrant way they are conducting their affair, and the tragedy is foreshadowed by the comment, "someday her hoosban' is killing him," predicted by Mr. Olsen.

Miss Simpson of the Charities, who is looking for Mrs. Hildebrand, who with her two children is about to be dispossessed, join the conversation, as does Maurrant and Shirley Kaplan. An argument springs up, carried on principally by Kaplan and Maurrant, concerning the efficacy of organized charity. It grows almost into a physical fight with Shirley Kaplan trying to drag her father away, and Mrs. Maurrant urging her pugnacious husband to quit. But the men are full of fight, Mr. Kaplan insisting on a reconstructed social order, Mr. Maurrant standing for the old-fashioned home and family honor.

Sam Kaplan, more interested in a book he is reading than in his neighbors or their interests, arrives home. Sankey stops awkwardly in passing and Maurrant stares pointedly at him, but the tension is relieved by Willie's return, scratched and torn from a fight, the reason for which he refuses to tell his father.

As the neighbors drift off, Rose Maurrant and Harry Easter appear. He is reluctant to bid Rose goodnight, and it appears he is her wealthy office manager who, although married, proposes that Rose set up in apartment with his help and try to get on the stage.

Maurrant returns from the saloon, berating Rose suspiciously. Mrs. Buchanan's time has arrived and the scene is punctuated by her screams. Vincent Jones, who lives in the house, makes a pass at Rose and Sam Kaplan gets pushed to the sidewalk for trying to stop him. Rose and Sam have a tender scene which shows her warm regard for him and his love for her, and Sam's despair at the pain of the world.

At daybreak the following morning, the tenement slowly comes to life. Sam and his sister Shirley argue about Rose. The neighbors argue and talk, Maurrant is ready to go to work, but before he goes he accuses Mrs. Maurrant of asking when he will be coming back because she wants someone to come calling on her. Rose remonstrates with him, but he departs with a threat.

Mrs. Maurrant explains to Rose that she's always tried to be a good wife, but that she has to talk to somebody. Rose simply asks her to be more discreet because she's afraid of what Maurrant will do if he starts drinking. Shirley Kaplan possessively pleads with Rose to let Sam continue with his school work, but their argument is stopped by Sam's arrival, and he voices his despair to Rose, who is more optimistic. Amid the general activity of the neighborhood, Sankey appears nonchalantly, and is invited up to Mrs. Maurrant's apartment. The City Marshal and his assistant are there to dispossess the Hildebrands, when Frank Maurrant suddenly appears, and starts up to the apartment. Sam Kaplan tries to stop him, and yells a warning to Mrs. Maurrant. There are two shots and then a heavy fall. Sankey tries to get out the window, is dragged back by Maurrant, and another shot is heard. In the confusion, Maurrant, having the crowd cowed with his revolver, escapes. Rose comes back in time to see her mother being carried away by the interns.

The next scene is mid-afternoon of the same day, the movers are taking away the last of the Hildebrand furniture, policemen are cleaning up the scene, and nursemaids read the afternoon tabloid about the double murder. Rose returns with crepe for the door, talks with Harry Easter and Shirley Kaplan, explaining that she will go away with Willie and that she doesn't want to be under obligation to anyone. As the neighbors discuss the violence of the tragedy, shots ring out, there are cries of "They got 'im!" and Maurrant is brought in. Rose goes to her father, and Maurrant pleads with the police to let him have a moment with his daughter. He tries to explain to her how he went completely out of his head when he shot her mother and Sankey. Sam and Rose are left behind as the police drag Maurrant away.

Sam begs Rose to go away with him, but Rose, realizing how young they are, and how tied down they would be if they wed now, tries to explain to him that loving and belonging aren't the same thing. They say boodbye, and Rose goes off, as a couple appear at the house to rent the apartment. The neighbors pick up the thread of conversation as usual, as the play ends.

<u>The Scarf</u>*

One Act

        In the kitchen of an isolated farmhouse, Miriam sits
at a spinning wheel, a long scarf of scarlet wool in her lap.
Reuel, her husband, sits on the bed watching her. She is
young; he is old. It is snowing outside and he pleads with
her to come to bed, but she remains impassive. She hears
the mailman coming, and reminds Reuel that a postman gets
well paid. Her husband accuses her of casting an evil spell
on the night, on the postman (who is lost), and on their marriage. He recounts the number of men who have stayed the
night in their house and suggests her having affairs with them
all. He calls her a witch, she discounts everything he is
saying, and he predicts a judgment on her soul. The postman arrives and asks to have a chance to get warm. She
gets him tea, and rouses Reuel to help the postman bring in
the mailbags. She asks him to then go out and stable the
horse, which he does. She tells the mailman of her youth
and how she grew up on this farm. Her father's been dead
two years and Reuel lived on the farm next door. Reuel returns from the barn and goes back to bed in a surly mood.
She again recalls her past, but Reuel finally speaks briefly
of her father's poor management of the farm. The postman
also speaks of his work and the tiresomeness of it all. Miriam sings a love song that is a kind of reminiscence and finally Reuel breaks in to wake the postman to remind him of
the work he has to do. Miriam wants him to rest, but finally the postman agrees that it is time to go. Reuel goes to
get the horse out and the postman sings lovingly to Miriam,
but they separate when Reuel returns to announce that the
storm has let up. As the postman leaves, Miriam takes the
scarf and puts it around his neck. When the two men leave,
she calls on the evil spirits to help her, the spirits she had
learned about from Darma. She calls on Lucifer, Satan and
Bael and offers her soul to them if they will bring back the
postman to her. She takes a small packet of feathers from

---

*Hoiby, Lee, music; Duncan, Harry, libretto, <u>The Scarf</u>,
(New York: G. Schirmer, 1959), no synopsis given.

beneath the spinning wheel and a votive light from beneath the picture of the Virgin Mary and a piece of chalk. She draws a circle on the floor and asks the red scarf to bring him back to her and falls to the floor. Reuel bursts into the room with the red scarf around his neck to stare in horror at Miriam on the floor. She blocks his way to the door and as he comes toward her, she strangles him with the scarf. She opens the door and calls for the postman to come back as the curtain falls.

The Devil and Daniel Webster*

The Devil and Daniel Webster is laid in New Hampshire, in the forties. It begins with a country festival--the
neighbors of Cross Corners celebrating the marriage of Jabez
and Mary Stone. The Stones were always poor, but Jabez
has prospered amazingly and they're talking of running him
for governor. Everything goes well at first--Daniel Webster,
the great New England hero, appears as a guest, and is given
a real New Hampshire welcome. But there is another guest,
too, and an unexpected one--a Boston lawyer named Scratch,
who carries a black collecting box under his arm. His appearance terrifies Jabez, the song he sings horrifies the
neighbors, and when a lost soul, in the form of a moth, flies
out of the collecting box, panic ensues. The neighbors realize that Jabez Stone has sold his soul to the devil, denounce
him, and flee. Left alone with Mary, Jabez tells how he
came to make his hideous bargain. They appeal to Daniel
Webster who promises to help them. But the devil--Mr.
Scratch--is an excellent lawyer too. When Webster demands
a trial for his client, Scratch summons from the Pit a jury
of famous American traitors and renegades and a hanging
judge who presided at the Salem witch-trials. It is a jury
of damned souls, and Webster seems about to lose, not only
the case but his own soul's salvation, when by his powers of
oratory, he finally turns the tables on Scratch and rescues
Jabez. The neighbors rush in to drive the Devil out of New
Hampshire, and the case ends with pie for breakfast, as it
should.

Wuthering Heights*

ACT I, PROLOGUE

It is England, 1845. Lockwood, a nearby tenant, enters from the storm, seeking shelter, as he has lost his way.
Heathcliff, the owner of Wuthering Heights, coldly offers him
a blanket beside the fire. Heathcliff's unhappy wife, Isabella,
gives Lockwood several books to read in case he can't sleep.
One of them is the diary of Catherine Linton. He is interrupted in his reading by a banging of a shutter which he tries
to close. But in reaching for the shutter a white arm extends through the window asking to be let in and she names
herself Catherine Linton. Lockwood's shrieking brings Heathcliff, and upon being told the name of the apparition, rushes
out into the night calling for Cathy.

SCENE 1

Fifteen years earlier, Cathy, her brother, Hindley,
and her father, Ernshaw, argue over the actions of Heathcliff, an orphan taken in by Ernshaw, who is a moody and
difficult boy. Cathy defends him against her brother who
wants him disciplined. The tutor, Joseph, also supports
Hindley, and the argument culminates in the father dying of
a heart attack. Cathy comforts Heathcliff and they vow eternal devotion.

SCENE 2

Cathy and Heathcliff are being read to by Joseph, their
tutor, but presently Cathy rebels and tears up the book. They
are punished by Hindley by being banished to the kitchen, and
they promptly escape to the crag on the moor. After a wildly, lyrical exchange, Cathy proposes that they visit the Grange
where the Lintons live. The scene changes to the Lintons',
and Heathcliff and Cathy are discovered looking in the window.

---

*Floyd, Carlisle, music and libretto, Wuthering Heights
(New York: Boosey and Hawkes, Inc., 1958), no synopsis
given.

They attempt to escape, but Cathy falls, hurting her ankle.
Cathy remains with the Lintons and Heathcliff returns to
Wuthering Heights to inform Cathy's family.

ACT II, SCENE 1

Four weeks later Cathy returns to Wuthering Heights
to the delight of Nelly, the cook, but to Heathcliff's sullen-
ness. He, however, finally combs his hair and makes a respectable appearance, but Edgar Linton makes a remark
about Heathcliff's manners which prompts Heathcliff to throw
tea in his face. Edgar and his sister, Isabella, leave quickly, and at the end of the act Cathy is comforting Heathcliff
who has been punished by Hindley for his display of anger.

SCENE 2

One month later, Cathy is preparing for a visit from
Edgar, and Heathcliff shows his jealousy to her. Edgar arrives and finally, after a display of temper followed by tears
on Cathy's part, he proposes marriage. She accepts, but
feels uneasy about the future and confides with Nelly. She
asks, finally, for Heathcliff but Nelly tells her that he has
gone. She frantically runs into an oncoming storm to look
for him.

ACT III, SCENE 1

It is now three years later at Thrushcross Grange
where Cathy is living with Edgar, as his wife, and with
Isabella, his sister. Nelly admits Heathcliff into the house
dressed in formal attire, very much the accomplished gentleman. A party is in progress, and when Cathy sees Heathcliff, she dances with him, to the chagrin of Edgar. Heathcliff states that he has returned and gambled Hindley, who
drinks too much, out of Wuthering Heights. Heathcliff will
now be a neighbor. After Heathcliff leaves, Cathy tells Nelly
that she will right matters with Edgar, who is unhappy to
see Heathcliff again. Nelly warns Cathy about Heathcliff's
ruthless nature, but Cathy is too happy to believe it.

SCENE 2

At Thrushcross Grange, four weeks later, Cathy and
Isabella argue about Heathcliff. Isabella confesses her love
for him and Cathy warns her of his hatred for her family
and his fierce nature. Heathcliff enters with Hindley, now

a broken man.   Cathy tells him of Isabella's love for him in
her presence.   Isabella, horrified at Cathy's forwardness,
grabs Cathy, but finally runs from the room.   In an argument Heathcliff calls Cathy's marriage a "sham and pretense."
Cathy orders him away and he goes out the door to find Isabella waiting for him.   They plot to run away to be married
that evening.   Cathy discovers them and, when Edgar arrives,
confronts him with the new situation.   But finally Edgar and
Heathcliff both incur the wrath of Cathy and she denounces
them both.   Left alone with Nelly, Cathy asks, in a long, incoherent speech, "What have I done?"

SCENE 3

       Cathy with Nelly, six months later, is expecting a
child which she doesn't want.   Heathcliff arrives and demands
to see Cathy, which he finally does.   Cathy begs him to carry
her to the moor after he accuses her of abandoning him.
But as he stands in the doorway holding her, she dies in his
arms.   Heathcliff places her back on the couch and cries out
that Cathy may never find peace.   He says that if he has
killed her, for her to haunt him the rest of his days.

He Who Gets Slapped (Pantaloon)*

ACT I

Tilly and Polly, clowns in Briquet's Continental Circus, are rehearsing their act when Briquet and Count Mancini enter arguing. Mancini, by threatening to remove his daughter Consuelo, the Bareback Tango Queen, from the circus, attempts to wheedle an advance on Consuelo's salary. Briquet's wife, Zinida, the Lion Tamer, enters and joins the argument; finally they agree on a small advance.

While they are involved in this transaction, a stranger, aristocratic in appearance, comes in quietly by the street door. When questioned by Briquet he expresses his wish to become a clown. Prodded by Zinida, Briquet reluctantly hires him as Pantaloon--He Who Gets Slapped. Consuelo and her partner Bezano enter and are introduced to Pantaloon.

Mancini reminds Consuelo of their luncheon date with Baron Regnard. When she says that she must rehearse with Bezano and cannot go, he stalks out, furious, and tells her to make her own excuses to the Baron. As Consuelo and Bezano start back toward the ring Zinida tries in vain to get the latter's attention.

Pantaloon tries to cover an awkward moment by asking whether the two young people are in love, but Zinida tells him to tend to his own affairs. Briquet asks Pantaloon for his real name; it is needed for the authorities. Reluctantly Pantaloon shows his credentials, which greatly impress Zinida and Briquet. Zinida tells her husband to show Pantaloon around the circus and to send Bezano in to her.

Zinida restlessly waits for Bezano. When he comes in she violently expresses her passion for him and her jealousy of Consuelo. Finally losing control she throws herself

_____

*Ward, Robert, music; Stambler, Bernard, libretto, He Who Gets Slapped (New York: Highgate Press, copyright 1959, 1961, Galaxy Music Corp., sole U.S. agent), n.p.g.

at Bezano, but he forcibly rejects her.   Bezano abruptly returns to the ring as Baron Regnard arrives for his date with
Consuelo.

        Zinida goes to fetch her, and the Baron, while wait-
ing, examines a fine string of pearls.   Consuelo arrives and
politely tells him that she cannot join him for lunch.   The
Baron, irritated and disappointed, finally offers a surprise
to Consuelo, who is naively pleased at the thought of a present.   He places the pearls around her neck, and then embraces her and pleads his love.   After a struggle, during
which the string of pearls is broken, Consuelo, in tears, is
forced to cry out that the Baron is repellent to her and that
she tolerates him only because of her father.

ACT II

        The chorus of circus artists, during an intermission
in their performance, sings of the splendors and excitements
of the circus with its animals, freaks, acrobats, and above
all, the daring tightrope walker.

        Pantaloon, Briquet, and Mancini enter.   The Count
commends the clown for his brilliant show, but Briquet
chides him for extending his mockery to the dangerous subject of religion, patriotism, and marriage.   Pantaloon, still
in the spirit of his act, extends his fantasies even farther by
bringing the world of the audience as well as that of the ring
into the play he improvises.

        As the bell rings, the chorus departs, singing once
more of the pleasures of the audience.   Mancini detains
Pantaloon, saying--as one gentleman to another--that he desperately needs money to buy off his latest mistress.   Pantaloon takes this chance to ask about Consuelo and about Mancini's antecedents.   The answers are impatient and vague,
but Pantaloon is able to gather that Mancini is a fraudulent
count and that Consuelo is not his daughter.   As guarantee
for his loan Mancini offers his certainty that the Baron will
marry Consuelo; the Baron, moved now not only by an old
lecher's lust but also by his desire to ally himself with a
genuinely noble title, has committed himself to the marriage
in a letter.

        The two are interrupted by Briquet staggering out of
the ring, unable to bear any longer Zinida's mad reckless-
ness with her lions.   The dead silence from the ring is

broken by a crash of yells and applause. Zinida comes
slowly down the ramp, in a mixture of ecstasy and shock,
having triumphed over her red lion but having been clawed
by him. She is followed by a number of the performers, including Consuelo and Bezano. Her words are only for Bezano: all that she has been doing is for proof that her red
lion really loves her, that she is capable of being loved.
When Bezano, without a word, turns on his heel and goes
off, her triumphant light is extinguished and she walks off
as though dead.

        Consuelo remains alone with Pantaloon. Saddened and
puzzled by what she has just witnessed, Consuelo starts to
ask whether love is always this unhappy thing that it seems
to be for Zinida or that it is likely to be for her in her
forthcoming marriage with the Baron. Before he can answer
she abruptly turns to playful questions. Pantaloon's response
embraces both the serious and the playful. He answers her
in terms of a palm-reading fantasy about her destiny, in
which he warns her about the destructive danger of marrying
the Baron. When she asks about Bezano, Pantaloon grudging-
ly admits that she might be happy with him. He then turns
to the mystery of her origin, and his fantasy becomes serious. In hypnotic tones he tells her that like Venus she rose
from the sea, and must return to the sea if she is not to be
doomed. Consuelo, caught up in the fantasy, asks how she
can return. Pantaloon, completely under the spell of his
own imagination, says that he, he is the old sea god come
down to carry her back--and attempts to kiss her.

        This abruptly breaks the spell for Consuelo: she
slaps him. At this he recalls--or realizes--that this fantasy
is only another of his plays, but before he can explain further
he is interrupted by Zinida, who had come back from the
ring and had been watching the end of this little scene.

        In a violent diatribe (yet somehow tinged with sym-
pathy), she mocks Pantaloon and reveals the frustrations of
his earlier attempts to reform the world about him. Consuelo, provoked by Zinida's attack, rises to his defense.
Sobered by this, Zinida finally wonders only why he has con-
tinually put himself into the position of being slapped. Pantaloon, seeming to reflect on his whole life can only reply:
"Am I not Pantaloon--He Who Gets Slapped?"

ACT III

    While the circus is being readied for a gala perform-
ance celebrating the forthcoming marriage of Consuelo to the
Baron, Pantaloon sings his ballad symbolically expressing the
fate of Consuelo and himself. The trumpets announce the
entrance of the wedding procession; he abruptly ends this
mood and pretends to be far gone in drunkenness. Against
the background of the wedding-chorus a quintet of the major
characters express their individual thoughts about this marriage: Consuelo her grief, Mancini his opportunistic triumph,
Zinida her cynical prophecy of the horns that await the Baron,
Briquet his disappointment at losing a star performer, and
Bezano his utter despair.

    Pantaloon breaks in saying that he has arranged a little
entertainment in the style of the medieval court ceremonies.
After a burlesqued overture, his play-within-a-play unfolds itself. Pantaloon takes the role of a slinking and conniving Mancini, while Tilly is an over-coy and simpering Consuelo to Polly's spiderish and lecherous Baron. The playlet farcically reveals the plots and deceptions of Mancini. When the real Baron
Regnard finally realizes through Pantaloon's play that Consuelo
is a nameless waif and that Mancini is a fake count, he lashes
out violently against Pantaloon, against Mancini and against the
whole trumpery circus--and then storms out.

    Mancini confesses his frauds, entrusts Consuelo to the
care of the circus folk, and departs. For a moment Consuelo is desolate, until she and Bezano realize that at last
they are free to seek each other. In a tango-duet they proclaim their love and hope.

    The performers jubilantly return to the ring, to give
a benefit performance for the Tango King and Queen. Zinida
and Briquet finally give full acceptance to the wisdom as well
as the clownish talents of Pantaloon, as they too go up the
ramp to the ring.

    Pantaloon, alone on the stage, sings to the poster
picturing Consuelo: she is the Queen of Beauty for whom he
is the fool, ever-loving and ever-deserving to be slapped.
Tilly and Polly come to fetch him, but he tells them that he
is leaving--there is nothing remaining for him here. He
takes off his clown costume, revealing his street clothes underneath, and quietly departs by the street door through
which he had first entered.

The Triumph of St. Joan*

One Act

SCENE 1

A parapet of the fortress. An English soldier expresses his wish that the imprisoned Joan of Arc would give in to her inquisitors and allow him to return to his love in England. Friar Julien tells him that, weary as she is, she still hopes for deliverance.

SCENE 2

A gloomy corridor. Friar Julien encounters Pierre Cauchon, who leaves him in no doubt that Joan is foredoomed. He instructs the Friar again to offer her woman's dress for her appearance before her inquisitors in token of submission to their wishes.

SCENE 3

Joan's cell. Her drunken jailor tries to seize and kiss her, and she fights him off. Only Friar Julien's timely arrival saves her. In a scene of combined tenderness and bitterness, he tries to save her soul as instructed by Cauchon. He is obviously touched by her sincerity and humility. He places the dress in her cell as he leaves for the trial chamber. In a soliloquy, she admits she is tempted to put it on. But rather than betray her guiding Voices, she resists the temptation.

SCENE 4

The great Trial Scene. Joan faces her inquisitors with dignity as they seek to entrap her. Again and again her

---

*Dello Joio, Norman, music and libretto, The Triumph of St. Joan, Reprinted from Stories of 100 Operas by Helen L. Kaufmann, copyright 1960 by Helen L. Kaufmann. Published by Grosset and Dunlap, Inc., p. 310-11.

simple honesty confounds the questioners.   Faced finally with
the threat of the stake, she shrinks from the sight of the executioner, and in a moment of weakness, recants.   But her
Voices speak to her, unheard by all save herself.   She gathers her strength, and holds out the dress to Cauchon in refusal.   As she does so, the chains fall miraculously from
her hands.   Nevertheless, she is condemned to be burned.
In a quick change of scene, she is led by the executioner to
the stake and the people surround her.   Clad in a white robe,
clutching to her breast a crucifix made of twigs, she sings
her last farewell, "O pray for me!"   A woman in the crowd
shrieks, "We are burning a saint," and the people, in a panic, run away, leaving Cauchon to see that justice is done before he, too, slowly walks off.

Six Characters in Search of an Author*

ACT I

As the cast and their director rehearse a new opera
on the bare stage of an opera house, six characters appear
suddenly--it is a family consisting of a father, mother, two
small children, a son, and a stepdaughter. It is apparent
that these people, although a family, are in deep discord.
However, they convince the rehearsing cast that they are also
a cast, but in search of an author who can finish their drama
for them. A substitution of the play in rehearsal for this
new play is proposed to the group and accepted. The family
problems are soon evident--the son despises his father, and
the other three children, it turns out, are illegitimate.

ACT II

As this new rehearsal proceeds, arguments develop
around the concept that the six characters be allowed to play
themselves. Members of the company take exception to this
and the Director points out the legal regulations covering the
performances in this opera house. However, the rehearsal
proceeds and when Madame Pace appears, all too abruptly,
the cast is amazed. The father points out the values of theatrical means and Madame Pace continues to perform much
to the amusement of the cast. Finally she leaves, insulted.
Now the stepdaughter insists that taking off her dress will be
an important aspect of her performance, but the Director for-
bids such an action in his theatre. She settles to just revealing one bare arm. As discord develops over these points of
rehearsal, the curtain is closed, much to the chagrin of the
Director. He insists that he was only speaking with the
prompter.

*Weisgall, Hugo, music; Johnston, Dennis, libretto, Six
Characters in Search of an Author (Bryn Mawr, Pa.: Merion
Music, Theo. Presser Co., 1957).

ACT III

    This disruptive rehearsal continues in the third act
with the son and mother arguing over the proper setting for
the next scene. After a chorus run-through, the argument
is finally resolved by the Director's stating that excessive
scenery is not possible. A garden scene is decided on and
as the stepdaughter sings, the scenic change is made. The
son, who has never agreed that this play should be given at
all, is appealed to to begin the scene, but in a fit of temper
slaps his mother. The cast is horrified and several leave,
threatening again a complete halt in the rehearsal. But this
is not the end of the unusual turn of events as the children
are missing. The son, rushing to the fountain, finds the
little girl drowned by the small boy who is now discovered
behind a tree. As she is carried off stage, the boy appears
with a gun and, despite the pleas of those around him, shoots
himself. There is a blackout. The cast is hysterical by
this time, and when the lights come on again the six characters are gone. Perhaps this was only something in the
Director's mind, suggest members of the chorus. Angered,
he declares an end to this rehearsal and the cast leave singing from the first piece they were originally rehearsing.

    As the Director attempts to sort out the events of the
day, the six characters suddenly appear far upstage, as in
a funeral. The Director, not seeing them, only hears the
laughter of the daughter as she runs across the stage. He
inquires as to who is there, but the puzzle remains. He
resigns himself to not finding answers and leaves. The
stage is again bare and empty and the piece is ended.

The Cradle Will Rock*

ACT I, SCENES 1 TO 6

The scene is Steeltown, USA; a night in 1931, during a union drive. The Moll is arrested by the Dick, for plying her trade. At the same time the over-zealous and clumsy Cop arrests, by mistake, the Liberty Committee, which consists of the elite of the town: Reverend Salvation, Editor Daily, Yasha (violinist), Dauber (artist), President Prexy and Professors Mamie and Trixie of College University, and Dr. Specialist. They are all hauled off to the Night Court, where the Moll makes friends with Druggist, a derelict to whom the Night Court is a second home. The Clerk reads off the names of the defendants. As they step forward, each appears in a scene showing his subservience to the Mister family, who own the town and its steel factory. The family if composed of Mr. Mister, Mrs. Mister, Junior Mister and Sister Mister. The act ends with the scene of Yasha and Dauber, rivals for the attentions of Mrs. Mister, their mutual patroness.

ACT II, SCENES 7 TO 10

Now Larry Foreman is brought into court. It was because of his speech that the Cop made the mistake of arresting the Liberty Committee; they had been listening with considerable antagonism to Larry, speaking in behalf of the union drive. More defendants come forward; each again has his scene with Mr. Mister, in flashback style. Now Mr. Mister actually appears in the Night Court, worried that the union drive seems to be succeeding. He makes a direct bid to buy off Larry Foreman, but is refused in no uncertain terms. We hear the sounds of bugles, fifes and drums; the union drive is a success.

---

*Blitzstein, Marc, libretto and music, The Cradle Will Rock (New York: Program Publishing Co., 1938), n.p.g.

The Wings of the Dove*

SCENE 1

In the ornate parlor of Mrs. Lowder in London, 1900, Mr. Croy, Kate's gambling father, enters to get needed funds from his daughter who lives with her wealthy aunt. He flouts her objections, but finally gets the money. Miles Dunster, a journalist, arrives to see Kate, but he is considered ineligible for her hand by Aunt Maude Lowder. He is invited to stay for dinner by both Kate and Aunt Maude, but he declines. Aunt Maude has made it clear to him that he is someone she would like to "count on" but he is not to entertain ideas of marriage to Kate.

SCENE 2

Several weeks later the parlor is now in readiness for a party honoring Milly Theale, a beautiful, frail American heiress touring Europe. Lord Mark, an eligible bachelor for Kate's hand, remarks on the similarity of a portrait between a Renaissance woman on an easel in the room and Milly. When she arrives, the similarity is apparent. She is asked to sing by Aunt Maude and does so, fainting at the conclusion of her recital. Miles is also present and helps her recover. They had met previously in America. Lord Mark also has been attracted to Milly and would like to marry her, but she is not interested. Kate expresses her concern for Miles' attraction to Milly, but she sees it as an advantage--a convenient third party that will be a meeting place for her and Miles.

SCENE 3

A few weeks later in the National Gallery, Milly and Susan, her travelling companion, meet Kate, and Milly proposes that they all go to Italy as her guests. Miles arrives and is included in the invitation. Milly and Susan leave and

---

*Moore, Douglas, music; Ayer, Ethan, libretto, Wings of the Dove (New York: G. Schirmer, 1961), no synopsis given.

and Kate points out to Miles the advantages of their all being together in Italy. She also points out that Miles can marry Milly and that when she dies he will be wealthy, enabling Kate and Miles to marry. Miles is shocked at this but Kate promises herself to him if he will go. He accepts her offer.

SCENE 4

Later that month at the Palazzo Leporelli in Venice, Milly and Miles are entertained by a group of players as consolation on Kate's departure back to London. The players perform a dance based upon the Janus theme of mythology-- the god with two heads. Miles leaves with a promise from Milly to visit him the next afternoon. After he is gone, Lord Mark steps out from behind a pillar and urges Milly to join him in a gondola ride. She begs to be excused, but before he leaves he tells her that Miles and Kate are lovers and the news leaves Milly stricken.

SCENE 5

Some days later in Milly's sitting-room she is ill and surrounded by flowers, Susan, and a Sister of Mercy. Milly has "turned her face to the wall" during the illness. Miles arrives and Milly and Miles exchange affectionate concern in wishing for each other's happiness. Milly feels she has come between him and Kate and asks him to send no more flowers. After she leaves he sings of their lost love.

SCENE 6

In Aunt Maud's parlor, several weeks later, Kate is reading a letter from Susan telling of Milly's death. Kate's father arrives to tell her of Miles' inheritance from Milly. Aunt Maude is also informed of this new turn of events, and then Miles enters. He tells her of his inheritance but that he won't take it and marry Kate too. She must decide if she will marry him under these conditions. She then asks if he loves her, and finally he says "no." She wilts and he leaves as she calls for her Aunt Maude. She comes in to comfort Kate by putting Milly's shawl around her, but Kate shrinks from it, and Aunt Maude assures her that "you'll be all right by tomorrow."

The Crucible*

ACT I

The curtain rises on the Reverend Samuel Parris kneeling distraught at the bed of his daughter Betty. She lies immobile and scarcely breathing, as she has lain since Parris came upon her and her cousin Abigail dancing in the woods the night before. Tituba comes to ask about Betty but is angrily sent away.

Abigail enters to say that the town is whispering of witchcraft and that Parris should go out to make denial. He bitterly turns on her to question her about the dancing and about her mysterious dismissal from the service of the Proctors. As she vehemently denies any wrongdoing, attributing her dismissal to Goodwife Proctor's arrogant desire for a slave, the Putnams enter to tell that their Ruth was stricken at the same time as Betty Parris and that they have sent to Beverly for the Reverend Hale, known for his skill in discovering witches.

While Parris, fearful of any suspicion of witchcraft in his own household, is anxiously doubting the need for Hale, Rebecca and Francis Nurse enter with Giles Corey. Rebecca is comforting, old Giles is flippant about the illness of the girls. When Putnam insists that witches are at work in Salem, Giles accuses him of using a witch scare to defraud his neighbors of their land. John Proctor's entrance only brings this quarrel to a higher peak. (Abigail, though silent in the upper room, visibly reacts with excitement to John's entrance.) Rebecca reprimands the men for this untimely

---

*Ward, Robert, music; Stambler, Bernard, libretto, The Crucible, copyright 1962 by Bernard Stambler and Robert Ward. Libretto and text for The Crucible copyright 1961 by Arthur Miller, Bernard Stambler and Robert Ward. Based upon the play The Crucible by Arthur Miller; copyright 1952, 1953 by Arthur Miller. All Rights Reserved. Highgate Press, publisher of vocal score and owner of publication and allied rights.

squabble in a house of illness, and calls them back to their
senses.   Giles departs with John.

They sing a psalm to beseech God's help.   As the
psalm proceeds, Betty begins to writhe on the bed and then
with an unearthly shriek tries to fly out of the window.   They
rush to her side.   In the midst of the commotion the Reverend Hale enters.   He calms them with his air of authority
and then methodically sets an inquiry under way.   He soon
learns that Tituba has played an important role in what has
been happening, having also been present at the dancing.
Ann Putnam asserts that Tituba knows conjuring.   Tituba is
sent for; at her entrance, Abigail, who has been under severe
inquisition by Hale, lashes out to accuse Tituba of compacting
with the Devil.   Tituba, overwhelmed by the sternness of
Hale and the malevolent intensity of Parris and the Putnams,
finally confesses that she has been visited by the Devil, but
denies that he has persuaded her into any wrcngdoing--for a
few moments she frightens Parris and the Putnams with a
heartfelt fantasy of the hellish power to bring them harm
that the Devil had offered her.

With Tituba's confession the spell over Betty is broken.
All return to the psalm in great thanksgiving, while Abby en-
vies the attention now being given to Tituba, hysterically repents her own compact with the Devil, and visibly receives
an answer to her prayer for forgiveness and for a call to
mark out others of the Devil's crew.

ACT II

John Proctor returns from a day's planting to find
Elizabeth listless and moody.   In her mind the witch trials
have become an aggravation of her domestic troubles, with
Abby at the center of both.   She insists that John expose
Abby's fraud to Judge Danforth; his reluctance to do this
convinces her that he still has a warm spot in his heart for
Abby.   John's self-defense is double: that he has no witness
to what Abby has told him, and that she will avenge herself
by revealing John's adultery with her.   And he is fed up
with Elizabeth's sitting in condemnatory judgment upon him.
She gently denies this but regrets the vanished sweetness of
their love.   Abby, she says, will not confess the lechery
lest she damn herself.   And what of those who suffer in jail
because of John's silence?   No, John _must_ tear the last
feeling for Abby out of his heart, or she will never give up
hope of some day having him for her own.

Mary Warren enters furtively from her day at court as one of Abby's crew of witchfinders. She tells, breaking into tears, that the number of those arrested has tripled-- and that Goody Osburn has been condemned to hang! She is truly troubled by this, and by her own part in it, but demonstrates how the mob excitement of the courtroom procedure turns her into an hysterical accuser even against her will. When John threatens to whip her if she ever returns to that court she blurts out that Goody Proctor herself has been mentioned in court and that only Mary's defense of her prevented an outright accusation.

Elizabeth is sure that Abby is behind this and is once more pleading with John to go to the court when Reverend Hale and John Cheever enter with a warrant for her arrest: that very evening Abby has charged Elizabeth with employing a witch's poppet to kill her. John makes Mary acknowledge it is her poppet, but Hale, although deeply troubled by these new directions of the witch hunts, feels that he must arrest Elizabeth for examination.

John is about to burst out wildly to prevent their taking Elizabeth away, but instead turns with intense but controlled passion upon Mary: she will tell her story in court even though it may provoke a charge of adultery from Abby and ruin both Abby and John completely--anything rather than that Elizabeth should be in danger for his sake.

ACT III, SCENE 1

Abby, with a mixture of scheming but passionate love for John and a mystical belief in her mission, tries to persuade John to abandon Elizabeth and to join her in the holy work of cleansing the puritanically corrupt town. He will not listen to this, but instead pleads that she free the town from the curse of her foolish wickedness, and then threatens to expose her fraud. She defies him: now any dire fate that descends on Elizabeth will be of his doing.

SCENE 2

Judge Danforth's invocation in court reveals the strength and fervor of his conviction that God's will is working through him to cleanse the land of a plague of witches.

As court opens, Giles Corey accuses Thomas Putnam, in his greed for his neighbor's land, of having bragged of

his role in the charges of witchcraft. Judge Danforth sends
Corey to jail and torture for refusing to name his witnesses
for this accusation. There is a great hubbub as Giles leaps
at Putnam as the man responsible for the arrest of his wife
and himself, and of Rebecca Nurse as well.

John Proctor presents Mary Warren's deposition that
the entire crying-out against witches started only as an exciting game for the girls--and is a complete pretense and
fraud. But Abby, he says, has continued the game in an effort to dispose of Elizabeth. Her encouragement to this
arose from the adultery that took place between Abby and
himself, which he is now confessing. When Elizabeth ordi-
narily incapable of a lie, is brought in and fails to confirm
John's confession; Abigail counterattacks, charging that Mary
herself has turned witch. Mary, helpless and then hysterical,
turns on John Proctor--accusing him of being the Devil's man
who has forced her into trying to confuse and overthrow the
court. All but the Reverend Hale close in on John Proctor
with sadistic vindictiveness.

ACT IV

Tituba and Sarah Good, crazed by the rigors of imprisonment, sing of the Devil and his broken promises to
them. Abby comes into the prison courtyard; she has bribed
the jailer to permit Proctor to escape. John, although broken by the months of prison and torture, scornfully rejects
the freedom and love she offers him. Abby runs off weeping.

Hale, and then Parris, try to persuade Judge Danforth
to postpone the executions of Proctor and Rebecca Nurse
scheduled for that morning: Salem may break into open re-
bellion at the execution of such respected citizens. Danforth
indignantly refuses, but agrees to ask Elizabeth to persuade
her husband to confess.

John is brought in and left alone with Elizabeth. She
tells him that Giles Corey has died, pressed to death rather
than say aye or nay to the charge of witchcraft, but that
many have confessed in order to save their lives. John reluctantly brings out his own wish to confess--if it will not
make her think ill of him for lying. Passionately she answers that it was her lie that doomed him--and that she
wants him alive. Exultant, he shouts that he will confess
to the charge of witchcraft.

Danforth, Hale, and Parris rejoice--for their various reasons--over John's confession, and Parris tries to persuade Rebecca, who has been brought in on the way to the gallows, also to confess. She refuses to damn herself with the lie. John is asked to sign his confession, that it may be exhibited before the town. But this is too much: he has deeply shamed himself by confessing, but he will not set his hand to the destruction of his own name--and the eternal shame of his sons. He tears up the document. In fury Danforth orders John and Rebecca to be led out to execution. Hale pleads with Elizabeth that she change John's decision while there is yet time. She refuses; "He has found his name and his goodness now--God forbid I take it from him."

The Golem*

ACT I, SCENE 1

Prague, in the year 1580. The Maharal, Rabbi Levi
Bar Bezallel, through mystical formulas deciphered in the
Caballah, derives the Pre-eminent Name of God, the SHEM
HAMMA FORASCH, said to be the secret of all Creation.
Believing himself counselled by Heaven to save his persecuted
people, he moulds from the clay of the riverbank, the figure
of a man. He will employ the Holy SHEM to create a being
with the superhuman strength to overcome their enemies.

In a vision, the Spirit of the Golem warns the Maharal
against creating an instrument of force. Determination over-
comes the Maharal's doubts. In a spiritual rite, aided by
his disciples, Yacov and Isaac, he injects the SHEM into the
skull of the clay figure, endowing his Golem with life.

SCENE 2

The Maharal brings the giant, cretin-like Golem into
his home, names him Yossef, and gives him his first lessons in human behavior. The Rabbi's wife views the Golem
with fear, but his granddaughter, Deborah, feels a compassion for the ungainly stranger. He is accepted in their midst
as a servant, a wood-chopper and water carrier. As the
Golem sleeps, the Maharal muses on how little he resembles
the Messenger of his dreams.

SCENE 3

Outside the Maharal's house, Yacov reads from the
BOOK OF PSALMS. Deborah, his betrothed, relates a
dream in which the Prophet, Elijah, appeared to her. Yacov
interprets this as a good omen, but Deborah feels a forboding
in her dream.

---

*Ellstein, Abraham, music; Ellstein, Abraham and Regan,
Sylvia, libretto, The Golem (New York: Program Publishing Company, 1962).

In deep distress, the old Rabbi Bashevi and several pious citizens inform the Maharal that their enemy, the fanatic monk, Tadeus, is preparing a new ritual murder accusation against them. Tanchum, the Ghetto mad-man, adds to their fears as he describes the death of his son in an earlier pre-Passover terror. Bashevi begs the Maharal to proclaim a period of fasting and prayer to help them. The Maharal taxes them with their dependence on prayer. In extremity they must use stronger means to defend themselves. As the Golem appears, axe over shoulder, on his way to chop wood, the Maharal knows the means he will use to save his afflicted people.

ACT II

The Fifth Tower, a desolate ruined castle, inhabited by the Jewish Beggars of the city. The Beggars huddle against the fierce cold, and plead to the God of Abraham, Isaac and Jacob to help them in their wretchedness. Tadeus appears with his Guards, a pair of soldiers-of-fortune who assist him in his iniquitous work. Unseen by the Beggars, he derides their disabilities and affirms his intention to destroy them.

The Maharal finds the Beggars chasing and mocking the Golem. Admonishingly, he sends them to the Ghetto to warn the people of their impending danger. Told to find safer shelter in the caves under the Synagogue, the Beggars leave the Fifth Tower.

Once again, the Maharal is assailed by doubt. In a vision, Elijah appears and offers to usher in the Messiah to help them. The Maharal renounces the age-old pious dream of the Messiah's promise to raise the dead. He will rely on his man of clay to watch over the living.

Deborah enters, seeking her grandfather. Out of compassion for the friendless Golem, she invites him to her impending wedding. As she describes its joys, the dancing, the wine, the Golem, overcome by her warmth and beauty, embraces her. Her cries attract the Maharal and his disciples. Yacov fiercely demands the Golem be driven out.

Alone with the Golem, the Maharal reveals to him the meaning of his existence, his wondrous powers. In a hypnotic trance, the Golem traces Tadeus and his false evidence, two sacks, holding the remains of a murdered Christian child

230   American Opera Librettos

and a flask of blood. Commanded to apprehend the enemy
and bring him the sacks, the Golem magically disappears to
carry out his mission. Exalted by the miracle, the Maharal
gives thanks to the Almighty One.

ACT III, SCENE 1

The underground caves beneath the Synagogue. Tadeus
and his cohorts emerge from a secret hidden tunnel, to plant
their false evidence. The Golem appears. Radiating with
the light of his new-found powers, he attacks the terrified
men. Routing them out, they leave behind the two sacks.
The Golem enjoys a moment of victory, but suddenly, as if
drained, the power goes out of him, and he is once again the
cretin-like Golem, afraid of his own shadow. Seeking a clue
to where he is and why, he opens the small sack, draws out
the flask of blood. Lighting up with recognition, he recalls
Deborah's description of a wedding. Certain the flask contains the wine she described, he puts it to his lips.

SCENE 2

Some time later, the Shames leads the Beggars down
into the caves. They find the Golem asleep, the empty flask
by his side, and mistakenly believe he is in a drunken stupor
from wine. The Golem wakes. He has tasted blood, and is
no longer the Maharal's docile servant. A wild power rages
in him. Enflamed beyond control, he strangles Tanchum before the horrified Beggars. In the ensuing commotion, he
disappears.

Confronted by the murder committed by his Golem,
the Maharal, in his growing madness, attempts to justify the
foul deed, revealing the Golem to be their savior. As the
old Bashevi and the Beggars go up into the Synagogue recit-
ing the prayer for the dead, Yacov confides to Isaac his
fears for the Maharal's sanity.

Alone with Tanchum's body, the Maharal once again
voices his inner doubts. In a vision of his now disordered
mind, the dead Tanchum suddenly comes to life. Thrice he
blows his rams-horn, signifying the coming of the Messiah.
Affirming he gave life to a stone, why not to Tanchum, the
Maharal is surrounded by many DEAD who arise to proclaim
him their Redeemer. In an apotheosis of his Messianic madness, the DEAD carry him off in a triumphal procession.

As the last wraithelike figure disappears, the Maharal is seen standing over Tanchum's body, lost in his dream.

ACT IV

The following day, just before the Sabbath. In the attic of the Synagogue, the Maharal searches in his books of mysticism for a means to bring the Golem once more under his control. The Rabbi's wife enters to tax him with the grim details of the destruction wrought by the Golem. In despair, she learns the extent of her husband's retreat from reality and reason.

A distressed Deborah recounts a dream in which she was a horrified witness to the Maharal's destruction. As she pleads with him to find a warning in her dream, frightened cries are heard from below. The berserk Golem has invaded the Synagogue and shattered the Eternal Light. Giving the Maharal the empty flash, the Shames attributes the Golem's destructive behavior to drunkenness. With sinking heart, the Maharal knows the flask contained not wine, but blood.

The frenzied Golem enters to attack the Maharal. In the anteroom, Deborah is a silent, terrified witness, as the two stalk each other, the Golem alternately threatening and pleading to be freed of the power that rages in him. Determined to hold the Golem under his command, the Maharal resorts to the supernatural, encircling him in an invisible wall of Holy Fire. Deborah runs in, beseeching her grandfather to release the Golem and sever the dreadful ties that bind them one to the other. As she attempts to free the Golem from his entrapment, he drags her into the circle. Suffused with the light of his destructive power, he strangles her.

In an agony of guilt, the brokenhearted Maharal cries out his repentance. This is his punishment for daring to equate himself with God and create a living being. Calling the Maharal to Sabbath Service, Yacov, Isaac and the Shames find Deborah dead. Devastated, Yacov carries Deborah off, as the now docile and bewildered Golem piteously asks where she has gone.

Restored to reason by the tragedy, the Maharal prepares the Golem for his final mission. Obediently, the Golem stretches out. With a gesture of finality, the Maharal

removes the SHEM from the Golem's skull.   Once again he
is clay.

From the Synagogue below, the voices of the congregation chant the opening prayer of welcome to the Sabbath.
The Maharal gently covers the clay figure with a prayer
shawl.   Filled with sadness, he starts off in the direction
of the voices, as the curtain falls.

Porgy and Bess*

ACT I

   A square in Catfish Row. The Negro workers whose
homes are in crowded Catfish Row sit or saunter outside
their houses. It is a hot summer night, and Clara sings
her baby to sleep with a lullaby, "Summertime." Her husband, Jake, meditates in song that "A woman is a sometime
thing." Somebody starts a crap game, and everyone gathers
round to watch. Porgy comes in, erect in a little cart
drawn by a goat. It is his only means of locomotion. He
too watches the game. But when the local bully, Crown,
enters the betting, the players start to squabble. Crown
gets ugly-tempered and there is a fight. Crown knifes and
kills Robbins and runs away, fearing the law. His girl,
Bess, is left alone. Sporting Life invites her to go with
him to New York, and offers her dope as an inducement.
But Porgy, who has secretly loved Bess, prevails upon her
to refuse the "happy-dust." As the women of Catfish Row
virtuously slam their doors in her face, she thankfully goes
into Porgy's house with him.

   In a room in the Robbins house, Serena mourns her
husband. The neighbors gather to sing over Robbins' body,
and to raise money for his funeral. "My Man's Gone Now,"
Serena keens, and the neighbors join her in deeply moving
spirituals, led for the most part by Porgy, who comes in
with Bess to give his share. A sinister note is struck when
two white detectives enter. They arrest the innocent honey
man, Peter, as a hostage, and roughly tell Serena that, for
sanitary reasons, Robbins' body must be underground within
twenty-four hours. This leads to a fresh outpouring of
prayer, which is partly answered when the undertaker agrees
to provide the funeral at once and accept his payment later.
Bess sings "Oh, the train is at the station," and all join in

---

*Gershwin, George, music; Heyward, DuBose and Gershwin,
Ira, libretto, Porgy and Bess, Reprinted from Stories of 100
Operas by Helen L. Kaufman, copyright 1960 by Helen L.
Kaufmann. Published by Grosset and Dunlap, Inc., p. 236-39.

as the curtain falls.

ACT II

    The square in Catfish Row, a month later. Jake and other fishermen prepare to go to sea, singing lustily, "It takes a long pull to get there." Porgy and Bess are as happy as the day is long. Porgy sings, "Oh, I got plenty o' nuttin', And nuttin's plenty fo' me" in a full-throated outpouring of happiness. He tells Bess that he has bought her a divorce from Crown, to whom she was not married in the first place. He chases off Sporting Life, who again tries to take Bess away. And then he and Bess sing a tender duet, "Bess, you is my woman now."

    The scene changes to the wooded island of Kittiwah, where a picnic is being held. Everyone but Porgy is there. Porgy has urged Bess to go and have a good time, though she offered to stay home with him. Sporting Life turns up again, and sings the enticing "It ain't necessarily so." Bess resists him, but when Crown comes from the thicket where he has been hiding, passionately embraces her and claims her for his own, she weakens. As the scene ends, she falls unconscious. He goes back into hiding, crying that he will come for her when he can.

    Back in Catfish Row, a week later, Bess still lies unconscious and near death, in Porgy's room. Porgy prays over her, joined by Serena and other neighbors, and as if by a miracle, she comes to. Porgy knows all, and forgives all, and when she confesses that she has promised to go with Crown when he comes for her, though she would rather stay with Porgy, Porgy promises to protect her against Crown and against herself. "I loves you, Porgy," she sings.

    The scene again changes to Serena's room. A terrible storm is raging, and the neighbors pray for God's protection. Can this be the Day of Judgment, they moan in terror. At this juncture, Crown threateningly enters, calling loudly for Bess, and sneering at their fright. He strikes Porgy when the cripple protects Bess. Clara cries from the window that she sees an overturned fishing boat. It must be her husband's, she feels. Crown alone goes with her to the rescue as the others are afraid.

ACT III

The same square in Catfish Row. It is quiet after
the storm, but Crown, Clara and Jake have not been heard
from; the women mourn them for dead. Sporting Life suggests that Crown may still be alive, as from Porgy's house
Bess's voice is heard singing "Summertime" to Clara's baby.
When the square is deserted, Crown appears, exhausted, and
crawls on all fours toward Porgy's door. As he passes under the window, Porgy quietly reaches out, closes two powerful hands around Crown's throat, and chokes him noiselessly
to death. There are no witnesses. When a detective enters
and asks someone to identify the body, Porgy goes with him.
Sporting Life, the tempter, again assails Bess with "happy
dust." Both her men are gone, he tells her. She may as
well go with him to New York. "There's a boat dat's leavin'
soon for New York," he sings, and poor Bess, a weak sister
despite her strong resolutions, agrees to go with him. When
Porgy returns, a week later, he finds his house empty. The
neighbors tell him that Bess has gone to New York with
Sporting Life. Porgy has no idea how far away New York is,
but bravely he sets out in his goat-drawn cart to find her,
wherever she is. "Oh Lawd, I'm on my way!" he sings as
the neighbors gather to wish him luck.

The Passion of Jonathan Wade*

SCENE ONE

At rise, a group of people are waiting for the return
of Confederate soldiers who are coming from the North with
the Union occupation forces. As they wait, they sing of the
war's devastation and their despair. The Confederate soldiers appear and are reunited with their families. They are
followed by the Union troops headed by Colonel Jonathan Wade.
Judge Gibben Townsend introduces himself and greets Jonathan. He introduces Wade to his daughter, Celia, who coldly
refuses to acknowledge the introduction. Townsend and his
daughter exit as Jonathan and his aide, Patrick, exit into
their hastily constructed headquarters.

EPISODE

A quartet of Negro boys sing and dance of their new-
found freedom. In somber counterpoint to their jubilation is
a maimed Confederate soldier who has returned to his deso-
lated home.

SCENE TWO

Jonathan is a guest of the Townsends. Townsend
proudly and nostalgically describes his home to Jonathan as
it existed before Sherman's pillage of the city. He is called
out of the room by Nicey, the Townsends' colored maid and
companion, and Jonathan is left with the silent, still-veiled,
Celia. He provokes her into conversation and she denounces
him bitterly, prompting him to angrily describe to her his
experiences with war and his passionate hatred of it. Celia
is stirred and chastened by his fervor and they each in turn
apologize for their outbursts. With an atmosphere of cordi-
ality established between them, Jonathan leaves and Celia
sings wonderingly at first and later exultantly of the stranger

---

*Floyd, Carlisle, music and libretto, The Passion of Jona-
than Wade (unpublished from files of New York City Opera by
permission of New York City Opera), no synopsis given.

who has come into her life.

EPISODE

As J. Tertius Riddle, a pardon-broker, is flamboyant-
ly describing the merits of obtaining a pardon from the President, he is interrupted by Lucas Wardlaw and his cronies
who taunt him in his attempts to sell pardons. Riddle, un-
daunted, approaches Townsend and is sternly rebuked for his
greed.

SCENE THREE

A party is in progress in the Townsend drawing room
where Lucas enters and cynically questions Jonathan on the
Negro's right to vote. After Townsend compliments Jonathan
and his men to the party guests, Nicey announces the arrival
of Ely Pratt and his wife, Amy. They enter and Ely confi-
dently tells Townsend of his function as head of the Freed-
men's Bureau in Columbia. Ely, to illustrate his point of
assisting Negroes to obtain an education, asks Nicey if she
wouldn't like to avail herself of their services. Nicey good-
naturedly rebuffs him and the party guests applaud her. Ely,
stung by their reaction, turns on them furiously, saying that
they, the Southerners, will be taught the War's lessons by
the North. The party guests, enraged by the overbearing
Ely, shout their defiance at him as the curtain falls.

ACT TWO, SCENE ONE

Jonathan is administering the oath, reinstating them
as citizens, to a group of tenant farmers as the curtain
rises. As he finishes, Lucas, who has watched the proceedings, scorns the taking of the oath and, to taunt Jonathan,
complains to him of having no Negro servants and of being
unable to keep Negro laborers on his farm. Jonathan, exasperated and angered by Lucas, threatens him and Lucas
exits. Patrick enters with an order from Washington. As
Jonathan reads the order with evident consternation, Ely enters and Jonathan tells him that he has been commanded to
remove Townsend as District Judge. He pleads with Ely to
intercede on Townsend's behalf but Ely refuses, saying that
he approved the order. Ely then exhorts Jonathan to forget
his allegiance to Lincoln and to join the Radical Party in
their efforts to raise the status of the Negro and thereby
hold political power for a hundred years. Jonathan rejects
his urging, refusing to condone the methods and aims of the

party and Ely obliquely threatens Jonathan with the loss of
his command.   As he exits, Jonathan sends a message, appealing the order.   Celia appears and announces that she has
come to take the oath even though it means risking the dis-
approval of her family and her friends.   She declares her
belief in Jonathan and, moved, he tells her he loves her.
As they are embracing, Lucas reappears and when he teases
Jonathan about his feeling for Celia, Jonathan, exasperated
beyond endurance, knocks him down.   Lucas, surly and
vengeful, threatens Jonathan by asking him if he knows of
the Ku Klux Klan as the scrim is lowered.

EPISODE

        A Union Leaguer is proclaiming to a group of colored
people that plantations will be divided and that they each will
be given forty acres and a mule.   J. Tertius Riddle reappears, this time selling bogus certificates to credulous Negroes.

SCENE TWO

        Riddle is arrested and sentenced by Jonathan to a
prison term.   Still protesting his innocence, he is carried
out as Patrick enters with the response to Jonathan's appeal.
Jonathan, disconsolate, tells his aide that he has been denied
and asks Patrick to bring Townsend to his office.   When he
is alone Jonathan sings of the conflict between his conscience
and his duty as an officer, pleading with his conscience to
sleep until he has completed what duty demands of him.
Townsend enters with Celia and Jonathan reluctantly tells him
of the order and of his efforts to have it countermanded.
Townsend retains his poise until Jonathan tells him that he
will be replaced by a Negro judge.   Townsend, his pride bitterly attacked, lashes out and, when Jonathan refuses to agree
with him that his honor has been impugned, Townsend turns
on Jonathan, accusing him of betrayal and saying that he is
never to see Celia again.   Jonathan asks Celia to marry him
and she pleads with her father not to make her choose between him and Jonathan.   He is implacable and Celia remains
with Jonathan as Townsend disowns her and exits.   When he
has gone Jonathan calls in Nicey, and Patrick appears with
the rector, who marries Jonathan and Celia in Jonathan's office.   When the couple are alone once more they listen to
Nicey and her friends who are huddled outside singing to
them.   Suddenly intruding into the song are the distant sounds
of the Ku Klux Klan.   The Negroes grow silent as the Ku

Klux Klan approaches and then they scream and run as the
Klan rushes on stage. Jonathan, alarmed, calls Patrick to
pursue the Klansmen and then he returns to comfort Celia,
pleading with her to forget the outside world and to belong
only to him. Urgently they profess their love for each other
as the curtain falls.

ACT THREE, SCENE ONE

The action begins some four years later. Celia is
rocking her child as Jonathan enters, followed by Amy and
Ely, who is arguing with Jonathan over the political motives
of the Union League. Ely warns Jonathan that his lack of
cooperation with the reigning political party may cost him
his job and then maliciously suggests that his lack of cooperation may be due to his Southern wife. Celia, angry and
hurt, sardonically tells Pratt of her ostracism in the city
during the four years and, bursting into tears, demands that
he leave them alone. She exits, followed by Jonathan, and
Ely, frustrated in his efforts to sway Jonathan, tells his wife
that he must be replaced and that he, Ely, must devise a
scheme to force him out of the Army. He seizes on the
idea of confiscation of Townsend's household goods to satisfy
a tax assessment as a means of coercing Jonathan into in-
subordination and calls Patrick in to help him in carrying out
his plans. Patrick, loyal to Jonathan, at first refuses, but
weakens when Ely threatens him by questioning his loyalty.
Ely instructs Patrick to watch for the order commanding
Jonathan to take possession of Townsend's property, and to
report all he sees and hears of Jonathan's reactions and subsequent behavior to him.

EPISODE

Two carpetbaggers approach a group of colored sen-
ators, questioning them as to whether or not bills which they
have bribed them to pass have been passed. A distinguished
colored man rebukes them and, when asked by a carpetbagger
to identify himself, he reveals himself to be Judge James
Bell, the man who has replaced Townsend.

SCENE TWO

Jonathan says goodbye to Bell who is resigning his
appointment as judge in protest over the corruption in the
state capital. Patrick brings in Ely's order which has been
sent from Washington and exits suspiciously, having seen

Jonathan's anger at reading it. Jonathan calls Celia in and
tells her that he refuses to execute the order and therefore
must decide what he has long postponed deciding: whether
or not he can continue to live with himself if he remains in
the Army. There is a long, agonized vigil in which Jonathan
struggles with his conscience, at the end of which he desperately announces his decision to desert. Celia attempts to
console him and he tells her plans for escape as the scrim
is lowered.

EPISODE

    Townsend is addressing a group of people at the un-
veiling of a Confederate monument. In his speech he reveals
the fact that the order to confiscate his household goods has
been carried out and swears vengeance against the tyrants
from the North. Celia, in the group, listens, alarmed, realizing that somebody else has known of the order and has
executed it.

SCENE THREE

    Jonathan, sensing a trap after hearing Celia's news,
sends Nicey for their driver so that they may leave immediately. As they are packing, Patrick appears with three
Klansmen who were discovered lighting a cross on Jonathan's
lawn. The Klansmen are ordered to unmask and Lucas is
revealed under the last hood. He laughs at Jonathan's astonishment and warns him that his men are coming to rescue
him and that their orders are to kill Jonathan on sight. Jonathan commands the Klansmen to be locked up and as they
exit, Nicey reappears with the driver. As the driver takes
their baggage, Nicey, the child and Celia follow him to the
carriage while Jonathan changes his clothes. In the distance
once again is heard the sound of the Ku Klux Klan. Jonathan
reappears on stage and as he hurries out to the carriage he
is shot and staggers back into the room. Celia rushes in,
followed by Patrick, Nicey, and the child. Immediately the
room fills with Union soldiers led in by Ely, and Ku Klux
Klansmen captured by the soldiers. Jonathan dies in Celia's
arms and the Klansmen and soldiers immediately begin to
accuse each other of his murder. At the peak of their argument, Celia screams that they are all murderers and commands them to leave. When they have gone, she says goodnight to her child and, left alone with the body of Jonathan,
she mourns the fact that there was no other time in which
they might have lived their lives as the CURTAIN FALLS.

Gentlemen, Be Seated! *

Gentlemen, Be Seated! is a history of the Civil War
in the form of a minstrel show.   We have tried throughout
the work to be as factual as possible.   For those of our audience who are not Civil War buffs we would like to offer these
few explanatory notes.

Picnic At Manasses: A series of gay luncheons did take
place on the Bull Run Battlefield given by Washington's social
set, who thought the war was going to be a one-battle affair.

The Ballad of Belle Boyd: Miss Boyd, after the War,
went on a theatrical tour of the United States recounting her
exploits for an enrapt audience.   This is an attempt to re-
create the kind of act she might have presented, basing it,
factually, upon incidents in her career.

Mr. Brady Takes A Photograph: This is the one piece
of fiction in Gentlemen, Be Seated! It is our own explanation of
a peculiar gap in the otherwise remarkably complete photograph-
ic documentation of the war by Mr. Brady and his assistant.

Atlanta To The Sea: The incident that forms the basis
of this number caused a wave of protest in the North when
news of it arrived shortly after Sherman and his Army entered Savannah.   Secretary of War Stanton went down to Geor-
gia along with a Commission of Inquiry to investigate the
facts.   In the end, they verified the happening but exonerated
Sherman's troops of malicious intent.

The Dialogues: All the jokes used in the dialogues
were culled from joke books printed during the Civil War.
We wish to thank the New York Public Library and the Library of Congress for generously allowing us access to their
collections.   Although you have been hearing these jokes for
the last hundred years, we hope you will not look upon them
as hoary chestnuts but as venerable jests.

---

*Moross, Jerome, music; Eager, Edward and Moross,
Jerome, libretto, Gentlemen, Be Seated! (From Playbill,
by permission of New York City Opera), p. 24.

Natalia Petrovna*

ACT I, SCENE 1

At the Islaev Estate in Central Russia, midsummer,
1850, various members of the Islaev family are whiling away
their time in the porch and garden. Natalia, a countess and
wife of the owner, is dreaming on the chaise; Rakitin, an
author in love with Natalia, stares at a book; and Anna, the
mother of Islaev, and a Doctor play cards. They discuss
their boredom and the Doctor approaches Natalia on the possibility of her niece, Vera, marrying a neighbor-landowner,
Bolisov. Natalia believes this to be a poor match as Bolisov
is old and boorish. Belaev, Vera, and Kolia enter playing
a game. Belaev is Kolia's new tutor whom Natalia is only
just meeting, and they talk. Natalia shows an interest in
him and the jealousy between Vera and Natalia over Belaev
is hinted at.

SCENE 2

The next day the Doctor, finding Lisavetta, Anna's
companion, coaxing Kolia to practice, asks her to meet him
alone. Bolisov appears and the Doctor reminds him of the
terms of payment due him if he lands Vera as a wife for
him. Vera enters with Belaev and they are finishing a kite
for Kolia. Vera tells Belaev about their winters on the estate, and their affectionate relationship grows. Natalia and
Rakitin enter and she is fighting with Rakitin and wishes to
see Belaev. She expresses her discontent and Rakitin and
she exchange sharp words. After this Vera approaches and
Natalia and Vera discuss Vera's growing womanhood. Of
course, Natalia is put off when Vera speaks of Belaev tender-
ly, and wonders at her own passions being truly awakened
for the first time.

---

*Hoiby, Lee, music; Ball, William, libretto, Natalia Petrovna
(New York: Boosey and Hawkes, 1965), no synopsis given.

ACT II

A few moments later Natalia is seated alone and the
sound of music and clapping is heard off-stage. Rakitin enters and discusses with her the new turn of events. He proposes to send the tutor away but Natalia is troubled by that.
Her husband, Arkady, and Anna, his mother, enter to discover Natalia and Rakitin embracing. Anna is disgusted but
Arkady tries to be understanding. Belaev enters and Rakitin
brooches the subject alone with him concerning his attention
to Natalia, suggesting that he is the one making the over-
tures. They exit to discuss this as the Doctor and Lisavetta
enter and engage in banter about their ages and their attrac-
tions for each other. Rakitin and Belaev enter as they exit
and Belaev has made his decision to leave. Rakitin exits and
Vera enters. Belaev tells her of his decision and at the end
of the scene, Vera realizes that Natalia wants him for herself. Natalia has overheard and Vera confronts her with
these facts and finally declares herself independent of Natalia
forever. After she leaves Natalia suggests that Belaev go,
but he stays to embrace her. When they see Rakitin they
separate and Rakitin seizes her wildly and kisses her brutal-
ly. Kolia enters after his mother has sunk to a chair and
puts a party mask on her and leads her off with a lamp in
her hand.

ACT II, SCENE 2

Late the next morning Anna and Arkady enter and
Anna urges him to confront Rakitin concerning Natalia. When
Rakitin enters Arkady is divided, and does not scold Rakitin.
When Rakitin tells him he is leaving, Arkady is sad and
urges him to stay. Belaev also enters and announces his
leaving. Vera watches Belaev start to go, and he gives her
the rose from his lapel that Natalia gave him. Arkady enters to tell that the dam on the estate is finished and the
Doctor reports seeing the tutor walking down the road. Vera
gives the answer "yes" to Bolisov's proposal and the principles in an ensemble sing of their preoccupations and discon-
tents. Afterwards Rakitin leaves and Anna, Arkady and Natalia are left on stage, much as at the beginning of the play--
sitting and playing cards.

<u>The Saint of Bleecker Street</u>*

ACT I

A poor living room in a flat in Bleecker Street. The
neighbors are gathered, praying, outside the door of the room
where Annina lies in a trance. They believe that by touching
them she can cure them of their illnesses. Two women fall
to quarreling, and the ensemble is growing noisy when Don
Marco, the parish priest, comes from Annina's room. He
says that her miraculous vision has begun, and that she will
be brought into the living room. No one, he warns, is to
touch the stigmata which may be expected to appear on her
hands. Deathly pale, Annina is carried in and placed in an
armchair. Barely conscious, she re-lives the Crucifixion in
a powerful aria, "Oh sweet Jesus, spare me this agony."
At the end, exhausted, she unclenches her fists, revealing
the bleeding stigmata. The neighbors, disregarding Don Marco's warning, struggle to be the first to touch the stigmata
and be cured.

In the midst of the confusion, the door is flung open
and Annina's brother Michele makes an angry entrance. He
orders the neighbors out. He savagely tells Don Marco that
it is a doctor, not a priest, that Annina needs. They argue,
but in the end, the priest departs and Michele slams the door
behind him.

The scene changes to an empty lot between two tene-
ments. Several months have passed. The neighbors are preparing for a parade in honor of the Festival of St. Gennaro.
Assunta sings an Italian lullaby, "Canta Ninna, Canta Nanna,"
to her baby. As she sits on her doorstep, the neighbors gossip. For the festival, Carmela and Annina dress little Con-
cettina as an angel. When they ask Annina if she is appearing in the parade, she realizes that her brother will not al-

---

*Menotti, Gian-Carlo, music and libretto, <u>The Saint of</u>
<u>Bleecker Street</u>. Reprinted from <u>Stories of 100 Operas</u> by
Helen L. Kaufmann, copyright 1960 by Helen L. Kaufmann.
Published by Grosset and Dunlap, Inc., p. 270-74.

low it.   When they have gone, she and Carmela have a touching scene, in which Carmela blushingly admits that she has
promised to marry Salvatore in the spring.   She will not become a nun with Annina, as they had planned.   Annina sweetly congratulates her, and asks her to promise to come to the
ceremony when she herself enters the nunnery.

        Assunta joins them.   Maria Corona rushes in, saying
that the Sons of Gennaro have vowed to take Annina to the
procession by force if Michele tries to stop them.   Michele
comes in at this point, and brother and sister sing a dramatic
duet, "Oh, dear Michele." He argues with her about her
supposed visions, her sainthood and her belief that the church
is her vocation.   But he cannot shake her faith.   They cling
to each other lovingly all the same.   The procession starts,
singing "Veglia su di noi" ("Watch over us").   A band of
young Sons of Gennaro appear, demanding their "little saint."
While four of them overpower Michele and chain him by the
wrists to a fence, the others carry off Annina on their shoulders to join the procession.   The street grows dark.   The
music dies away.   Desideria the siren comes from her house.
She compassionately releases Michele, takes him in her arms,
and presses her lips to his in a sultry kiss as the curtain
falls.

ACT II

        An Italian restaurant in a basement on Bleecker
Street.   The wedding of Carmela and Salvatore is in full
swing.   The guests improvise toasts, "There never was such
a pair." Annina instructs the groom to be kind to his pretty
bride, and all go in to the banquet room for the wedding
feast.   Only the bartender remains behind.   Desideria enters
sullenly.   She insists that he call Michele.   When Michele
comes, she works herself into a towering rage because she
has not been invited to the wedding, and demands that Michele
take her into the banquet room with him.   He refuses.   She
goes on to complain of his devotion to Annina, always Annina,
which comes between them, and in the end, with a shrug of
despair, he leads her to the entrance of the banquet room.
The priest Don Marco blocks their way, and Michele is about
to come to blows with him when the guests come pouring out.
Michele turns on them.   "I know that you all hate me," he
begins, and in a magnificent aria, he tries to explain himself as an Italian who wishes to be a true American yet re-
tain the best of his Italian heritage.   This breaks up the
party.   Everyone goes home except Michele, Annina and

Desideria. Again Desideria taunts Michele, and this time
she accuses him of being in love with his sister. This is
too much. He shouts at her to be quiet. "You love her!
You love her!" she retorts. He snatches a knife from the
bar and plunges it into her. She falls to the floor, dying.
Annina takes Desideria's head to her bosom, and prays with
her. Michele runs into the street to escape the police.
Desideria dies in Annina's arms weakly repeating Annina's
prayer. A policeman enters as the curtain falls.

ACT III, SCENE 1

A subway station. The priest brings Michele to meet
Annina at Maria Corona's newsstand, warning him that Annina
is very ill. Annina tells Michele that her dearest wish is to
become a nun before she dies. Michele again loses his temper, and churlishly refuses his permission, though she says
she believes that her prayers will save him. He curses her
but she defies him. "This is good-bye!" she cries. He
dashes away, and she falls senseless to the ground.

SCENE 2

A few months later, Annina sits in the armchair in
her apartment, deathly weak. Carmela, Assunta, and others
kneel in prayer. Angelic voices have assured Annina that
today she will become a nun, but the message from Don
Marco's superior giving permission has not been received.
Agitatedly, she worries because she has no white dress and
veil for the ceremony and Carmela, weeping, promises to
lend her her wedding outfit. The message finally arrives.
In a transport of joy, Annina asks to be left alone to pray,
and sings her final aria, imploring Death to delay long enough
for her to take the veil. She walks weakly from the room
with Carmela. The priest, in an aside, tells those nearest
the door to watch out for Michele, who has been seen in the
neighborhood. He is to be kept out if he tries to enter. The
ceremony then is solemnly conducted. Annina, all in white,
totters weakly in. She prostrates herself on the floor, her
arms in the form of a cross, as the priest intones the words.
When he proclaims, to triumphant music, that she is now
Sister Angela and that Annina is dead to the world, a nun
covers her with a black veil. At this moment, Michele
breaks in and implores Annina for the last time to listen to
him. She kneels, silent and unresponsive. He watches,
frustrated, as she weakly staggers toward the priest to receive the ring of Christ. All kneel. The ceremony con-

cludes. At the end, she falls lifeless to the floor, and Don
Marco presses on her finger the ring which signifies that she
is the bride of the Church. Michele's heartbroken sobs sound
over a triumphant chorale as the curtain falls.

Lizzie Borden*

ACT I, SCENE 1

In the Andrew Borden home in Fall River, Mass., in
the 1880's, Lizzie Borden, Andrew's daughter, directs the
children's church choir rehearsal under Rev. Harrington's
watchful eye. We learn of Andrew Borden's wealth, of Lizzie's mother's death, and of his remarriage to Abbie. Andrew enters--a stern and unforgiving man--who is mostly interested in his wealth, and upon his arrival the Reverend and
the children leave quickly. He is unsympathetic with Lizzie's
need for a new gown for a speaking engagement at the church
and tells her to "make do." He lectures her about excesses
and they argue about Abbie's expensive dresses. Dinner is
announced and Abbie and Margaret, a younger sister of Lizzie's, join Andrew and Lizzie in what is a strained relationship.

SCENE 2

In their room the two girls discuss Jason's arrival that evening and his possibly asking their father for
Margaret's hand in marriage. A lyric passage ends the
scene with Margaret dreaming of the day she will leave this
house.

ACT II

After dinner in the living room, the same evening,
Abbie is playing the harmonium and she and Andrew discuss
the need to repair the instrument. Abbie wants a piano but
he isn't interested and Abbie speaks accusingly of the girls'
over-concern with their Mother's possessions. She sings
again and Lizzie and Margaret enter and Lizzie works on the
needlework of the Garden of Eden picture. The doorbell
rings and Jason and Reverend Harrington enter. After rather

*Elmslie, Kenward, libretto; Beeson, Jack, music; Plant,
Richard, scenario; Lizzie Borden (New York: Boosey and
Hawkes, 1966), no synopsis given.

severe pleasantries, Andrew leaves to lock up the house, and
the rest remain to talk and finally play a game in which they
declare "what they hope to harvest." When Andrew returns
he is offended that the minister should suggest that Andrew
give money for a new steeple on the church and urges him
to leave. After he does leave, Jason asks for Margaret's
hand, but Andrew offers him Lizzie instead. Andrew de-
grades Lizzie to her face, and Jason taunts Andrew and
leaves. Lizzie and Andrew exchange sharp words about what
Lizzie is forbidden, and when Abbie attracts Andrew's attention, he leaves for bed. Lizzie remains to sing a long aria
about her anguish and her half-formed plans for revenge.

ACT III, SCENE 1

    The following morning in the room and garden of the
two girls we hear Andrew's voice forbidding either Margaret
or Lizzie to see Jason. Abbie interrupts because it is their
wedding anniversary and wants a pleasant day. After Abbie
and Andrew leave, Lizzie encourages Margaret to plan her
departure with Jason as she works on her Mother's wedding
dress for Margaret's wedding. Jason's voice is heard and
he has come to take Margaret away. After some doubt she
decides to go. Lizzie becomes more and more obsessed
with her own fantasies of her old age and barrenness. Jason
tells her he will return for Margaret's belongings, and Margaret says they'll return for Lizzie soon. After they leave
Lizzie puts on the wedding dress and imagines herself as
Jason's bride. Abbie returns and tries to ignore Lizzie but
ends in taunting her and ripping the wedding dress open to
shame her. After Abbie leaves, Lizzie looks at herself in
the mirror and then pounds the mirror with her fists, breaking it.

SCENE 2

    In the girls' room later in the afternoon, Lizzie sits
quietly when Jason enters to gather Margaret's things. Lizzie is barely aware of him, but then tries to make Jason
promise to write her as he wrote Margaret. Abbie, who
has been resting, speaks to them briefly and Jason leaves
soon after. Then Abbie goes back into her room and Lizzie
follows her. A scream is heard. Andrew returns and calls
for Abbie. Lizzie meets him on the stairs, and follows him
to the bedroom as the curtain falls.

EPILOGUE

Lizzie, several years later, is working on the account books when Reverend Harrington enters to return her church pledge. The church members voted not to accept it after the murder of her parents. We learn that Margaret is happy and has children, but Lizzie seems hardly interested in this news, and coldly ushers the minister to the door. Outside we hear children singing a taunting song about Lizzie murdering her parents with an axe.

Miss Julie*

ACT I

Christine, the cook, is in a reverie, dreaming of a man who'll love her now that it's midsummer's night. A chorus of revellers is heard off-stage. Miss Julie, daughter of the Count, enters with Niels, her fiance, and she taunts Niels who is rapidly growing to dislike her more and more. She prefers the servant's company to his, he tells her and walks out on her. She sings of her boredom and dreams, and of her wish for a real lover. John, the valet, enters and discusses Miss Julie's unconventional behavior with Christine. Miss Julie enters and wants to dance with John and he finally agrees. After the dance they talk and Christine pretends to sleep by the fire. They speak in French and finally in English when she proceeds to tease John. They become less and less guarded, telling each other their dreams and discuss if either one has ever been in love. He tells her of observing her from afar and thinking "dirty" thoughts about her. Revellers are heard approaching and they hide in John's nearby room where, despite her objections, John begins to seduce her as the revellers dance and drink in the kitchen.

ACT II

A few hours later as dawn is about to break, the revellers are gradually exiting and John and Miss Julie get up. They discuss the events that have taken place and John suggests that they must go away as far as they can, as everyone knows what has happened. He discusses their going to open a hotel on Lake Como, but they have no money. This leads to an argument about the seduction and to John's disdain of her. He makes fun of her and she finally tells him of her family's background and of her mother's hatred of men. He finally convinces her to go to her room and get dressed for the trip and also to find money. She goes and Christine enters; she soon determines what has gone on and

---

*Rorem, Ned, music; Elmslie, Kenward, libretto, Miss Julie (New York: Boosey and Hawkes, 1965), no synopsis given.

thinks it is high time that she and John get married and
leave this estate.   Miss Julie returns with her traveling
clothes on and carrying a bird cage.   John says that the
bird can't go and takes it out of the cage and chops its head
off.   Christine enters ready for church, and, as John shaves,
all three sing of the conflicting emotions.   Christine leaves
for church and the sound of the Count's carriage is heard
returning from a trip.   Miss Julie is frightened at the pros-
pect of seeing her father and asks John what to do.   He is
now busy reassuming his role of servant.   Finally he hands
her his shaving razor, suggesting that she kill herself.   As
she practices with the razor on her wrists John goes to the
speaking tube to answer the Count's call.

The Servant of Two Masters*

ACT I, SCENE 1

In the house of Pantalone, Clarissa and Silvio are plighting their troth. The two fathers are present and also, as witnesses, Clarissa's maid Smeraldina and the innkeeper Brighella. After the clauses of the marriage contract have been confirmed, Pantalone offers a toast in memory of Federigo Rasponi. Clarissa had been contracted in marriage to him--only the report, recently come, of Federigo's death in Torino had released her from marrying a man she had never seen.

As they are drinking the toast, Truffaldino enters and stands agape. His astonishment comes from having just this moment arrived at Pantalone's door with his master--and at then hearing that master, Federigo Rasponi, saluted in a toast.

Federigo enters and, in a lordly way, accepts introductions to the stunned assemblage. He makes his demands: for money, as Pantalone's business associate; and for Clarissa's hand.

Consternation turns to turmoil. In an elaborate fugue, Clarissa, Silvio, and Lombardi converge upon Pantalone to cajole, reproach, appeal, revile--to prevent him from fulfilling the contract with Federigo. At the same time, apart from the others, Brighella, who has recognized the newcomer as Federigo's sister, Beatrice, learns the motive for her disguise: only with a man's freedom of action can she hope to find her lover, Florindo Aretusi, who had fled Torino after wounding her brother in a duel.

Pantalone caps the protesting storm by shouting that the contract with Federigo will be fulfilled.

---

*Stambler, Bernard, libretto; Giannini, Vittorio, music, The Servant of Two Masters (New York: Franco Colombo, Inc., 1967. Used by permission of Belwin-Mills Pub. Corp.) p. iii-iv.

SCENE 2

Truffaldino, waiting for his master, grows hungrier
by the moment. He is struck by the great law of Nature
which always manages that men are born either with money
or with an appetite. Upon these meditations enter a young
gentleman (we soon learn that this is Florindo Aretusi) and
an overburdened porter. Florindo asks Truffaldino to carry
his bags into the inn in return for a meal; liking his silent
and willing behavior, Florindo offers to take him on as servant and sends him to pick up the mail.

Before Truffaldino can decide what to do, Beatrice-
Federigo enters--and also sends Truffaldino after the mail.
At this point all that Truffaldino wants is just one good meal
--but then the great idea comes. Why not two jobs, two
masters? If he can carry it off, think of the splendors of
two salaries, two dinners every evening, and perhaps other
desirables in double! Even if he can get away with it for
no more than a day, his name will live for ever in the annals of servantdom.

At this moment Smeraldina enters. She fits perfectly
into his prospects--that is, if she can measure up to his
newly elevated standards. He puts her through a little catechism, but all her responses are flippant or evasive. Finally she tells him that she came only to deliver a purse of
money for his master, throws it to him, and runs off.

SCENE 3

Clarissa is in tears, Pantalone is regretful but determined: she must live up to his word and marry Federigo.
Beatrice-Federigo enters and, seeing Clarissa's tears, asks
for a moment alone with her, to try for a kind word.

Failing to persuade Clarissa that this marraige is
equally undesired by both of them, Beatrice finally reveals
that she is a woman. But she reminds Clarissa how power-
less she herself had been to get anywhere in a man's world
and obtains Clarissa's promise to keep the secret until Florindo has been found.

Pantalone enters to find them in a friendly embrace:
the wedding, he decides, must take place immediately. Before this can be straightened out, Lombardi and Silvio enter.
Silvio wants only his bride; Lombardi asserts that by law the

second contract supersedes the first. Pantalone will hear
none of this; for him, honor is higher than the law. But
love is yet higher than honor--and he had seen Clarissa in
Federigo's embrace. In agony to tell the truth, but bound
by her word to Beatrice, Clarissa must admit that her father
has told the truth. Silvio violently attacks Clarissa with
words and Beatrice-Federigo with his sword. The servants
push the two interlopers out, and the two tearful women can
only hope that finding Florindo soon will put an end to their
problems.

ACT II, SCENE 1

    At the inn, Truffaldino, who never managed to get to
the post office, fails to persuade Florindo that it is time for
dinner. Florindo himself goes after the mail. Beatrice enters, despondent over not hearing from her lover, and tells
Truffaldino to have dinner served.

    Brighella says that because of the lateness of the
hour there is barely enough for the gentleman; Truffaldino
will be lucky to get some fragments for his own dinner.

    Florindo comes in, hunger awakened by his walk, and
requests dinner. Truffaldino's ensuing job calls upon his
highest talents at being servant of two masters. From the
kitchen he fetches the first trayful of courses for Florindo's
dinner. His faith in the tiny appetite of gentlemen is sustained: after he has fetched the second tray to Florindo, a
slight rearrangement of the first tray makes it servable to
Beatrice. And so through the entire meal--with everything
kept in good order by three signal bells, of recognizably different tones and timbres.

    In the midst of this feat of serving, Smeraldina comes
with a letter from Pantalone. Truffaldino seizes this occasion for a more elaborate catechism and proposal. This
time Smeraldina cooperates perfectly. They find themselves
soulmates, and dream out a future in which, both of them
weary of being servants, they soar to an idyllic livelihood--
a shop of delightful delicacies. But the awakening comes in
the midst of the dream: Smeraldina is bound as servant for
six more years; they have no way of getting the capital needed
for their enterprise.

SCENE 2

Florindo has decided to return to Torino and has told
Truffaldino to be ready to leave immediately. Beatrice decides to transfer her search to Naples, and so informs Truffaldino.

Florindo sees Beatrice's luggage at the door--recog-
nizes a case and a portrait. Under his intense questioning
Truffaldino first flounders and then invents a story: the luggage, the case--these things belonged to the dead master of
his friend. In his grief Florindo is barely able to get to
his room.

Beatrice comes in and recognizes Florindo's luggage
and portrait. This time Truffaldino is quicker with the story
about Pasquale. Heartbroken, she goes to her room. A
moment later she comes out, with uplifted dagger, for a last
look at the luggage, the only surviving token of her lover.
Florindo, with his dagger uplifted, comes out of his room at
the same moment. As they turn, they see each other and
rush into an embrace.

In the midst of their joy they happen to discover the
dual role of Truffaldino. Called to account, he is taken
aback but not shamefaced: life provides opportunities but
does not insure that all will pan out. The two cannot really
reproach him; he has, after all, brought them together. He
takes advantage of their good will to ask their help towards
the dream he shares with Smeraldina.

While Beatrice-Federigo has gone to transform herself into woman, Pantalone enters, with Clarissa and Smeraldina, to fetch Federigo to his wedding. Lombardi enters
with notice of a lawsuit against Pantalone, and Silvio comes
with a challenge, to Federigo, of a duel to the death. Beatrice's entrance with Florindo clears up all these contentions.
Then, Pantalone willingly releases Smeraldina; Beatrice, with
some byplay about "Pasquale," bestows the bag of money upon the young shopkeepers-to-be.

The two fathers depart to prepare for a triple wedding. Truffaldino, in the mode of commedia dell'arte, addresses the audience directly--asking them to remember for
themselves, as in the concluding sextet of the opera, the
gleaming and redeeming gifts of love.

Carry Nation*

PROLOGUE

In a Topeka bar at the turn of the century men and
their "girls" laugh about Carry Nation and her attempt to
"clean up" Topeka saloons as she claims drinking to be il-
legal. Carry and her women appear with hatchets to smash
the bar. The marshal strides in and arrests Carry.

ACT I, SCENE 1

We return to 1865 and the parlor of Carry's father in
Belton, Missouri. He is reading the Bible and Carry is
cleaning and day-dreaming. Her father notices her day-
dreaming and asks her to recall her religious conversion.
They discuss a boarder they are taking because of their lack
of money. Her Mother comes in and talks of her pre-Civil
War life of hunts and servants. She can't accept the idea of
a boarder and considers him a "visitor." Carry's Father
speaks of his wife's failing mind and his faith in Carry's
good sense. Dr. Charles Lloyd, the boarder, arrives and
meets the family. Charles is faint and Carry suggests
brandy, which her father refuses to serve. She brings
Charles water instead. At the sound of bells all four drop
to their knees for evening prayer.

ACT I, SCENE 2

The following spring on a Sunday morning a church
service is in progress off stage. Charles, carrying a flask,
wonders about the punishment in the religious message and
expresses his hatred of man's treatment of man. Carry enters and they discuss a passage from Shakespeare which
Charles contrasts to the hard attitudes of the churchgoers.
He then appeals to her of his need for someone to love.
Carry's Father enters and berates their behavior and points

---

*Moore, Douglas, music; North, William Jayme, libretto,
Carry Nation (Unpublished score, New York City Opera.
Copyright 1968 by Galaxy Music Corp.) no synopsis given.

out tombstones in the graveyard of people who've paid for
their sins. He orders Carry back into church while Charles
speaks of his "natural" love for Carry. Her Father accuses
him of drinking too much. Charles drinks from his flask in
defiance.

ACT I, SCENE 3

       That autumn at a barn dance the chorus sings of the
harvest moon's effect on them and then they dance. Charles
tells Carry he has a new medical practice in another town
and proposes to her. Carry's Mother and Father arrive.
Her Father tells Carry how sick her Mother is and almost
succeeds in telling Carry how bad Charles is when Charles
interrupts to ask for Carry's hand. Her Father refuses, but
Charles makes a public announcement anyway, partially drunk,
and her Father assures Carry that Charles loves his bottle
more. She answers, who are we to judge, and accepts his
hand.

ACT II, SCENE 1

       In Charles and Carry's home a local auxiliary of la-
dies read Emily Bronte to each other. Carry goes to make
tea and the ladies gossip about Charles' poor practice and
his drinking. Charles enters and the ladies leave; Carry argues with him about his drinking. She speaks of her loneliness and tells him of a forthcoming baby.

ACT II, SCENE 2

       Carry's Mother sings to her dolls and toys in her in-
sanity. She tells Carry's Father of Carry's approaching baby.
They read a letter from her asking their help. Her Father
decides to go to Carry and her Mother accuses Carry's Father of destroying everything.

ACT II, SCENE 3

       The next day at a men's club in Holden a quartet, of
which Charles is a member, sings. Charles is very drunk
and tells a war story of his allowing a soldier to bleed to
death. Carry enters to urge Charles home. Soon her Father appears and he urges her to go home with him. Charles
also pleads with her. She leaves with her Father as Charles
slumps down.

Appendix B

ACT II, SCENE 4

The following spring in the churchyard, Easter Sunday morning. An old caretaker puts flowers on graves from the morning Service. Carry enters, wheeling a baby carriage with her Mother following. She reads from Charles' letter and he tells of his getting better. Her Father enters to warn her not to get her hopes up--that Charles has just died. Alone, she prays for her guilt and asks God to possess her soul: "For someone has to pay." As the scene changes to a lecture hall, she sings and she speaks directly to the audience of their guilt.

Nine Rivers From Jordan*

It is the second World War and a British soldier, Don
Hanwell, who is stationed in the Near East near the Dead
Sea, is visited by an apparition-like woman. She warns him
that he is not to carry a gun or kill anyone in this war. He
agrees and subsequently he allows a German soldier to escape. The German later reappears in the story as a guard
at the Nazi Todenwald concentration camp.

Shifting to the site of the fabled Walpurgisnacht in the
Brocken, a trial is being held to determine the responsibility
for the Todenwald crimes. The result of this trial is to establish that we are all guilty for the war. Don Hanwell,
sharing this feeling of guilt, feels that he must correct an
old wrong--that of allowing the German soldier, Otto Suder,
to escape and serve at Todenwald. As the result of the trial,
it is pointed out by the judges that if Suder is killed, everyone else will be forgiven. With this in mind Don begins his
search with a bomb to kill Suder.

When Hanwell finds Suder at the near-conclusion of
the war, Suder tricks him. He is disguised as an English
soldier attempting to escape into Italy, and when he learns
Hanwell's purpose, Suder takes Hanwell's papers and convinces the nearby group of D.P.'s that Hanwell is a Nazi.
Don's companion, Copperhead Kelly, makes no move to defend Don, and a woman in the crowd takes Don's bomb and
gives it to Suder. However, Suder fouls his attempt to
throw the bomb and kills himself.

Don, who is puzzled by these events of betrayal,
speaks to God (who replys in the voice of Copperhead Kelly).
Don is made to realize that we have personal responsibility
in this life as well as in areas of life that we cannot control.
And although we are all guilty in this world we are still not
damned.

---

*Weisgal, Hugo, music; Johnston, Dennis, libretto, Nine
Rivers From Jordan (Bryn Mawr, Penna.: Theodore Presser
Company, 1969).

Help, Help, The Globolinks!*

SCENE 1

On a country road a school bus filled with children is
stalled by Globolinks, creatures from outer space. Anxiously the driver honks his horn, which frightens them away for
the moment. The radio tells the Driver and children that
only the sound of music will prove an effective weapon against
the Globolinks. Upon asking the children, Tony, the driver,
discovers that only Emily has her violin with her. She is
sent ahead to reach the school for help, playing her violin.

SCENE 2

In the Dean's office of St. Paul's school, Dr. Stone,
the principal, worries with a student, Timothy, about the
late arriving children. Madame Euterpova, the music teacher, enters offering her resignation, as she is convinced the
children aren't interested in studying music but quiets down
when she hears that the children are long overdue. She exits and Dr. Stone lies down to be awakened by Globolinks.
As a result of the Globolinks touching him, Dr. Stone can
only utter electronic sounds. Timothy calls the teachers for
help and Madame Euterpova organizes everyone into a musical band to ward off the Globolinks.

SCENE 3

Back on the country road the children wonder when
Emily will return. The Globolinks are getting bolder, but
as they approach threateningly a trumpet fanfare is heard
scaring the Globolinks away. There is a joyful reunion of
teachers and students, but Emily is still not back. They appeal to Dr. Stone who now has Globolink powers to help them
and he flies off with Madame Euterpova and children following him.

---

*Menotti, Gian-Carlo, libretto and music, Help, Help, The
Globolinks! (New York: G. Schirmer, Inc., 1969). No
synopsis given.

SCENE 4

  In a Forest of Steel Emily is still playing her violin.
When she stops to rest the Globolinks seize and destroy her
violin. Dr. Stone arrives to reassure her, but can only say
"la." As he turns into a Globolink, Emily faints. The children and the teachers arrive and dispel the Steel Forest.
Madame Euterpova moralizes to the children on the need for
music in the world and they then march off. A little Globolink appears to pull the curtain.

The Most Important Man*

ACT I

        In an African "white state" Toimé Ukamba, a pupil of
the scientist, Dr. Arnek, returns after a long absence to
Arnek's laboratory. Toimé, in his absence, has gained a
new sense of his place as a black person in a white world.
After much pleading, Arnek convinces Toimé to stay with
him and be accepted as his son.

        Cora, Arnek's daughter arrives for a visit and meets
Toimé. Her Mother, Leona, enters and orders Toimé to
leave them alone. Leona complains of Toimé living with
them and of his being treated as an equal. She continues
her objections to Arnek and tells him of her own attempted
suicide and finally threatens to leave him.

        Later Toimé and Cora discuss Toimé's position in the
house and she speaks of her admiration of him. He warns
her of playing with fire.

ACT II

        Two years later in the nation's capitol, a group of
scientists have just been shown Dr. Arnek's discovery and
they are truly amazed. They speak of how best to handle
this discovery and cannot agree on a course of action. Toimé
is introduced to the group and Dr. Arnek gives Toimé full
credit for the discovery. To the shocked group of white scientists Toimé announces that he is unwilling to give them his
secret, and the meeting ends without a decision. The scientists and Leona discuss the ramifications of this discovery
and the power that Toimé potentially has. They agree that
it was really Dr. Arnek who made the discovery.

        Mrs. Akawasi, a native witch doctor, and Leona dis-

---

*Menotti, Gian-Carlo, music and libretto, The Most Impor-
tant Man (Unpublished score, New York City Opera) no
synopsis given.

cuss the changes the discovery has brought to the local village. Mrs. Akawasi finally asks to speak to Dr. Toimé.
He quickly tells her he wants nothing to do with her and that
he's not a black man but a man who belongs to the world.
He finally calls Dr. Arnek who supports him in asking her
to leave. Leona returns to chide the men for their action
and predicts more trouble.

Leona and Arnek argue about the discovery and Arnek
still fully supports Toimé. Eric, another assistant, also
pleads with Arnek to explain the problems to Toimé. Toimé
and Arnek talk and Arnek asks about Toimé's relationship
with Cora. They argue; Cora enters and Toimé tells Arnek
of Cora's pregnancy. Eric enters as Cora and Toimé leave
and Arnek gives the safety vault number containing the formula to Eric, and immediately regrets it.

ACT III

Toimé discovers that Eric has the combination to the
vault and Eric threatens to shoot him. But Toimé kills
Eric and then calls Cora. The two of them decide to escape
into the forest.

Toimé and Cora are hiding and Toimé begs Cora to
burn the papers. Intoning words to Hymen and Apollo, she
sets fire to the papers. Dr. Arnek calls to them but Toimé
asks why Arnek tried to make a man of him and then betrayed
him. But Toimé is shot by other men searching him out.
As Toimé dies, Dr. Arnek asks his forgiveness.